And Grace Will Lead Me Home

And Grace Will Lead Me Home

The Jerry Evenrud Collection of Images
of the Parable of the Prodigal Son

by Robert M. Brusic

with essays by Jerry A. Evenrud, Sarah Henrich,
Wilson Yates, and David Morgan
Introduction by Richard Bliese

Lutheran University Press
Minneapolis Minnesota

And Grace Will Lead Me Home
The Jerry Evenrud Collection of Images of the Parable of the Prodigal Son
by Robert M. Brusic

Edited and designed by Lucy Brusic
Photography by Rick Souther
Cover design by Jesse Hubbard

The image on the title page is *Le Retour de l'Enfant Prodigue* (ca. 1900) by Jean-Louis Forain. More information about this etching is on pages 112-113.

Library of Congress Cataloging-in-Publication Data

Brusic, Robert M.
 And grace will lead me home : the Jerry Evenrud collection of images of the parable of the Prodigal son / by Robert M. Brusic ; with essays by Jerry Evenrud ... [et al.] ; introduction by Richard Bliese.
    p. cm.
 Includes index.
 ISBN-13: 978-1-932688-18-4 (hardbound w/ dust jacket)
 ISBN-10: 1-932688-18-8
 1. Prodigal son (Parable) in art. 2. Christian art and symbolism--Modern period, 1500- 3. Art--Private collections--United States. 4. Evenrud, Jerry--Art collections. I. Evenrud, Jerry. II. Title.
 N8110.B78 2007
  704.9'484--dc22
                               2006033744

Lutheran University Press, PO Box 390759, Minneapolis MN 55439
Printed in Hong Kong

This book is dedicated to the memories of Avis and Kirsten Evenrud and Matthew Brusic.
Their deaths left spaces in our lives that art could partially fill.

Table of Contents

Weathervane

Weathered metal
(26 x 15 ins.)

One of the side effects
of collecting images
of the Prodigal Son is
that people have sent
Jerry Evenrud pigs in
many forms.

Luther Seminary and the *Art* of Witness

by Richard Bliese

The simple story of sin and forgiveness in the parable of the Prodigal Son has deeply captivated and inspired the imaginations of millions of readers since Luke first put the parable to page. In other words, this simple story isn't really so simple. It reads us as much as we read it. One quick perusal through the pages of this book will confirm that the parable is complex in structure and rich in meaning. The parable preaches—even as image! One person whose imagination has been particularly captivated by this story for many years is a friend of Luther Seminary, Jerry Evenrud. Years of wrestling with this text have led him on a fascinating quest to gather a unique collection of art works, musical scores, and artifacts around the theme of the Prodigal Son. The resulting collection has been shown and admired all around the country in various art galleries, museums, colleges, denominational headquarters, and churches. These works of art are truly a witness to the incredible richness and power of this story to inspire, challenge, disturb, and comfort.

I first experienced these art works years ago at Jerry's home when I was given a personal tour of his collection. The collection *completely* filled his house from top to bottom. Every room contained large and small paintings, bookshelves brimming with books and art objects, and hidden treasures stashed away in closets and bathrooms. I have never felt so surrounded and embraced by one biblical text! This unique collection is also a testimony to the incredibly rich diversity of interpretations Christians have given to this story. Each piece of art lifts up different themes from the narrative: the contrasting roles of prodigal son and loving father, the context surrounding their reunion, the nature of the sin involved, the relationship between the two sons. Even the pigs get a special place of honor in Evenrud's collection!

The mission of Luther Seminary is to educate leaders for Christian communities, called and sent by the Holy Spirit to witness to salvation through Jesus Christ and to serve in God's world. We believe that God is calling and sending the church of Jesus Christ into apostolic mission in the twenty-first century. We have been called and sent to be both light and salt in a world that God loves. Is there any more powerful story that relates to our present mission and context than the Prodigal Son? And is there a better medium for the new evangelism at the beginning of the twenty-first century than art? This parable captures the mission of Luther Seminary like few other verses in scripture.

Luther Seminary has discovered the power of art on its campus to shape, mold, and educate future leaders. The Seminary owns five hundred fine art pieces in addition to three thousand artifacts in the Mission Heritage collection. This art is rotated regularly throughout our buildings on campus in order to make a strong spiritual impact on the community. These art pieces preach and teach every day. Given the thematic power and scope of these works, it was with great excitement that Luther Seminary agreed to become the permanent home for this "prodigal collection." Jerry Evenrud felt that Luther Seminary would provide the proper setting and backdrop to make this collection more visible both to future leaders in the church and the wider community. The gift of his collection also provides the seminary with an important legacy of connecting its mission with Luke's parable.

Our appreciation as a community to Jerry Evenrud for this amazing gift is profound and heartfelt. We expect that the witness of this collection —like the parable itself—will only grow and deepen as its images influence generation after generation of church leaders.

Editor's Introduction

by Lucy Brusic

This introduction has two purposes: one, to explain how this book is organized, and two, to thank the people who were involved in producing it.

The Evenrud collection contains over two hundred original works of art. The first task was to figure out which ones would be included in this book. At first, we simply selected those of which Jerry Evenrud was particularly fond. Gradually the selection process became more refined so that there would be groups of pictures to illustrate the various themes that can be discerned in the story of the Prodigal Son.

Our initial aim was to select forty pictures for commentary. Eventually, we expanded the number of selections to fifty-one. (The thought behind this decision was that if a reader included the reflection by David Morgan on his work [found on page 35], then one could read a commentary a week for a year.) The reader is of course welcome to read at his or her own pace.

Once the reflections were written it became necessary to put them in some kind of order. Scenes of homecoming and reunion have been much more popular with artists than scenes of departure, debauchery, and despair. We decided to group the three D's in one section and expand the homecomings into Return, Reconciliation, and Celebration. Happily, with only a little manipulation, the homecomings divided fairly evenly into three sections. Within the sections, we began by arranging works alphabetically by the artist's last name. This decision nicely mixed the works by style, type, and period.

Works that came in a series or covered all of the episodes of the parable challenged this arrangement, however. In the end, we decided to distribute these artworks throughout the book. Usually our decision was based on what we felt was the strongest work in the group. Obviously, though, the problems of arranging pictures (particularly groups of four or six) so the commentary always fell on a left-hand page meant that the alphabetical system was somewhat compromised.

The sizes of all the pictures are listed in the captions, with width preceding height. We have made each picture as large as possible given page constraints, but no work is reproduced larger than its actual size.

Early on, we decided to treat *Prodigal Son* as a proper name and have therefore capitalized it to avoid confusion.

While we were attempting to produce a proper catalog of selected works from the Evenrud collection, it also became apparent to us that the story of the Prodigal Son, while well known to all of us, was not necessarily familiar to people outside of the church. In fact, many people could not define the word *parable*. Therefore we engaged Sarah Henrich, professor of New Testament at Luther Seminary, to write an essay on the parable. In the same vein, we asked Wilson Yates, president emeritus of United Theological Seminary, to describe the proper and profound uses of religious art.

The Evenrud collection also contains many items that do not hang on walls. Some of these pieces, like porcelain plates and book dust jackets, are works of art in their own sphere. What to do with a veritable farmyard of porcelain and stuffed pigs is perhaps best left to the reader's imagination.

The title suggested itself early in the process—during a conversation between Luther Seminary's Fine Arts Committee and David Tiede, the then-president of Luther Seminary. Since Jerry Evenrud and Bob Brusic are musicians, it seemed only natural the title of the book might derive from a hymn. Their common knowledge of the power of hymnody led them to feel that the concluding line of one of the stanzas of "Amazing Grace" summed up much of what the parable is about for the reader, the writer, and the artist.

Although this book does not catalogue every work in the collection, the appendices represent a serious effort to cover the range of items and instances of the use of the parable of the Prodigal Son in art, music, and literature.

Acknowledgements

Numerous people deserve thanks for bringing this book into being. Jerry Evenrud himself was an instigator and participant and deserves most of the credit—for he was the person who created the collection. He had the initial vision for the book and made many editorial suggestions along the way. In every sense, though other people wrote most of the words, this is really Jerry's book.

Luther Seminary has been consistently supportive of this project. David Tiede, president-emeritus of Luther Seminary, was the first person who saw the possibility that an arts collection in general—and the Evenrud collection in particular—might find a home at the seminary. Paul Daniels, the archivist and curator at Luther Seminary, was instrumental in arranging for the Evenrud collection to be given to the seminary. Nina Bliese, Robert Brusic, Sheri Booms Holm, Cindy Beth Johnson, and Mons Teig served on the Arts Committee of Luther Seminary that arranged for the donation. Various legal and financial aspects of the acquisition were capably handled by Kathy Hansen and James Peterson. Kathy also affirmed the book's value as a resource to the larger constituency of Luther Seminary. Kari Bostrum and Don Lewis from the seminary attended numerous meetings as we discussed publication of the book. Maria Thompson from the seminary assisted with the promotion. Laura Kaslow graciously proofread the manuscript at a final phase.

We also owe timely thanks to the Museum of Biblical Art (MOBIA). Without the impetus of planning for the show to take place from October 4, 2007, to February 17, 2008, this book might not have been written. We are indebted to Ena Heller, executive director, and Holly Flora, curator, of MOBIA for taking the initiative to approach Jerry Evenrud and starting the process.

Leonard Flachman, publisher of Lutheran University Press, has been most helpful in working with us to design the book. He graciously offered to secure permissions for the art works; we are glad he had the staff and the resources to take that daunting task off our hands. The cover was designed by Jesse Hubbard of Lutheran University Press. Sarah Kammerer of Lutheran University Press designed the promotional materials.

We spent several intense but pleasant days with Rick Souther photographing the collection in Jerry's living room. We were all sorry when the task was done because we had so many engaging conversations while we were lining up the shots. Rick also worked with us to make sure that the color was correct on the pictures and on our computers. All the photography not otherwise credited is the work of Rick Souther.

Cindy Beth Johnson, Henry Horn, and Mark Throntveit read portions of the book at various stages of its development. Jim Boyce, Jim Limburg, and Mary Preus helped with translations from Latin and German. Tim Johnson helped with translating Swedish. Sarah Henrich clarified a few Latin words.

Adam Brusic participated in the project by photographing, scanning, and solving the computer problems that inevitably arise in the production of a book.

Although the opinions represent those of the writers, we have checked facts and dates carefully. If any errors remain, we accept the responsibility for them.

Part 1

Essays about the Collection

Robert Hodgell

The Prodigal (1960)

Linoleum block print
(34 x 24⅜ ins.)

The Evenrud
collection of Prodigal
Son images began
when this image of
the Prodigal Son
was displayed at a
church in Eau Claire,
Wisconsin, where
Jerry Evenrud was
serving as director of
music.

How The Prodigal Son Collection Came to Be

by Jerry A. Evenrud

The Prodigal Son collection is a witness to the continuing appeal of the parable in Luke 15, to the inventiveness of artists in representing it, and to the importance of "visual exegesis" in the history of art. The collection also reveals the desire of artists to delve into the meaning of the parable for themselves and to convey that meaning to others.

The catalyst for focusing this collection of art, music, and books relating to the Prodigal parable can be traced to a linoleum block print exhibit by University of Wisconsin-Madison artist, Robert Hodgell, at Grace Lutheran Church, Eau Claire, Wisconsin, in 1960. The exhibit was sponsored by the church's "Art for Faith's Sake" committee. Hodgell included several works inspired by Old and New Testament texts. One print featured the parable of the Prodigal Son. Crouched between two large Iowa sows was the forlorn son. On the cuff links of the son's shirt Hodgell etched the hedonistic symbol of the Playboy Club—bunny ears—and placed in his back pocket a whiskey flask. This contextual update for the first-century biblical parable prompted one member of the congregation to say, "Every time I pass that damn pig picture I think, but for the grace of God and AA, I would be there myself." I realized this provocative insight affirmed the exhibition theme, "Art for Faith's Sake."

In 1983 I had the privilege of a six-month sabbatical study leave. I spent six weeks at the Royal School of Church Music (RSCM), Croyden, England. Needing to write a report about my sabbatical journey, I reflected again about the 1960 encounter with the AA member from Grace Lutheran Church. I decided to make an inventory of what composers and artists had created who were inspired by the parable of the Prodigal Son. This quest not only engaged me, but fascinated a number of other people along the way. One discovery led to another in a series of eye-opening surprises.

When I mentioned my quest to a retired curator from the British Museum

Don Hunt

Three vodka bottles (1996)

Ceramic (12½,11, 9½ ins. high)

After an exhibit of the Evenrud collection at Bethel Lutheran Church in Madison, Wisconsin, a member of the congregation wanted to use his skill as a ceramic artist to relate the story of the Prodigal. The image of the pig and the lettering degrade to indicate the descent of the Prodigal into misery.

who volunteered in the library at the RSCM, he said, "I think you should meet the curator of the Warburg Institute at the University of London." (The institute is based on the personal library of Aby Warburg (1866-1929) and exists principally to study symbols and images of the classical world. Formerly based in Germany, the institute moved to England in 1933 and became part of the University of London in 1944.)

In my interview with the curator, his first words were, "I understand that you are very interested in art that has been inspired by the Prodigal Son parable. What period?" Novice that I was at the time, I said, "Well, I'm just interested." He said, "We don't have anything before 1300. You'll have to go to Princeton University in the United States for material before 1300." Indeed I did, and I was amazed at the number of works recorded before 1300.

Eventually, from Princeton, I went to New York; I had lived in New York from

Banner based on an image by Hans Georg Annies

(1997)

Silk screen
(24 x 72 ins.)

The Evenrud collection has been displayed at over thirty sites throughout the United States. This banner, created by the Valparaiso Art Department, advertised the exhibit at Valparaiso University in 1997. The decorative pigs are called Hamlet and Pygmalion. The image on which this banner is based was a gift from an organist from Karl Marx City (Chemnitz), Germany.

1951 to 1953 when I attended the Union Theological Seminary School of Sacred Music and often went to the Metropolitan Museum of Art to see paintings and sculpture. I did not realize at the time that there was a Print and Drawing Department. Appointments are required. A staff person handed me a pair of white gloves and said, "Aren't you from Minnesota?" He was a member of Holy Trinity Lutheran Church on Central Park West and had attended a national Lutheran convention where I had directed the music. He was intrigued that I was focusing on art inspired by the Prodigal Son and took the time to share many examples of works in their collection.

He also made an appointment for me with Edmund Wolf II, the director of the Library Company in Philadelphia, the oldest cultural institution in America. (It was founded by Benjamin Franklin.) At a luncheon meeting Mr. Wolf gave me a book, *Eighteenth-Century Prints in Colonial America: To Educate and Decorate,* edited by Joan Dolmetsch (Williamsburg: Colonial Williamsburg, 1979). Wolf had written a chapter in the book: "The Prodigal Son in England and America, a Century of Change." This chapter documented a collection he had assembled of eighteenth-century prints inspired by the Prodigal parable.

In discussing the sets of prints of the Prodigal Son narrative that adorned the walls of eighteenth-century American homes, Wolf wrote, "As visual prayers, the sets of prints flowered on the walls of English middle-class homes, redolent with the smell of candle wax and roast beef. And, since English middle-class virtues and vices had widespread appeal for colonial and later national Americans, they bought English 'Prodigal Sons' and created their own versions long after the craze for them had died down across the Atlantic" (Wolf, pp. 151-152). Many of the works in my collection are indeed these visual prayers, in which the son, dressed in clothing of the period, either leaves or returns to an eighteenth- or nineteenth-century home. In many cases it would be hard to recognize the parable without a title or quotation in the margins.

When I returned to Minneapolis, I met with the Rev. Richard Hillstrom, the curator of what was then the Lutheran Brotherhood Collection of Art. He gave me a list of five dealers in New York with whom he had worked. I returned to New York, where I visited one of the galleries Hillstrom had recommended. Imagine my surprise when the owner replied affirmatively to my question: Do you have any art inspired by the Prodigal Son parable? The week before he had been at an estate sale and he had a work from 1636 —a small Rembrandt etching. That etching became the first work in the collection. Rembrandt (1606-1669) did several works based on Luke 15, the best known of which is the large painting in the Hermitage in St. Petersburg.

Since then I have been adding works to the collection. In 1986 I was asked by the art committee at Central Lutheran Church in Minneapolis to have an exhibit. At that time I did not have enough items for an exhibit so I borrowed from the Lutheran Brotherhood Collection, from Augsburg College, and from an editor at Augsburg Publishing House. After the exhibit at Central, I was asked to exhibit at Luther Seminary and at United Seminary, both located in the Twin Cities. The first exhibit away from Minnesota was at Fourth Presbyterian Church, Chicago, Illinois. On the last day of that exhibit a visitor from Louisville asked if I would exhibit in Louisville. Two weeks later I had an invitation from the Roman Catholic Cathedral in Louisville, Kentucky. A listing of thirty-nine exhibits can be found in the appendix of this book.

Visitors come to see the collection

Since 2001 I have been the in-house docent for tours of the collection at my home. This activity has indeed enriched my retirement. One of my visitors shared this insightful statement from W. H. Auden:

No collection is ever truly realized or completed; each is a final

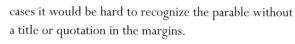

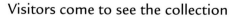

vision of sorts at any particular moment, fixed while still in flux, a clear expression of an ongoing determination of sensibilities. When formed by luck, certainly, but also with taste and judgment, and with a growing refinement of imperatives, a collection can furnish the reader, viewer, the beholder, a new set of conjugations, parallels, alternatives, and even understandings. [I have not been able to find the exact source of this quotation.]

Visitors to the collection often respond by sending Prodigal-related items. A woman from Oslo, Norway, sent me a picture of a mosaic mural (1920) by Emanuel Vigeland (1875-1948) from the Gjerpen Church in Tellemark, Norway. She remembered seeing a photo of the mosaic on the jacket cover of *Norsk Kirke-Historie* by Carl Wisloff, a gift to the collection from the Luther College Library. Photos, sermons, bulletin covers, hymns, and musical scores and, of course, gifted pigs abound.

John August Swanson, an artist from Los Angeles, shared his experience of visiting the collection with his mother (Magdalena Velesquez Swanson), who in turn sent a *Soviet Life* magazine (February 1987) with an article on the Russian painter Ilya Glazunov (b. 1930). Included was a photo of his painting, *The Return of the Prodigal Son*. In this painting, a young man in jeans (presumably the Prodigal) kneels before and is welcomed and blessed by a figure who seems to be Jesus. Behind the Jesus figure are fifteen recognizable portraits of Russian leaders. When asked why he considered this painting to be one of his major works, Glazunov replied

> I used the well-known biblical theme of a son leaving his father's house. After squandering everything he had and after being reduced to eating with swine, the son remembers he has a father and a home. By father and a home I mean the self-awareness and the spiritual culture of the people. That's why I put Andrei Rublyev, St. Sergius of Radonezh, Rachmaninoff, Scriabin, and the great defenders of the land in my picture. My painting is about being true to one's roots. If the roots of a tree are dug up or chipped off, the tree dies. Everyone, every country has a national culture and all people, all nations should be encouraged to cherish it.

Foreign travel enhances the collection

Foreign travel was often an opportunity to enrich the collection. After reading an article in the Summer 1992 issue of *Art and Antiques* by Sir Steven Runciman on "The Forgotten Frescoes of Romania," I shared the information

Image used by permission of the artist

Ilya Glazunov

The Return of the Prodigal Son (1977)

Oil on canvas (approx. 78 x 117 ins.)

This painting, showing the Prodigal returning to his fathers (famous Russians such as Gogol and Dostoyevsky), is illustrated in *Ilya Glazunov* by Valentin Novikov (Moscow: Sobor, 1992). The work is in a private collection.

with friends Marcel and Hana Sulicanu who had emigrated from Bucharest, Romania. They had visited the painted church at Humor (1530) where an outside wall has a fresco with eight panels depicting the Prodigal parable. The last panel features five dancers dancing the hora on the return of the Prodigal. After visiting Humor, Romania, I met Marian Zidaru who created a triptych and an icon for the collection. Is it possible that the three angels are dancing the hora on the Prodigal's return?

Adolphe Léon Willette

L'enfant Prodigue
(c. 1890)

Score for a pantomime by Michel Carré fils; music by André Wormser (Biardot, Paris: no date but around 1890). (7½ x 10 ins.)

This illustration (page 87) shows a teardrop reflecting the son stealing from the father's safe. The music is romantic and melodramatic, and the pantomime introduces many characters who are not in the biblical narrative.

An interesting discovery on a trip to London was the piano score by André Wormser to accompany "L'Enfant Prodigue," a Pantomime in Three Acts by Michael Carré fils. Years later I also acquired a poster announcing a performance of this work in Paris.

On a visit to Vienna, Austria, I discovered a beautiful art gallery across from the church where I sang in a volunteer choir for the Easter service. I returned on Monday at 10:00 A.M. and inquired if they had any art inspired by the Prodigal parable. As it happened, a week earlier the owner of the gallery had bought at auction in Holland a fifteen-foot-long fabric depicting the Prodigal parable. A local curator indicated that the work was Swedish from the eighteenth century but had no more information.

I bought the work and included it in the Rockford, Illinois, exhibit and then had it installed at my home. Several years later, while I was visiting the Swedish Institute in Minneapolis, I met a tourist from Sweden, Gunnel Wennerholm. I told her about the lack of information on the fabric work. She replied, "I am a retired dental surgeon; I'll do research for you." Her most useful information is from an academic treatise by Elizabeth Berglen, "A Peasant Painter and His World, Johannes Nilsson of Breared." The author has registered two hundred forty-eight works by Nilsson.

The collection continues to evolve. It now encompasses works from 1540—*Parable of the Prodigal Son Surrounded by Swine* by Hans Sebald Beham—to 2005—James McNeill Mesplé, *Prodigal Son Receiving his Patrimony*. The media range through etchings, paintings, ceramics, sculpture, and fabric.

The historical span of the collection affirms the continuing resonance of the parable. Helmut Thielicke captures some of this resonance in the introduction to his book, *The Waiting Father: Sermons on the Parables of Jesus* (New York: Harper & Brothers, 1959). The German title of the book is *Das Bilderbuch Gottes (The Picture Book of God)*.

> When we read the parables, we are surrounded by the scenery of a world that is very near, *our* world. But everything depends upon our finding the right entrance from which their meaning is discovered. (p.12)

The artists who tell the story of the Prodigal Son are doing "visual exegesis"—giving a close reading and a critical interpretation of the scripture. They are finding an entrance to the meaning in the story and revealing it by their interpretations and their visual skills. Some artists create a series or a sequence that covers the whole story, such as John August Swanson or, my favorite, Hieronymus Nadel. (Nadel includes in the background an image of Jesus relating the story to the Pharisees.) Sometimes a visual rather than a verbal delivery of the story prompts the viewer to investigate other biblical stories, leading to a better understanding of the Christian faith. I call this an aesthetic encounter rather than a crusade.

Some artists depict the entire narrative in a series of prints, usually four to six segments. Some artists focus on just one aspect, such as the pig pen or the return. There is a whole genre I refer to as "non-Sunday-School material," which in many cases turns out to be autobiographical on the part of the artist.

The segment most frequently portrayed by a single print is the homecoming embrace by the father, who, as Thielicke says (p. 22), has kept the son in his thoughts. The homecoming scene represents the most meaningful aspect of faith—that of grace and forgiveness. The story as told by Luke serves as a catalyst for the exploration of faith and forgiveness, and artists stretch their imaginations, their artistic skills, and their experience to portray and convey the emotions felt by the participants. Sometimes artists add mothers, sisters, daughters, and additional brothers to the scene of the return or use clothing or other ethnic props to bring the story of the Prodigal Son into our world. As in the case of my parishioner from Eau Claire, the props supplied by the artist identify and intensify the experience of the Gospel.

In addition, artists often convey more than a visual retelling of the story; they invest the story with a wealth of human detail. The details in these works also convey something of the lifestyles of the rich and famous in the sixteenth and seventeenth centuries, or details of life in the Great Depression and the Dustbowl, or a graphic picture of the effects of substance abuse.

Reflections on the donation to Luther Seminary

Two more thoughts come to me, now that I am giving my collection to Luther Seminary. First, I think of this quote from *A Self Portrait with Donors: Confessions of an Art Collector* (Boston: Little/Brown, 1974) by John Walker, the first director of the National Gallery in Washington, DC:

> Why do collectors continue to search for and to acquire great and noble works of art? There are many inducements. There is the excitement of the chase; there is the prestige of ownership; there is the intrinsic joy of looking at beautiful objects; and though perhaps an illusion, there is the security of investment in an inflationary period. But at least in America, there is a deeper motive, one that only a cynic would ignore. I believe a fundamental incentive is the desire to add to the cultural heritage of this country through the enrichment of our museums. American collections remain private for only one generation. In the United States, it is axiomatic that the undertaker and the museum director arrive almost simultaneously! (p. xvii)

But I also think of this quote from J. Irwin Miller, the philanthropist who endowed the move of the Union School of Sacred Music to Yale University.

> Most seminary education today gives no more than a passing nod to one of the most important treasures of Christianity. Art is treated as an *ornament* not a *necessity*. Few pastors use their adult lives to remedy this omission from their education. Is it any wonder then that sensitivities atrophy and finally disappear, that worship services abound in third-rate music and liturgy which touches no one, and in embarrassing poetry which is no more than a chain of clichés?
> (J. Irwin Miller. "Today's Church as Seen by One Layman," Hugh Thomas Miller Lecture No. 2, Christian Theological Seminary, March 16, 1983. In *More than Worlds Can Alone: J. Irwin Miller, The Hugh Th. Miller Lectures.* Indianapolis: Christian Theological Seminary, 1983, pp. 31-32.)

"And grace will lead me home"

The story of the Prodigal Son continues to inspire all kinds of artistic expression. At this writing, for example, the musical "And Grace Will Lead Me Home" with lyrics by Herbert Brokering and music by Daniel Kallman has not been completed, but it is a work in progress—inspired by the collection.

The concluding song includes this festive text:

> Grace is all the gift we take
> Which we can never make
> So sing and dance and love
> Give praise to God above
> We'll be home, we'll all be home in time.

Final thoughts

I didn't set out to create a collection; it just happened. Nurturing and shepherding the collection has enriched my life and particularly my retirement. But now it seems a seminary that has begun to collect and incorporate art as part of its educational mission is a place where the collection might be used. The collection has a potential for sharing the gospel; it is visual evangelism, speaking where words cannot. It is my hope that for as long as the story of the Prodigal Son is told, the collection will continue to inspire people's lives and enrich their faith.

Hans Sebold Beham

Parable of the Prodigal Surrounded by Swine (1540)

Burin original (4 x 2½ ins.)

This work is the oldest art piece in the Evenrud collection.

The Parable of the Prodigal Son

Luke 15: 11-32

This version of the parable is from the *New Revised Standard Version of the Bible.* (Grand Rapids: Zondervan, 1989).

Then Jesus said, "There was a man who had two sons. [12] The younger of them said to his father, 'Father, give me the share of property that will belong to me.' So he divided his property between them. [13] A few days later, the younger son gathered all he had and traveled to a distant country, and there he squandered his property in dissolute living. [14] When he had spent everything, a severe famine took place throughout that country, and he began to be in need. [15] So he went and hired himself out to one of the citizens of that country, who sent him to his fields to feed the pigs. [16] And he would gladly have filled himself with the pods that the pigs were eating: and no one gave him anything. [17] But when he came to himself he said, 'How many of my father's hired servants have bread enough and to spare, but here I am dying of hunger! [18] I will get up and go to my father, and I will say to him, "Father I have sinned against heaven and before you; [19] I am no longer worthy to be called your son; treat me like one of your hired hands." [20] So he set off and went to his father. But when he still far off, his father saw him and was filled with compassion, he ran and put his arms around him and kissed him. [21] Then the son said to him, 'Father, I have sinned against heaven and before you; I am no longer worthy to be called your son.' [22] But the father said to his slaves, 'Quickly, bring out a robe—the best one— and put it on him; put a ring on his finger, and sandals on his feet. [23] And get the fatted calf, and kill it, and let us eat and celebrate, [24] for this son of mine was dead and is alive again; he was lost and is found.' And they began to celebrate.

[25] "Now his elder brother was in the field; and when he came and approached the house, he heard music and dancing. [26] He called one of the slaves and asked what was going on. [27] He replied, 'Your brother has come, and your father has killed the fatted calf, because he has got him back safe and sound.' [28] Then he became angry and refused to go in. His father came out and began to plead with him. [29] But he answered his father, 'Listen! For all these years I have been working like a slave for you, and I have never disobeyed your command; yet you have never given me even a young goat so that I might celebrate with my friends. [30] But when this son of yours came back, who has devoured your property with prostitutes, you killed the fatted calf for him!' [31] Then the father said to him, 'Son, you are always with me, and all that is mine is yours. [32] But we had to celebrate and rejoice, because this brother of yours was dead and has come to life; he was lost and has been found.'"

Luke 15:11-32: A Parable of a Father and Two Sons

by Sarah Henrich

Introduction

How shall we name this story that appears only in the gospel according to Luke (15:11-32)? It has been known most often as the parable of the Prodigal Son, less often as the parable of the waiting father. Almost never has it been identified by its third major character, the elder son whose story occupies its second half and its culminating scene. Just these few suggestions for possible titles for this story put an artistic and theological truth squarely before us. That truth? Parables beget interpretation by their very nature. Let us see why this is so before we focus on this particular parable, that of "a certain father who had two sons" (Luke 15:11).

What is a parable?

For nearly two millennia Christians have handed down teachings of Jesus in the collection of writings called the New Testament. Parables constitute a considerable proportion of that teaching. Parables have, therefore, been important to Christians trying to understand Jesus and live a Christian life. Yet, it is clear that even within the gospel stories, Jesus's earliest followers struggled to understand what parables might mean.[1] Like those early followers, later preachers, teachers, artists, and followers of all sorts have tried to make sense of parables for their own time and place. What a parable is and how to interpret it are bound tightly together.

We can begin to define parables by describing some features of a parable that would have been familiar to first-century audiences as well as to contemporary readers. Parables are brief narratives. They depict everyday events and are set in everyday locations. Usually the characters in parables do not have proper names. The combination of everyday events and locations with unnamed characters makes it possible for hearers to imagine themselves or those they know as participants.

Most importantly, parables tend to be short and allusive. Parables use familiar settings and generic characters to describe briefly and in terms of human actions the extraordinary reality of God and the reign of God. In what way does a farmer sowing his seed speak truly to us of God? What connections, what interpretations do we make when ordinary human actions are intended to help us imagine what we cannot fully know? Parables force us to wrestle for meaning. As a literary form, a parable inherently provides meaning that is not obvious, clear, or singular. The lack of clarity about meaning is exacerbated for those living lo these many centuries after the time of Jesus; we don't find even the "ordinary," everyday world of the parables easily intelligible.

How have parables been understood?

Early on, within the New Testament and for fifteen hundred years afterward, parables were understood as allegories. Each character and action of the parable corresponded to some other reality which correct interpretation would reveal. Saint Augustine (354-471 C.E.) writes about our story of a man with two sons in this way. Although allegory with its exact correspondence of every aspect of the gospel story to some other reality strikes us as strained, sometimes even nonsensical, this way of understanding the meaning of Jesus' stories was popular. Why, folks wondered, would *Jesus* tell stories about farmers and bakers, family life and vine-keeping? Surely these stories must have had a deeper meaning. Surely these were stories about God and God's work in the world. As time went on folks came to see in the parables Jesus speaking in a coded way and prophetically of his gathered people, the church. Notice that this kind of interpretation did not invite ordinary hearers to understand the parable in an immediate way. Instead, interpretation was left to experts, usually preachers, who could de-code the story.

In the late nineteenth century, a New Testament scholar, A. Julicher, insisted that parables were not to be understood as allegories. Instead they were short stories carrying one main point or idea. Julicher's convictions led

[1] See Luke 8:9; Matthew 4:10; Mark 4:10.

to a tendency to "boil down" parables to one meaning. That meaning was often understood to be a challenge to prevailing customs. For Julicher, a parable was a story with a "twist," usually designed to teach a truth or moral. But, parables resist this sort of reduction to one meaning. Since the 1950s students of the Bible have moved away from both allegory and from "one main point" as adequate means of understanding parables. Interpreters have striven to let the story speak, used the setting of the story in the gospel itself to understand the story more fully, and learned more about how first-century audiences would have understood the behaviors in the parable. We will bring all these techniques to bear on Luke's longest parable, the story of the father who had two sons.[2]

The whole parable (Luke 15:11-32)

This parable is the longest and most complex of all parables in the New Testament. One reason for its astounding popularity over nearly two millennia is that it is a lengthy and well-developed story. It has substance, suspense, and surprise. The story begins by mentioning two sons, but concentrates on the younger of the two for the whole first half of its length. The parable almost seems as if could end with Luke 15:24, the return and joyful reception of the younger son. In fact, for many interpreters, visual as well as verbal, the second part of the story does not receive attention. If we name this text as "the parable of the Prodigal Son," we fall into this truncated way of reading the story. To stop with Luke 15:24 would leave us with the story of only one son. The rest of the parable—eight verses— is required for resolution of this story, if resolution there is to be.

Another reason for the parable's popularity—and complexity—hinges on attention to the elder brother. In Luke 15, Jesus offers three parables one after another (verses 3-7, 8-10, and 11-32). All the parables are about losing, finding, and the great joy and celebration that mark that finding. The elder brother, at the end of all these stories, introduces the first discordant note. Because Luke includes the elder brother's point of view, our parable represents two very distinct behaviors, attitudes, and modes of engagement with the father. Interpreters are able easily to cast opposing points of view into whatever version of "us" and "them" is suitable for their own contexts. Such dualistic interpretations seem to have been almost irresistible. You will see this kind of contextualizing in many of the artistic renderings of this parable.

Because Luke's Jesus teaches by telling a story we will begin by engaging our parable as a story. We will look at the setting, the characters, the scenes, and the customs that are assumed. Then we will look at the "gaps." By necessity, all literature, like all art, is filled with gaps. No one can ever say, paint, or sculpt everything that she or he experiences. Choices about what to leave in and what to leave out are made in every artistic project. Interpretation is, at least in part, the art of filling in gaps in a meaningful way. We'll talk more about that as we move along in the story.

Setting

We can begin as Luke does, setting the parable in a particular context, as a response to a particular audience. In Luke 15:1-2 some Pharisees and scribes were grumbling about Jesus' habitual meal companions, namely tax collectors and sinners. Luke is the only writer to use this word "grumble" in the New Testament, but it is common in *his* scripture, our Old Testament. Biblically, "to grumble" is to complain (often to or about God) because of a profound lack of understanding about God's activity. When we hear about grumbling among Pharisees and scribes, whom Luke has already described as troubled by Jesus and hostile to him (Luke 11:53), we know that they are failing to understand how Jesus uses these parables to remedy their failure to understand. Verse 3 announces that Jesus "told this parable (and this refers to all three of the parables in Luke 15) *to* them. The "parables of the lost," including the parable of the man with two sons, are directed primarily to the Pharisees and scribes, dedicated defenders of the faith.

Part of the setting of this parable includes the two short stories that precede it. These two are very similar one to another. In each a single character loses a precious object, searches diligently for it, finds it, and celebrates with neighbors over the find. Jesus draws explicit connections (vv. 7, 10) with the joy and celebration in heaven when one repentant sinner is "found," a joy greater than that felt over the righteous who have not been lost. Then Jesus moves to the longer story of the father with two sons. We expect a similar story highlighting the joy and celebration, and that certainly seems to occur in 15:22-24. Yet, we are left to come to grips with the remainder of this long parable, a remainder that has no parallel in the two preceding stories. An alert hearer might catch some similarities between the "grumbling" in the beginning and the older son's bitter complaint at the end.

[2] One broad definition of a parable is this: a metaphor or simile drawn from nature or common life, arresting the hearer by its vividness or strangeness and leaving the mind in sufficient doubt about its precise application to tease the mind into thought. For this definition and a brief overview of parable interpretation, see Charles W. Hedrick, *Many Things in Parables: Jesus and His Modern Critics* (Louisville: Westminster John Knox Press, 2004) pp xiv-xv.

Characters

Our parable has multiple characters explicitly mentioned and an array of others that we can imagine (as artists usually do). We are told of a man (the father), an older and a younger son, a citizen of a far country, pigs, hired hands and slaves of the father's household, including a particular slave who speaks with the older son. We must imagine those among whom the younger son lived dissolutely, those invited to the feast, musicians, cooks, a mother perhaps, and any other women of the household. This simple listing immediately requires us to imagine our way into the story. Who are these people? What do they look like? What attitudes and relationships might they have to one another? How do their faces look when the younger son asks for an inheritance, leaves, and returns? These details are all "gaps" that readers and hearers fill in for themselves or have filled in by others. The tale is animated, that is, fleshed out and made lively by whoever tells it verbally, visually, in music, or dance.

Each character has an important part to play that influences how we understand the point of the parable. Choices are made, often unconsciously, about how we "picture" each individual and the relationships that bind them together in this story. In addition, in the back of our minds, we always have Jesus, the Pharisees, and the scribes, for we must imagine how they participated in the telling of this parable—speaking it and receiving it—in order to begin to make some sense of it for ourselves.

We are not left clueless about these relationships, even though we are not, nor can we be, told everything significant about them. We learn something about the relationships and the characters in three important ways:

> The language used to describe characters and relationships
>
> The unfolding of the scenes
>
> How these events would have been understood in their own time and place, that is, historically.

Scenes in the story

Let's begin with the scenes in this parable. Along with the number of characters, the number of scenes is remarkably large for a New Testament parable. There is an introductory scene in which we learn of the family's existence and of the younger son's desire to claim his inheritance and leave home (15:11-12). In a second scene, vv. 13-16, the younger son traveled, spent his inheritance in "dissolute living," and was reduced to miserable labor (feeding pigs[3]) and to desperate hunger. In a third scene (15:17-20), the young man realized that he would have plenty to eat back home, even as one of his father's hired hands. After setting out a confession of his sin and a plea for being hired, he went home. Verses 20-24, scene four, portray the homecoming of the younger son. After his father has run out to welcome his son home, filled with compassion and joy, he commands a feast of rich food and the giving of rich adornment for the son. No hired hand here! The son comes home as son. Clearly the family was still at the farm and still able to manage a big party. The ending of this scene is reminiscent of the joy and celebration of the "finders" in the preceding parables.

Along comes the second half of this story. In scene five (vv. 25-32), the elder son who had been working in the field, came home, heard the sounds of celebration, and had to ask a slave what was happening. When he refused to enter the house out of anger, the father came out also to him. Their dialogue concludes the scene, the parable, and the chapter in Luke's gospel. It is a painful dialogue, with the older brother unable to understand why his father rejoices so heartily over a wastrel who has come home when the father never seemed to notice, let alone celebrate, the on-going hard work that the elder son had put into the family. Note that he will not even identify the younger son as his brother, but refers to him as "this son of yours" (v. 30). He goes beyond the narrator's description when he says that the younger son had used up the family property "with prostitutes." How does he know?

To this outpouring of anger and a deep sense of injustice, the father responds with a promise that is often neglected by interpreters, "Son, you are always with me and all that is mine is yours." The father does not change one whit in his insistence on celebration, the celebration of a dead son come to life, of a lost son being found. Nor does he allow the elder son to distance himself from the younger one. In 15:32, the father says, "this brother of yours" to his older son and implies that the joy and value in one being found belongs to the whole family.

The parable ends promptly. We do not know what happens. Each scene leaves us with questions that are not resolved in the end. We do not know if the elder brother "comes to himself" and joins the party. We do not know any of the feelings that shaped the relationship of elder to younger before they parted or after. We do not and cannot know whether the younger son

[3] Feeding pigs indicates that the young man has gone far from home and kin, for no Jewish farmer would raise pigs. That this young man is now tending pigs tells us to what level of despair he has sunk.

was sincere as he planned his speech in scene three, or simply chastened and savvy. Did the father show favoritism to the younger son? Had he done so all his life? Did the elder son speak the truth or did he exaggerate? What does all this have to do with God's reign and with Jesus, let alone with the Pharisees and scribes?

"What do you read there?" (Luke 10:26)

Although we are not left clueless about reading this parable and coming to some defensible understanding of it, interpretation is not easy. Many able and honest interpreters have come to quite different understandings. We cannot review the full history of interpretation of this parable, but I will offer a method and an interpretation that I find persuasive. Just to say it once more, many understandings are possible, given the open-endedness of the parable as well as its great distance from us in language and custom. Most importantly, perhaps, parables are stories designed to engage, even tease, their hearers into a new imagination of "how things really are." While everyday settings are used, the parables often lead to places where one wouldn't go in the everyday world. What is "ordinary" is used to help us stretch our limited conceptions to places that we can only imagine, towards the reign of God. When parables rely on our moving from the known to the unknown and indeed, to the unknowable, they must be open-ended, able to continue to woo us toward that which we may have dimly perceived or that about which we have never thought.

The first conviction I bring to parable interpretation is that Luke and Jesus wanted their hearers to engage these parables, to find them renewing, perhaps even disconcerting. That means that parables must operate in a world and with customs, language, and behaviors that are relatively familiar to those early audiences. In fact, we can imagine the characters in most parables as "stock characters" or "types." It is not a particular father that is brought to mind in this story, but a character "father" to which folks brought their own customary ideas of what fathers were like, how they behaved, and spoke, what, in a word, could be expected of them. The same can be said for the equally nameless sons, slaves, and citizens of a far country.

It is true that this family is likely to be a Jewish one. Luke puts the parable in the mouth of a Jewish preacher, Jesus. Jesus speaks it to a Jewish audience who are adherents of their faith. Understanding the family as Jewish makes

the tending of pigs all the more a serious departure from custom. The younger son works with unclean animals and might himself be designated unclean or a sinner on the basis of this work. That point is never made in the parable. When he comes to himself it is not in terms of religious faith or custom, but in terms of not being trapped in the miserable reality that was doing him in.

It is also true that the behavior of the younger son would have fallen somewhere on a scale of distasteful to reprehensible for young men at the turn of the first millennium. It was customary and respected to work for the household unit, obey the father, and support one's family to the best of one's ability. Honoring the father was key to maintaining stable families, cities, agricultural work, and well-being in general. At the same time there exist a significant number of ancient stories of young men leaving home for a variety of reasons. (Note that Luke does not specify the reason in this story.) Therefore, while it would not be looked upon as a right and proper thing to do when the younger brother claimed his inheritance and took off with it, it may not be quite as dastardly a deed as some interpreters have imagined. The family seems to continue to function at a fairly high level in the absence of the son and his share of the money.

By studying very carefully conventional behavior and language in fictional narratives that remain from the ancient Mediterranean world, scholars have learned a great deal about how audiences in that time and place were likely to "read" human behavior. Study of ancient texts contemporary with the parable has shown us that the behavior of the father and the sons is within the range of normal behavior for the situation. Neither the father nor the sons were outrageously out of sync with their times.

Reading the parable in light of other ancient stories helps us see that the parable is about God's joyous and emotional response when God receives back those God loves. The father's running toward the younger son, the one he had presumed thoroughly lost or even dead, would have been seen as an appropriate response by the original hearers of the parable. Interestingly, twentieth-century Middle Eastern women were interviewed about the behavior in this parable independently of the study of ancient stories. They were not surprised by the impulsive behavior of the younger son, the anger of the older one, or the father's eager welcome. To read the parable of the father and two sons with insight from ancient texts corroborated by contemporary women from this very-slow-to-change culture is to place the emphasis in a distinct way. The parable says, "See, God is like this—joyful and ready to celebrate the return of someone deemed lost." The similarity of this parable and the preceding two parables in Luke 15 is in the joy expressed by the one who finds or receives back that which had been lost.

This leaves us with the elder brother who does not exhibit joy when his brother is being feted, but anger. Why is he so angry? There are many possible reasons. Is it because he was not summoned home from the fields to share even in the welcome reception, let alone the party? Is it because he had to ask a slave what was happening, thus diminishing his intimacy with the father and sense of honor and value in the household? Was he angry because the reappearance of his brother might have negative consequences for his own inheritance? The parable itself suggests that the son was angry because he had been and remained—obvious from his presence in the fields that very day—a hard-working contributor to the family's well-being, quite unlike his brother. It seemed to him that his own contribution had been trivialized by the generous acceptance of his less productive, self-centered brother. His honor had been diminished; he had been devalued in the sight of all, including himself.

The elder brother experiences grief, anger, even astonishment, that his own fidelity has gone unrewarded[4] while his brother's mere return has been extravagantly rewarded. As one hears the eldest son's complaint, one harks back to the first parable and to the setting. How and why would there be more joy in heaven over one repentant sinner than over ninety-nine just ones? This statement made and makes no sense in worldly economies, nor would it seem to make sense in a heavenly one where the just are praised (Luke 1:6) and the unjust excluded (Luke 13:27; 16:25-29). The first two parables seem to demean the desire of the Pharisees and scribes to be faithful. One might indeed wonder at such a God who disregarded the very people who strove to serve and remain faithful. Such folks are the very group to which the lost ones are returned. One might likewise wonder at a father who did not show honor to his faithful son. How can joy be compared so that there is more over the returnees than over the ones to whose company they are returned?

The final verses of the parable provide an answer to the narrative audience of verses 1-2 and to the surprised hearers of verse 7—as well as to the elder son. All that the father has belongs also to the elder son, including even the father's presence. Celebration is required because of the younger son's return. The need to celebrate suggests the sadness of time away from the father, the "faithful" one. Joy is intense at return, but in no way diminishes the shared joy that has belonged to the faithful all the while. The parable is about the joy God experiences, rather than God's annoyance, impatience, or judgment, at the return of one of God's lost ones. It is also about the joy in the *shared* relationship with God that is also *shared* among the faithful.

We do not learn in the parable if the younger brother was sincere or manipulative in his repentance. We do not discover whether the elder brother "came to himself" and entered the house to feast in the presence of his father and brother.[5] To enter into the feast requires both men to acknowledge one another as brothers of the same father. Can they do it? We do not know. The open-endedness of this tale allows us, rather, forces us to enter it and imagine the outcomes. It is certainly fair to say that both Jesus and Luke tell these stories with a point that goes beyond entertainment. What does this story have to do with the story of God and humanity as Jesus tells it? Although it is not unusual for characters to pick up this very question after hearing parables in Luke's gospel,[6] no character does that in Luke 15:11-32. The story moves on with a quick shift of audience to the "disciples" in 16:1, and the interpretive task is left to us.

As you will see, through nearly two thousand years of "filling in the gaps," artists have presented us with innumerable possibilities for understanding. Interpretation is shaped by context, just as the original story must be. This volume and the collection of artistic renderings of the parable of the man with two sons will press you to interpret the story, the art work, and finally yourself. Look, listen, and celebrate.

[4] Note that the father does not contradict his claim that not even a young goat had been barbequed for him.

[5] Note that the elder brother denies his relationship to the younger by referring to him as "your son" in conversation with the father (v. 30). The father will not allow this misidentification of relationship: in v. 32, he says, "this brother of yours."

[6] See Luke 8:9; 9:44-45; 10:28-29, (the questioner does finally understand the parable; 12:41; 16:14; 16:31; and the like.

Magdalena Hinedziewicz

Prodigal Son
(2003)

Oil paint on glass
(4 x 5½ ins.)

This image is the only work in the Evenrud collection in which the father is wearing a yamulka.

The Prodigal Son Through the Artist's Eye

by Wilson Yates

The absence of the parables in the art of the church

The Prodigal Son, as a biblical parable and literary work, has been a part of the church's life since its beginnings. But the parable does not appear in the visual arts in any significant fashion until the Reformation. Robin Jensen in her study, *Understanding Early Christian Art,* lifts up the significant images that were most common to the early church: the Good Shepherd, an orant or praying figure, the teacher/philosopher, Jonah, Noah, Adam and Eve, Moses, Abraham and Isaac, Daniel and, from the New Testament, John baptizing Jesus, the raising of Lazarus, the loaves and fishes, the healing of the paralytic, the turning of water into wine, and the woman at the well.[1] Images that would later become the primary subjects of medieval and Renaissance art, such as nativity-related scenes and the passion cycle, were not generally found in the early church. Visual images of the crucifixion, for example, did not appear until the fifth century, and the parables received little attention in art that we can document. Jensen observes, regarding New Testament images, that "while specific healings and miracles appear frequently, other scenes from Jesus' life . . . appear surprisingly late, given their relative popularity in the entire history of Christian art, including representations of the nativity, transfiguration, Last Supper, passion, and resurrection."[2] To this list, one could add the parables and, particularly, the parable of the Prodigal Son.

In the early centuries of the church the visual image was officially both in and out of favor as iconoclast movements developed, waned, and reemerged. An edict from the Synod of Elvira, around 315 C.E., stated, "There should be no pictures in the church building, lest what is worshipped and adored might be painted on the wall."[3] Restrictions, however, loosened as supporters of visual images grew stronger. Pope Gregory's letter on art, which accepted the legitimacy of the arts in the church, was a moment of much import. Around 600 C.E. Gregory wrote, "Pictures are used in the church, in order that those who are ignorant of letters may by merely looking at the walls read there what they are unable to read in books."[4] In 730 an edict from Emperor Leo III appeared opposing the use of images. Still later the second council, held in Nicea in 787, lifted the ban. In 843 Empress Theodora restored the veneration of icons and decreed the icon imperative for Christian worship. With this action the matter was largely settled in the Eastern Church. In the Reformation period we will see both iconoclastic and open positions regarding the use of images.

The church of the first eight centuries, therefore, moved back and forth between periods of uneasiness and prohibition followed by greater acceptance until the ninth century when the use of the visual image in the church—on its walls, in its liturgy, and for its congregants' devotional life—was given official acceptance.

Early visual images

The earliest visual images were fresco wall paintings found in early churches and in the catacombs. The oldest extant Christian church, located in Dura-Europos in Syria and destroyed in 256 C.E., had wall paintings including images of Adam and Eve, the Good Shepherd, Jesus walking on water, the healing of the paralytic, the woman at the well, and a remaining figure of a woman who may have been one of the three Marys.[5] Sculpted stone carvings appeared on sarcophagi—one of the best known is that of Junius Bassus (359 C.E.)—and visual works hung in wall niches, as we see in the catacombs. Mosaics adorned the ceilings, domes, and walls of churches such as the Ravenna churches and tombs to which S. Appolinaire in Classe, San Vitale, and Galla Placidia give full testimony. But the selected biblical images did not include the parables, much less the parable of the Prodigal Son.

[1] Robin Jensen, *Understanding Early Christian Art* (London: Routledge, 2000), p.64-65. See particularly chapter 3, "Pictorial Typologies and Visual Exegesis."

[2] Ibid. See also Jensen's study *Face to Face, Portraits of the Divine in Early Christianity* (Minneapolis: Fortress Press, 2005) for an excellent discussion of early Christian art and the question of how the church treated the matter of imaging the divine.

[3] Wilson Yates, *The Arts in Theological Education* (Atlanta: Scholars Press, 1987), p. 97.

[4] Ibid., p. 100. For a discussion of the iconoclastic theological battles see Leonid Ouspensky, *Theology of the Icon,* (Crestwood, NY: St. Vladimir's Seminary Press: 1992), vol. 1, ch. 8.

[5] Jensen, *Face to Face,* op. cit., and Robert Milburn, *Early Christian Art and Architecture* (Berkeley: University of California Press, 1988), for discussions of the earliest forms of Christian art as well as Dura Europos. See also Graydon F. Snyder, *Ante Pacem, Archaeological Evidence of Church Life Before Constantine* (Macon: Mercer Press, 2003).

[6]See major art history texts such as Frederick Hartt, *Art, A History of Painting, Sculpture, Architecture,* for an easily accessible work that offers illustrations of both early Christian and medieval art with excellent reproductions. Hartt's work includes one of the major early Christian works, the Sarcophagus of Junius Bassus (359 C.E.)—a work with carved scenes drawn from scripture: the sacrifice of Isaac, Peter taken prisoner, Christ enthroned between Peter and Paul, Christ before Pilate, Daniel in the lions' den, and Paul led to martyrdom.

[7] See Francesca Flores D'Arcais, *Giotto* (New York: Abbeville Press, 1995). This study offers excellent reproductions of the cycles and commentary on the frescoes.

The medieval era of the church, stretching roughly from 750 C.E to 1350 C.E., included Carolingian, Ottonian, Byzantine, Romanesque, and Gothic periods of art and the beginning time of the transition to the Renaissance. A rich mixture of art forms emerged in this era, including new forms that were absorbed by the church—such as mystery and morality plays and medieval dance (though they were later excluded from the sanctuary). The extensive development of the visual arts included paintings, frescoes, illuminated manuscripts, stained glass, sculpture, tapestries, mosaics, and church architecture. The subject matter of visual images, however, was limited in large part to scenes related to the nativity (including the annunciation through the flight to Egypt), icons of mother and child, scenes of the baptism of Jesus, events of holy week with a particular focus on the crucifixion, the saints and events in their lives, the hierarchy of Christ as Pantocrator, and the last judgment. There were exceptions—most notably in illuminated manuscripts where there was a more extensive use of biblical images—but, still, few biblical scenes received sustained treatment beyond those related to the nativity, the baptism, and the passion of Christ.

In the late medieval period, from roughly 1250 to 1350 C.E., such artists as Duccio, A. Lorenzetti, Cimabue, and Giotto elaborated traditional biblical subjects with greater attention to narrative and the details of story, but neither they or any other major artists took the parables as their subject.[6] The parables remained outside the artists' canon.

Early Italian Renaissance art, 1350 to 1500 C.E., expanded the artistic canon and offered treatments of nature, historical scenes, secular figures, mythological stories, and ecclesiastical events, but the major focus remained, when treating biblical scenes, the events of the nativity and scenes from the life of Mary, selected scenes from Jesus' public ministry, his baptism, and the passion cycle. Sculpted scenes including major door sculptures, such as those in the baptistery doors in the Cathedral in Florence, and illuminated manuscripts were most apt to treat a wider range of biblical events than any other art of the time; they often drew heavily on Old Testament scenes.

Renaissance artists extended narrative painting and historicized the biblical narratives by placing events in an historical context—usually the period and locale of the artist. Tuscan hills and cities with Renaissance houses, churches, and costumes defined the settings of the paintings from Tuscany. Such was the case for all of the Renaissance artists from both the south and the north; France, Flanders, Holland, Germany became their settings. One could wish that this process of elaborating religious scenes, engaging narrative themes, and locating events within historical contexts, had invited the treatment of the parables, but there was little or no such treatment.

This medieval and Renaissance world reflected an ethos in which events in Mary's life, Jesus' birth, the baptism, the passion, the last judgment, the saints, and significant historical moments in the church's life were the primary religious subjects that the church asked artists to paint. In the medieval period these images, whether treated in Byzantine, Romanesque, or Gothic styles, served to point the Christian, through symbolic participation in the work, to the eternal—to the otherworldly. In Byzantine work there was little or no reference to historical reality or settings such as countryside or city. Our eyes were to be cast heavenward.

From the late medieval period into the early Renaissance—the fourteenth century—one begins to see a transition to a more this-worldly focus where the Spirit of God is seen moving within history. The focus changes from a full vision of the divinity of Christ to a greater recognition of the humanity of Christ, from Christ as the Lord of history to a greater understanding of Jesus relating to the people. In turn, human beings are seen more in relational terms with the implication that God is active in history. Saint Francis (1181-1226) and his form of Christian humanism laid the foundations for this understanding, and such artists as Giotto (1267-1337) brought this historical focus to life in his Assisi and Padua fresco cycles of Saint Francis' life.[7]

The parables and the larger trove of biblical narratives, however, still do not enter the picture, literally or figuratively. They do not do so in the Catholic world until the Counter-Reformation and the Council of Trent (from 1545 until 1563 C.E.)

Finally, in the northern Renaissance and the Reformation of the sixteenth century, biblical material became primary subject matter and the parables, including the parable of the Prodigal Son, entered the canon of subjects. Scripture was central to the Protestant movements and their faith; accordingly, we see among Protestant artists an emerging and finally dominant use of

biblical subjects in hymns, poetry, and the visual arts. The iconoclastic spirit, however, which had woven its way through the history of the church was also given new life by certain of the reformers. In a parallel to the iconoclast movement of the early centuries of the church, concern over idolatry and the fear that artworks might function as graven images flared up. The responses of different Reformation traditions and their theologians were markedly different—ranging from very positive to highly rejective positions.[8] Martin Luther had little trouble with the visual image so long as it spread the Word of God, though music remained his dominant interest among the arts. As he observed, artists could paint on the sides of barns if it spread the Word. The artist Albrecht Dürer, while he did not paint on the sides of barns, reflected the Protestant spirit of Luther in his work as an artist. Luther responded to the fear set forth by some Protestants regarding the concern over idolatry by stating: "I suppose there is nobody, or certainly very few, who do not understand that yonder crucifix is not my God, for my God is in heaven, but that this is simply a sign."[9]

Andreas von Karlstadt, on the other hand, mounted a sharply etched iconoclastic response to Luther's openness to visual images and set forth one of the major Protestant objections to the use of images. Calvin was uneasy with visual images in the church because of their potential for becoming graven images, though historical scenes were acceptable and could be instructive. It is somewhat paradoxical that the Calvinist ethos in Holland and Rembrandt's own affinity for Dutch Calvinism produced one of the greatest of western artists. But Calvinist thought down through the Puritans never easily embraced the visual arts. In the case of Zwingli there was rather strict prohibition against not only the visual image but against musical instruments and hymn singing as well. Nonetheless, in the Left Wing of the Reformation, and particularly in the tradition of Menno Simon, artists readily provided images. For the Mennonites, works were portrayed in the book *Martyrs Mirror* (printed in 1660 and reissued regularly: 1668, 1685). *Martyrs Mirror* presented the persecution of Christians by secular rulers, Roman Catholics, Lutherans, and Calvinists—including the special history of Anabaptist persecution. Jan Luyken's 104 copper plate etchings tell the story in powerful fashion; the etchings represent an important contribution to Reformation art.

So the Reformation response to the visual arts was mixed, but the visual expression of biblical narratives emerged with great power and influence as a means of proclaiming and experiencing the Christian message.

The church's art and its inclusion of the Prodigal Son

The Reformation focus on the authority of scripture—in Luther's case *sola scriptura*—led to a weaving of scripture throughout the Christian experience. Preaching and liturgy were turned towards scripture, and Christian piety and the moral life were to be shaped by scripture. This expectation was given great impetus with the development of the printing press which led to the dissemination of the Bible and permitted scripture reading to become a pivotal act in deepening and living out one's faith.

In the arts this emphasis on the authority of scripture was reflected in the use of biblical narrative, images, metaphors, and symbols as primary subject matter. While subjects came from both the Old and New Testaments, the gospel stories, the baptism of Jesus, nativity scenes, and the passion became common sources of subject matter. The Evenrud collection of the art of the Prodigal Son provides work from a representative number of such artists and moves us into the seventeenth and eighteenth centuries.

Why artists chose the Prodigal Son as subject matter would obviously vary from artist to artist. Emotional affinity, personal piety, financial arrangements, social recognition, donor expectations—each played a role. But there were also factors more related to the subject itself. I want to highlight three: the historicizing of the Christian faith, the dramatic character of the parables, and the rich possibilities for interpretation.[10]

Historicizing the Christian faith and the role of the parable

I have spoken of the shift in which the church took into greater account the human drama and the world in which it was being played out. This movement affected the style and subject of art. In the Renaissance, this change of direction was fueled by the recovery of Greek philosophy, the rise of science, and the shift of theology to a more this-worldly focus on the life of faith.

In the Reformation, the presence of God to the faithful and the sense of Christ working in human history was accentuated even more. The focus on

[8] See Carl C. Christensen, *Art and the Reformation in Germany* (Athens, OH: University of Ohio, 1979) for an excellent discussion of Luther and Andreas von Karlstadt. See also John Cook, "Picturing Theology: Martin Luther and Lucas Cranach," in *Art and Religion: Faith, Form and Reform, 1984 Paine Lectures in Religion* (Columbia, MO: University of Missouri, 1986). ch. 2; George Heyer, *Signs of Our Times* (Grand Rapids: Eerdmans, 1980) for a consideration of John Calvin; The Herald Press English translation edition of *Martyrs Mirror* edited by Robert Kreider; John S. Oyer and Robert S. Kreider, *Mirror of the Martyrs* (Intercourse, PA: Good Books, 1999), for a discussion of this text and the reproduction of the 104 Luyken copper plate etchings; and John Dillenberger, *Images and Relics, Theological Perceptions and Visual Images in Sixteenth-Century Europe* (New York: Oxford Press, 1999). Dillenberger's study offers an exceptional analysis of theological perspectives on the arts in both the Continental and English Reformations.

[9] Christensen, ibid., p. 56.

the individual, the centrality of justification and grace through a person's relationship to God, the assumption that all Christians had a calling to live a disciplined life of religious and moral response to the world, and the importance of the Christian's direct relationship to God as a part of the individual's religious pilgrimage—all engaged the Christian as they proceeded on this pilgrimage.

Using the parables and scripture generally for both understanding and forming a life of faith fit well into the frame of Protestant theologies. The parables, more than many other biblical narratives, provided expressions of human experience and faith within history. The Christian could see both what and how Jesus taught, how God offered the individual justifying grace, and what manner of human response was possible in an actual moment of history. It followed, therefore, that artists treating religious subjects turned readily to scripture and the parables, since this is where the church and its theology focused.

The parable offers the artist dramatic and complex scenes

This parable has a particular fascination for artists because its story is multi-layered and complex. Each of its five scenes has dramatic—even theatrical—possibilities that, as storylines, offer powerful explorations of our relationship to God. One only need note the scenes to see how.[11] Scene one opens with the younger of two sons seeking to take his inheritance, leave the family, and embark on an independent life (Luke 15: 11-12). Scene two shows the son living high off his inheritance and then falling into misery, hunger, and destitution (verses 13-16). Artists have made much of prostitutes and the pigs as symbols of his fallen condition; he is often pictured in rags without hope—a person in crisis. At other times the scene is treated with a touch of whimsy, if not ridicule, often manifest on the face of the pigs. Scene three (verses 17-20) finds the son sorting through what to do. Theologians and artists treat in different ways his decision to return home, confess his sins, and seek acceptance. Some have regarded his actions as a simple scheme to get himself out of a run of bad luck. He is, after all, seemingly weighing what will work to his advantage in his encounter with his father. Others accept his decision as the first step towards repentance; they maintain that, while there is a calculation in his reasoning, he is also aware of his moral

and familial failure at some personal level. Still other interpreters point out the ambiguity of his actions and caution that finally we cannot get inside the figure fully enough to understand the nature of his motives; indeed, even he cannot grasp the ambiguity of his own thought and action. Scene four (verses 20-24) is the return with the father running out to kiss and embrace the son with expressions of joy and compassion, the son confessing to his father and entering the family setting. Some artists treat this action by focusing on the father with the son's back to the viewer, while others allow us to see both figures and their faces as they embrace each other. The father calls the servants to kill a fatted calf, prepare a feast and bring a robe, a ring, and shoes that all might celebrate the return. The son who was lost has been found.

Scene five (verses 25-32) is about the older son's response. He returns from the field to discover the celebration and must ask a servant what is happening. He is told of the brother's return and the father's joyful response. The older son's response is anger and hurt; consequently, he refuses to join in the feasting and celebration. His father comes out and they speak. The son responds to the father by speaking of his loyalty and obedience but observes that such virtues have never merited the killing of a fatted calf or a celebration such as this. The last words in the scene are those of the father who tells him that he is with him always and all that is his is his son's as well. They must celebrate, for the brother who was lost has been found, was dead is now alive again.

Sarah Henrich, whose essay on this parable is in this volume, makes the point that the father does not "allow the elder son to distance himself from the younger one." In response to his older son, who at the beginning of the conversation has in anger called his brother "this son of yours," the father speaks of "this brother of yours" and, as Henrich states, "implies that the joy and value in one being found, belong to the whole family."[12] That artists have seldom treated this scene is strange given its dramatic possibilities and the very human responses that one might argue are necessary if the full meaning of the parable is to be understood. (The older son is occasionally treated as part of the fourth scene where he appears anguished at God's reception of the Prodigal Son. Jan Shoger's 1959 picture (page 95) in this volume offers us a unique image where the older son takes center stage).

10 See Wilson Yates, chapter IV, "The Case for Integration" in *The Arts in Theological Education* (Atlanta: Scholars Press, 1987), where nine different roles the arts play in the life of the church are spelled out. In an article entitled "The Intersection of Art and Religion," in *ARTS, The Arts in Religious and Theological Studies*, vol. 10, no.1, 1998, there is an article by the author that explores five primary roles including the three above as well as the role of the arts in worship and the prophetic role of art.
11 Sarah Henrich in her essay in this volume, "Parable of Father and Two Sons," offers a rich explication of the five scenes of the parable and raises crucial questions of interpretation.
12 Henrich, ibid., p. 25.

The emotions in the parable range from happiness to misery, from bewilderment to anger, from compassion to joy. The theological themes are equally rich: we glimpse the character of God, and we encounter the human need for love and justice, for repentance and forgiveness, and the reality of sin and grace, reconciliation and celebration. Dramatic elements of order and conflict, loss and recovery, rejection and acceptance are here, as are unresolved questions that act as counterpoint to what appears to be happening. The scenes themselves move from the high points of freedom and adventure to downfall and despair. Love permeates the father's response to the returned son, yet seems to elude the elder son's experience. The denouement closes the lines on stage, but does so in such a fashion that the viewer/listener/observer is left with an unsettled question of why the parable ends as it does.

It is a dramatic parable that invites dramatic presentation on canvas, panel, and paper. The church had made the narrative of scripture central to faith, and artists extended their reach to the portrayal of parables. In so doing, they moved beyond the traditionally painted subjects and opened up a new world of images to nurture the faith of Christians.

The parable offers a richness of interpretive possibilities

When artists approached the parable they found that the story not only eschewed a single interpretation, but was complex enough to invite a range of interpretations partially determined by the particular scene or scenes on which the artist focused. The artist did not view the parable as a fable that would have suggested a rather obvious conclusion regarding its meaning. Its plot was not simple, as we have observed in the discussion of the scenes, and it invited artists to embellish the story with figures beyond those in the text. Indeed, artists' treatments have included servants, family members, friends, laborers, servants, clergy, townspeople, prostitutes, money changers, innkeepers, and party makers. Furthermore, artists have often presented only one scene, as if the message of the complex story can be captured by a single incident. Images of the father receiving the returning son are the most common. What is arguably the greatest of the Prodigal paintings, Rembrandt's *Return of the Prodigal Son* (in the Hermitage in St. Petersburg), reinforces the return as iconic for artists' treatments of the story. (Rembrandt does not show the son's face in the Hermitage painting. However, the etching in the Evenrud collection [page 129] shows the faces of both the father and the returning son.)

Certainly the dominant theological meaning of the parable concerns God's forgiveness. But throughout the history of artistic representations of the parable, the son's "fall" becomes paradigmatic and pigs and prostitutes vie for dramatic attention. Furthermore, the first scene has its share of artistic treatments with varying presentations of the younger son as innocent, as naïve, as self-centered, as adventurous.[13]

Some artists have painted the scenes in a series of works as in the case of James Mesplé and James Tissot, or, as in the case of Marten de Vos, put four scenes in one picture. But whether we view a series or an artist's choice of a single scene or a portrayal of all scenes in one scene, a theological interpretation is present in the work itself. The artists provide us a *visual theology* of the story. With the subtle marks of pen and ink, brush as well as etchings, and later lithographs, artists offer their theological statements in the way they create the images and give them form and expression. This volume—a testimony to Jerry Evenrud who has spent a lifetime creating this collection—has taken fifty-two works and allowed us to see what the artists interpreted as the theological crux of the narrative.

An important example of these varied interpretations is brought to light by Doug Adams in his essay, "Changing Perceptions of Jesus' Parable through Art History: Polyvalency in Paint." Adams lifts up in excellent fashion the contrasting Protestant and Roman Catholic interpretations of the Prodigal Son in his analysis of Rembrandt's painting (1668-69) and Murillo's painting (1667-70) both titled *The Return of the Prodigal*. Rembrandt, who lived in a Dutch Calvinist ethos, and Murillo, who lived in Roman Catholic Spain, each accented their own religious worlds' understanding of forgiveness. The sharpest difference Adams finds in Rembrandt's returning Prodigal is the absence of repentance—which is central in Murillo's work. Rembrandt's focus reflects a Protestant view of God as one who receives back the lost child unconditionally—quite apart from repentance. As Adams writes:

> Rembrandt portrays the Prodigal Son as undeserving and unrepentant, and as deceitful as Jacob when he knelt before his

[13] See William H. Halewood, *Six Subjects of Reformation Art: A preface to Rembrandt* (Toronto: University of Toronto Press, 1982) Chapter 4, "Prodigal Son"; Hidde Hoekstra, *Rembrandt and the Bible: Stories from the Old and New Testament* (Weert, Netherlands: Magna Books, 1990); Gary Schwartz, ed., *The Complete Etchings of Rembrandt* (New York: Dover, 1994); Arthur Wheelock, Jr., *Rembrandt's Late Religious Portraits* (Chicago: University of Chicago, 2005), for discussions of Rembrandt and his treatment of biblical imagery.

father. . . . Rembrandt emphasized the Reformation insight that God's acceptance of us is not deserved by any merit of ours, but is a gift of God's grace and God's faith in us—however unjustified we are by our own actions or unfaithfulness. Justification by faith through grace does not refer to our faith, but rather the faith that God has and that Christ has in God.[14]

In contrast to Protestant theology, with its focus on the father as symbolic of God, Catholic thought focused on the son and the son's repentance. "A portrayal of him as genuinely repentant was a way to encourage the sacrament of penance, a sacrament the Protestants disputed."[15] In Rembrandt we have the father facing the viewer with the son's head only partially visible. The accent is on the father's act of forgiveness, not on repentance. In Murillo we have a full profile of the son with the father's gaze directing us to the repentant son. A small dog, often used as a symbol of faith, is looking up in excitement at the son. Surrounding the father and the son are joyful people preparing for the feast. The scene suggests that the son has returned repentant and that repentance leads to the father's forgiveness.

In this present volume of works, both Protestant and Roman Catholic theological emphases are manifest in the dramatic scenes the artists choose to treat. Works that focus on the father's acceptance and forgiveness of the son apart from whether repentance or deep self-awareness by the son is expressed offer a more Protestant perspective; this is evident in the case of twentieth-century works by Sadao Watanabe (1983) and Sybil Andrews (1939). Works that provide strong images of the son coming to some sense of his own need for repentance reflect a more Roman Catholic perspective. Jerome Nadel's work published in 1595 after his death provides a good Counter-reformation interpretation as does Adolphe Marie Timothée Beaufrère's study from 1921.

When we move beyond the sixteenth and seventeenth centuries, there emerges a broader treatment of the Prodigal. The personal interpretation of the artist comes more into play. The son's fall into depravity is treated whimsically as well as seriously; the settings are painted to suggest an everydayness as well as more dramatic backgrounds reflecting the drama of the scenes. Some works made the parable into a morality tale of God and the question of good behavior; others pointed the viewer to the character of God's forgiveness.

By the nineteenth and twentieth centuries, the concept of the Prodigal Son was embedded in western culture. To refer to the Prodigal Son—even in a secular setting—communicated to all present. The sons and the father became cultural points of reference for people in general. Francis Bacon, the English twentieth-century artist, was once asked why he used the crucifixion in his works when he was far removed from any relationship to Christianity; indeed, he could be antagonistic towards it. Bacon responded by saying that the crucifixion has become in western culture an "armature of feeling" that can be used without necessary reference to its specific religious context or meaning. In certain respects, the Prodigal Son has likewise become an "armature of feeling" in culture generally; it is used to remind us of or point to a certain archetypal experience. We immediately recognize it as a religious parable in works that bear profound meaning such as Prokofiev's Fourth Symphony and Ballet, *The Prodigal Ballet in Three Scenes;* Benjamin Britten's choral work, *The Prodigal Son, A Parable for Church Performance*; and Samo Hung's film, *Prodigal Son*. It also has a cultural meaning when it is used to describe disgraced sports stars returning to the team, the name for a blog, the title for an episode of *Miami Vice*, the name for a bar and grill in Chicago, and the title of a Dean Koontz novel that treats the Frankenstein theme.

But if such latter uses in relative degree distance themselves from religious meanings, they retain a glimpse of the seriousness of the claim of the parable on us. The name is treated with irony, humor, and whimsy, to refer to a son who left the family and now returns, after having dissipated his life, in the hope of being forgiven and accepted back into the family. (In this collection there is reference to some of the disparate uses the term has accrued in addition to the explicitly religious ones. See pages 173-178.)

The last five hundred years have left a body of work that present the parable as an "armature of feeling" for the creation of serious and profound interpretations and for references that maintain only a suggestive relationship.

Art of the parable and the Christian's response

The arts in the life of the church can engage and challenge, nurture and deepen the Christian's religious life. This is true of the artists' renditions of the Prodigal Son.

[14] Doug Adams, "Changing Perceptions of Jesus' Parable through Art History: Polyvalency in Paint," in Ena Giurescu Heller, ed., *Reluctant Partners, Art and Religion in Dialogue* (New York: American Bible Society, 2004), p. 76. See also Adams' essay on "Changing Patterns and Interpretations of Parables in Art" in Kimberly Vrudny and Wilson Yates, eds., *Arts, Theology, and the Church, New Intersections* (Cleveland: Pilgrim Press, 2005) for an elaboration of his view of the parables in art.

[15] Ibid.

There are a number of primary ways that the arts can speak to the church. I want here, to note three with reference to this parable. Art can raise existential questions that call us into religious explorations of the meaning of our lives and faith; it can educate us to the history of the Christian community and the church's understanding of its own scriptures; and it can be sacramental in our lives, that is, call us onto holy ground and become a means of grace.

Existential questions

Art can pose questions about the meaning of our life and our relationship to God, our destiny, our need for reconciliation and forgiveness, our participation in human sinfulness and the need for repentance. Our entrance into the story through the work's images and the artist's interpretation will vary from artist to artist. The parable, as I have noted, is made up of brief scenes with a few specific actions on the part of principal figures, but they leave open the possibility of adding actions between the scenes or in the scenes— of filling out the story with gestures, expressions, people who are not in the text—all of which shape the artist's and the viewer's interpretation and the religious questions the work raises. As Sarah Henrich suggests, artists can "fill in the gaps." They can and often do elaborate and embellish the scenes, or in the case of modern artists, offer simple lines and abstract portrayals that reduce the actions to core gestures. We can see this in a number of works in this collection. In nineteenth-century works we see elaborate detail and the addition of many more figures than the text includes. In the case of Lutz Haufschild, we see the son's departure expressed in only a few gestures. Each artwork poses its own questions for us. In certain works the focus is on the nature and character of God's forgiveness and how we are to open ourselves to that forgiveness. In other works the exploration is more about the human condition of the Prodigal and the morally ambiguous character of decision-making. Still other works probe the interplay of alienation and reconciliation. However artists portray the scene, they provide us a rich set of questions to enter into and engage as we seek understanding.

Insights into historical understandings of the church

We have already noted one theological issue that emerged in the sixteenth century—that of repentance and forgiveness and how Protestant and Roman Catholic artists presented their traditions' different perspectives.

Another historical and theological example is related to artists who include additional figures at the scene. In some works the mother is present. In other works, at the moment when the father receives back the son, there are figures in the background, one of whom might be the brother of the Prodigal. Rembrandt may be doing this in his large canvas, *The Return of the Prodigal,* where individuals are gathered a short distance from the father. Most commonly, however, the background figures remain ambiguous. This treatment of the parable introduces an important historical question. Did the artists' inclusion of the family and community reflect only their peculiar interpretation or did it reflect the understanding that the church, itself, had of the parable? (Here the exploration of sermons, hymns, and poetry would be in order to determine whether the church's treatment of the parable was simply being corroborated by the artist's work.) It is also significant, if we are to use artistic interpretation to understand the church's past interpretations, to note what is not treated. Where artists treat a range of scenes, the last scene with the older son's encounter with his father is routinely ignored. (I have mentioned this lacuna before.) The historical question raised here is whether the artists' tendency to ignore the last scene was actually reflecting the church's tendency to ignore the last scene, and, subsequently, its potential theological significance for understanding the story as a whole.

Sarah Henrich in her contemporary interpretation of the parable raises questions about the older son in an illuminating fashion and in so doing gives richness to the figure and his importance for the story as a whole. She does what the artist might have done. She fills in "the gap." She invites us to explore the brother's situation and invites us into the scene's complexity.

But artists embellish the story at other points. There is an amazingly diverse treatment of the Prodigal's indulgence of himself and his own "fall." For dozens of artists, of whom selected ones are part of this book's collection, the pigs have rooted their way to center stage and the prostitutes have little resistance in practicing their trade. The Prodigal's religion would not have allowed him to deal with pigs, for pork was forbidden. Nor would he have been allowed to visit prostitutes. Only when the older brother enters the story do we hear that the younger brother had been with harlots. How the older brother would have known this is unclear. Was it simply a foregone conclusion in the culture of the time that a young man who left home, wasted his money in frivolity, and ended up destitute had been with prostitutes? Or did the older brother have knowledge along the way about the younger brother's escapades?

The artists approach the matter as settled. If one can ask how the older brother knows, the dancing pens of the artists tell us that this was the fact of the case and then they show us in what fashion it took place. In eighteenth- and nineteenth-century works, artists who portrayed the dreaded marks of syphilis lent an even more tragic dimension to the story. Artists provide scenes of the texts that fit their time and in so doing allow us to enter into an understanding of how their time perceived the scenes.

Sacramental possibilities

An artwork may become a means through which truth and grace are mediated. A human construct that is profane in form, art may become that through which we experience the holy, through which we glimpse the face of God. Again and again a work of art is the burning bush that turns common ground into sacred ground and when it does so our spirituality is nurtured. We do not control the possibility of art becoming sacramental, for grace is a gift of God that we receive in a moment of response. But when it occurs we do know God.

In the artistic representations of the parable we encounter the deepest of human matters: the questions of freedom and our destiny as human beings; the power of betrayal by a son of his father and the father's hopes for him; the shape of sin and our ambiguous response to it; the need for repentance and forgiveness. We encounter a God whose love never forsakes us; the human experience of moving in a labyrinth of anger, jealousy, and a sense of injustice; and moments of forgiveness and acceptance, moments of grace by living through what the artist presents. We enter into and become the son who is forgiven; we experience the father who forgives.

With the drawings of the pen, the stroke of the brush, an artwork may well pull us into a full awareness of repentance and forgiveness in our own lives. When it does, the work has entered our imagination and become a part of us. It is there as the assurance of grace that whoever we are in the drama at any given moment we still rest within the arms of God. We still encounter God's Spirit offering us the mysterious and amazing assurance that we are never forsaken.

An artwork of the parable may, indeed, invite us onto holy ground where we have never been.

No One Gave Him Anything

by David Morgan

"And he would gladly have fed on the pods that the swine ate; and no one gave him anything" (Luke 15:16).

The experience of repentance is a corporeal one, that is, it is one we feel in our bodies. We know repentance with our skin, with our lungs, with the muscles that stretch across our chest. Forgiveness is an explosion, a burst of light, a radiant shout of joy that moves in visceral waves of warmth.

But to know repentance and forgiveness, we first must experience despair and abandon. I suppose this is because we refuse to recognize the offer of forgiveness until we have no alternative, no way to extricate ourselves from the mess we make of our lives. Forgiveness means nothing until you have a debt held against you, until you feel the world closing about you.

The revelation that forgiveness brings is that you are not alone, that as hard as you try, you cannot make yourself alone. Your father and your mother, your brothers and sisters, your friends, and God await you. You may not know it. You may choose to ignore it. But their presence is a steadfast one.

And they may never be so close to you as when you are mired down in the pigsty of your despair. Look closely. They are a word away. But you may not see them until your soul has emptied itself entirely into the darkness of the hour.

At that moment a radical new vision of the world unfolds before you. Everything is bathed in a new light, the light of a soul reconciled to the family he or she had abandoned but has now rejoined.

I have sought to visualize this bottoming out in the parable of the Prodigal Son. At the very depth of his despair, when "no one gave him anything," when he realized how terribly alone he was, he turned to recognize the mercy of his father and went home. The fall from grace was reversed, and the very universe changed for him.

no one gave him anything

David Morgan

"No one gave him anything" (1983)

Photogravure of a collage (16½ x 21 ins.)

From "Seed from the Sower," Responses to the Parables of Jesus, Concordia College, Seward, Nebraska, 1983

Used by permission of the artist

Part 2

Commentaries on Selected Works

Leaving home . . . is a denial of the spiritual reality that I belong to God with every part of my being, that God holds me safe in an eternal embrace, that I am indeed carved in the palms of God's hands and hidden in their shadows. Leaving home means ignoring the truth that God had "fashioned me in secret, moulded me in the depths of the earth, and knitted me together in my mother's womb." Leaving home is living as though I do not yet have a home and must look far and wide to find one. . . .

I am touching here the mystery that Jesus himself became the Prodigal Son for our sake. He had left the house of his heavenly Father, came to a foreign country, gave away all that he had, and returned through his cross to his Father's home . . . as an obedient son.

Henry Nouwen, *The Return of the Prodigal Son*
(New York: Image Books, 1994), pp. 37, 55

Facing page: August-Louis Lepere, *The Prodigal Son* (see also page 60-61)

Departure, Debauchery, Degradation

The foolish son asks for his money

Certain games from childhood have a way of establishing playful patterns that carry over into adult life. One of these youthful exercises consists of comparing and contrasting two similar pictures: what are the similarities, what are the difference between them? This pair of German lithographs from the nineteenth century invites the adult viewer to enter into the game, for they are about the same size and they portray the same subject. In each we see a domestic drama which, by its title, tells us that the Prodigal, having received his inheritance, is in the process of leaving home. Both scenes indicate this imminent departure by the piles of luggage, the footman and waiting coach, and the gestures that move the interior action toward open space.

Aside from these and other superficial similarities, which make the game enjoyable, significant differences prevail. In one (dated 1830-1840, henceforth called Departure A), the father in his olive brown robe stands and gestures in a left-handed kind of blessing. In the other print (dated 1896, Departure B) the father is seated and dressed in a period day suit; he gestures with his left hand, palm upwards (a sign of supplication rather than blessing). In Departure A the bearded older brother stands off to the side and looks on with a hooded expression, a little like a villain in a Victorian melodrama. In Departure B the beardless brother (who actually looks younger than the departing sibling) affects a more open, wide-eyed look.

Each print incorporates descriptions in two or more languages that tell what is going on—each description being a liberal paraphrase of the initial part of the Lukan story, from chapter 15, verses 11-13a. One of the explanations (from the French at the bottom of Departure A) reads: "A father had two sons, of which the younger asked for his maternal inheritance. In spite of sage advice from his father, the son persisted in his foolish plan. The family could foresee the unhappiness that the ungrateful son would encounter. The broken-hearted father gave the son his inheritance, and he departed."

This information both interprets and elaborates the original story. For one thing, Luke says nothing about a *maternal* inheritance. There is no mention of the father offering sage advice, though we might suppose he had some to give. Future misfortune to the son may be inferred, but it is not mentioned at this point in the parable. And, while the father may have been broken-hearted, that condition is not noted in the Bible story either.

The emotional state of the father, mentioned in the lithographic text, is quite apparently belied in the picture itself (the text in Departure B speaks of "the tears of the old man"). Yet, in neither print—even under inspection with a magnifying glass—can we see any sign of broken-hearted tears. The dignified father, in both prints, appears calm, collected, and dry-eyed. The son, who looks more as if he is packed to go off to college or to music camp, is sent off with a composed farewell. On the whole, these portrayals have more the feel of a scene from a novel like *Buddenbrooks* than the foreboding approach of *Sturm und Drang*. Perhaps if we had access to other scenes from the series—if they existed—we could get a better sense of the whole, for here we see only in part.

Because we do know the rest of story, however, we may well infer the underlying emotions in this drawing room departure. Both lithographs make it clear that something significant is happening in the lives of these three contained characters. They are well dressed and well mannered; but a break in their family structure is in fact taking place. Even if the son *were* only going off to college, he would come back a changed man. All departures contain the possibility of changed condition, even heartbreak. As it is, we look at these prints on their own terms and know that the youth is leaving to embrace immediate profligacy and eventual ruination. In that sense we, like this prosperous bourgeois family, can foresee the unhappiness that the ungrateful son will encounter. We watch the son now depart in peace; but we know the Prodigal will eventually return, his life in pieces.

L'enfant prodigue reçoit son héritage.

Der verlorene Sohn erhält sein Erbtheil.

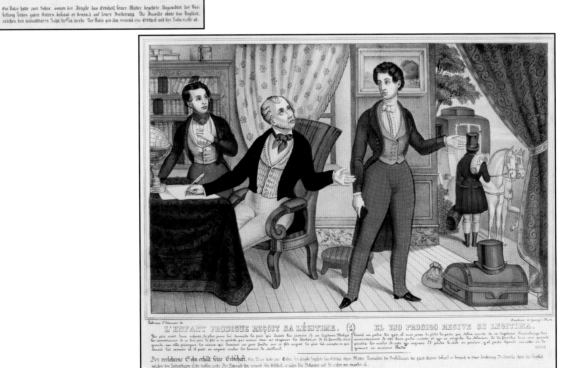

L'ENFANT PRODIGUE REÇOIT SA LÉGITIME. EL HIO PRODIGO RESIVE SU LEGITIMA.

Der verlorene Sohn erhält seine Erbschaft.

1 A–B

Anonymous German

Two colored lithographs

A (left)

L'enfant Prodigue reçoit son heritage
(The Prodigal receives his inheritance)
(1830-1840)

Executed by Georg Balthasar Probst; published by the Brothers Wentzel at Wissembourg
(12 x 9½ ins.)

B (right)

L'enfant Prodigue reçoit sa légitime
(The Prodigal receives his legacy)
(1896)

Dembour et Gangel, Vienna
(12 x 9½ ins.)

The Prodigal says goodbye

Ambiguity can be disconcerting for people who prefer things straight and simple in their lives. Viewers of art with a low threshold for ambiguity might be inclined to look at this painting of the Prodigal Son by Lutz Haufschild (b. 1943) and be content to view the father on the left addressing his wayward son. Puzzled, perhaps, by the coloration and lack of physical detail, they might nonetheless see a scene of homecoming in which the two tall figures clasp hands in welcome.

Other viewers, however, might regard this work in a more equivocal way. They might look at this work and raise some questions. How can we be sure, they might ask, that the father is the figure on the left? Perhaps the father is the one on the right, with open lips expressing welcome to the returning son. The blue-headed father-figure could be registering surprise (maybe even mild rebuke) to the marginally taller son on the left. Could it be that the taller, browner figure has his lips compressed in an adolescent, pouty manner?

During the time this work was exhibited at a seminary, theological students were inclined to pause, look, and revel in its perceived ambiguity. Some, noting that the title is simply *The Prodigal Son*, speculated that perhaps it is a scene of departure rather than return. After all, one figure could be placing inheritance currency in the other figure's hand preparatory to his leaving. It could be, therefore, that the son on the right has his mouth open to say "Thanks, Dad; see you later." Or, upon further reflection, the son could be the closed-mouthed one on the left, shaking hands with his father who utters a departing sigh: "Safe journey, son; I truly hope that I *will* see you later."

One viewer, having speculated on who was doing and saying what in the scene, offered an observation on the white space between the two figures. Taking a cue from one of the great textbook optical illusions, this observer concentrated on the shaft of white as it moves upward to a complex and open-ended curvature at the top. Whereupon this viewer reported that he saw a large vertical candlestick or an elongated goblet with its base extending below the blue horizontals near the bottom. This thoughtful observer proceeded to interpret that white space symbolically, suggesting that light and/or drink might well accompany the festivity of return—or even, come to think of it, the melancholy of departure.

Whether Lutz Haufschild intended this range of ambiguity is uncertain and, in any case, cannot be ascertained. The painting is an anomaly for him, for Haufschild is known as a sculptor and glass artist. Born in Germany, he is now a highly respected Canadian artist who has completed over 200 commissions in Canada, Europe, India, Japan, and the United States. His work invites viewers to contemplate what is going on aesthetically. Haufschild wants his work to have a visual impact that respects rather than assaults the viewer. Such an artistic invitation seems to allow for both certainty and ambiguity in perception and interpretation.

One of Haufschild's most impressive works is a 48-foot by 18-foot glass wall at the Skydome in Toronto. Created in 1989, it is called *Tribute to Baseball*. A work that sparkles in the light, it catches frozen moments of the game's grace and form, the perceived essence of baseball. In accepting and executing the work Haufschild acknowledged that baseball fans needed art to which they could relate.

Of lesser dimension (25 inches wide and 59 inches high) *The Prodigal Son* is still an imposing work, depicting the grace and form of a different kind of game, that of parable. Because of its almost life-size height, it must be viewed by looking *up* at the figures who wear coats of many colors. Nonetheless, whatever the level of certainty or ambiguity in the scene, we are drawn into their relationship. Whether they are taking leave or coming home, they are bonded, something we can detect in their facial profiles and in the touching of their hands.

It may not be easy—or possible—to resolve what is happening between the two figures (and in the defined white space between them); but we can tell that things are more complex than they appear on the surface. This complexity (and the attendant ambiguity) is consistent with what Haufschild once articulated. "In art, like in life," he said, "rarely do good things come easily. But things that are well-cared for, and nurtured like one nurtures children, well, like those well-nurtured children, they are sources of endless joy. What could be more rewarding!" To contemplate and speculate on this prodigal work: What could be more rewarding?

2

Lutz Haufschild

The Prodigal Son
(1997)

Oil on canvas.
(25 x 59 ins.)

The Prodigal departs jauntily

Ride a Cockhorse to Banbury Cross
To see a fine lady upon a white horse.
With rings on her fingers and bells on her toes
She shall have music wherever she goes.

In this nursery rhyme we travel to see Queen Elizabeth of England (the fine lady) who herself had ridden to Banbury on a white horse to see the huge stone cross recently erected there. Her fine jewelry, of course, was the rings on her fingers, while her curved slippers would be ornamented with little musical bells. Since Banbury was atop a very steep hill, we would need the services of a huge stallion (a cockhorse) to climb the slope.

Something of the cantering rhythm of the nursery rhyme is suggested by the departure of the Prodigal Son in this painting by Birgitta Hedengren (b. 1947). Erect in the saddle and dressed in his finest traveling clothes, the jaunty youth might be riding a prancing Swedish cockhorse as he leaves home to make his way in the world. We know, however, that the fine lady (or ladies) he will eventually encounter will be from a much earthier social stratum than the queen. These ladies will meet him, treat him, and finally deplete him.

Those eventualities, however, are beyond the margins of the picture. In this scene we see him confidently set out, his mother and father gamely waving their left arms in farewell. We may deduce an undertone of sadness; but we discern on the surface a sunny scene. Arcs of green explode like vegetal fireworks from the four-story house. Kites of flowers soar in the sky. Puffs of white and roundels of red enframe the scene above and below like well-wishing clouds and flowers. And, like a supertitle at the opera, the Swedish text invokes the Luke 15 text: "The Prodigal Son goes to the far country."

The fanciful quality of the scene is influenced by the national folk art style of Sweden called *Dalamälning*. Originally this style of art grew out of a simple desire to decorate the homes of townspeople where there was little light and plenty of draft. Artisans painted colorful works on canvas to hide the soot and damaged walls, particularly on special occasions. In time the rolled canvases were replaced by mounted boards that served both to insulate and decorate. The *Dalamälning* style became so popular that it was used to paint furniture and decorative objects like cabinets, doors, and wooden horses. Eventually, in a bit of artistic irony, this humble style of painting became popular with the wealthy who wanted their houses festooned in this fashion.

Hedengren adopts this folk art style in her depiction of the prodigal's departure. In the fashion of *Dalamälning* artists, she paints a biblical scene with the characters, one of whom rides a colorful horse, dressed in seventeenth- and eighteenth-century Swedish dress. Floating in the air are kurbit leaves— a stylized cucumber leaf—that spring out of rooftops, rise over the horse, and even burst out of nowhere.

In the company of floating floral arrays, the kurbit leaf has a symbolic meaning. Some Swedish art historians claim that the kurbit represents the gourd vine God provided to shelter Jonah (in Jonah 4) while the disgruntled prophet was resting and grousing outside of Nineveh. The association of the kurbit, the prophet, and the Prodigal in this particular painting is felicitous, for Jonah, like the son, went off to a far country and there found adventure. Bright and happy coloration, of course, masks the more serious business of proclamation (for Jonah) and departure (for the son).

The creamy white background, the floating green and red shapes, and the towering house give an airy, breathy quality to the scene. The cocksure and rosy-cheeked son on his prancing horse sets out on his journey. Wedged between his waving parents and a huge leaning flower, he jauntily sets out wearing white breeches, dark coat, and top hat. The horse seems to be on parade with two legs poised in the air; its darting eye and upturned mouth are a horsy parallel to the confidence displayed by the son. The plethora of kurbit leaves and flowers intimate the kind of dazzle we customarily associate with festive parades.

Our eye may be diverted by the sparkle; but our mind's eye might be directed to the more somber side of the story. Departures are always mixed occasions, often containing some degree of wistfulness and sorrow. In the case of the Prodigal Son, we know that he is riding his cockhorse in the direction of profligacy and humiliation; whores and pigs will have their way with him. We anticipate that much later, sobered and wiser, he will make his way back to home and family. At that point he is likely to be horseless, hatless, and feckless. With luck, though, he might also find himself once again surrounded by floating kurbits, raging floral arrays, and embracing love.

Den förlorade sonen reser bort i främmande land. Luk.15.

3

Birgitta Hedengren

The Prodigal Son Leaves Home

(1997)

Oil on canvas in the manner of traditional Swedish Dala painting (35 x 42 ins.)

The Prodigal loses his purse

In the mind's eye (though certainly not in reality) we like and admire the figure of Charles Dickens's genial pickpocket, the Artful Dodger. In the novel *Oliver Twist*, the young scamp was one of Fagin's most apt pupils, having successfully been taught to make a living by lifting goods from unprotected pockets.

The Artful Dodger is not the only notable cutpurse in the arts. Paintings of pickpockets became popular during the seventeenth century. In these works, an unsuspecting youth, distracted by fast women and men who tell fortunes or deal cards, often has his pockets picked. Examples of this artful dodging may be seen in Georges de La Tour's *Fortune-Teller* (about 1630) and in his *Dice Players* (1650).

Such scenes of gambling, carousing, and debauchery enjoyed a vast patronage. The common theme was of a benighted youth who blithely fell in with worldly company only to be relieved of his fortune. It is not surprising that such works were associated with the parable of the Prodigal Son, for he too experienced a period of high life that ended with his pockets being picked.

This anonymous seventeenth-century engraving, *L'Enfant Prodigue dine en Joyeuse Companie*, after Abraham Bosse (1602-1676), coyly tells the story, complete with sexual innuendo, vast quantities of wine, and a French precursor of the Artful Dodger. The latter, urged on by a floozy belted with a cincture that trails a bag and keys, obediently lifts the prodigal's purse from his pocket.

The pudgy-faced and mustachioed wastrel is in no position to notice his loss, however. He is being pressed and cosseted by three courtesans; and while he doubtless feels a great deal, he doesn't seem to feel the lifting of his purse. The company is enjoying such an intimate moment that they pay no heed to other appetites, for they ignore the savory-looking apple tart on the table.

We know that the French Baroque engraver, Bosse (on whose work this print is based), had a keen eye for fashion. It is said that his etchings enlighten us regarding the life styles and fashions of French society in seventeenth-century Paris. The clothing of all the characters in this work suggests the height of fashion. Bosse was also known as a master of perspective. He plays with our perception as we take note of the glass of wine held in the woman's extended left hand. The glass of wine is probably no bigger than it ought to be; but, when lifted and seen alongside the tower in the distance, it looks huge. No wonder the party is in such high spirits.

There are other arousing spirits in the back room on the left. A dandy is clearly unbuttoning for amorous activity, with a bowl of pyramid shapes (sweets, perhaps?) and a roaring fire in the background. A female figure lying on a bed invites the young man's advance, though, if this is foreplay, there is something singular about the positioning of her legs. That is, one foot, likely her right foot, points upward. If that it is so, one wonders how the other foot could be pointing downward toward the floor in an opposing manner. My wife, when asked to replicate this fancy piece of footwork, painfully observed, "That would be hard." A crouching dog, with its back to this awkwardly wanton scene, looks out at the viewer with what might be an embarrassed expression on its human-like face.

The blatant carnality of this engraving is doubtless intended to convey a moral message to the viewer. It might be said that if you get yourself in a compromising position, you should not be surprised if you get your pocket picked by some predatory artful dodger. The beginning and the end of the poem at the bottom of this prurient but moralistic picture put the matter this way:

> In this place where Venus makes an infamous commerce
> This slave of sense and voluptuousness miserably lost
>   his body and soul . . .
> All their flattery is just a trick; all that they are doing is for his purse.
> For it is only money that they have for a lover.

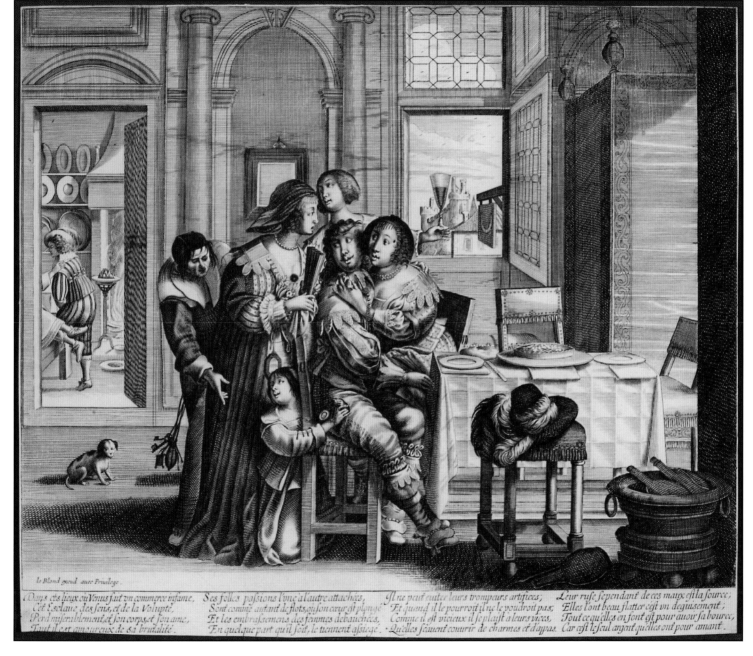

Anonymous engraver, after Abraham Bosse

L' Enfant Prodigue dine en Joyeuse Companie (The Prodigal Son Dines in Happy Company) (undated)

Engraving (14½ x 12 ins.)

The Prodigal gets drunk

Adam and Eve, Romeo and Juliet, Gilbert and Sullivan, Currier and Ives: These pairings are so linked in our minds that it is difficult to think of one without the other. Yet it is obvious that each must have had separate lives and experiences. We know, for instance, that Eve engaged in a private conversation with the serpent without Adam. Juliet took faux poison in Romeo's absence. Arthur Sullivan wrote the tune for "Onward, Christian Soldiers" without the poetic help of William Schwenck Gilbert. And Nathaniel Currier (1813-1888) was in the printing business, producing hundreds of prints long before James Ives (1824-1895) joined the firm in 1852.

By the time Currier and Ives ceased production in 1907, they had produced more than seventy-five hundred different titles, totaling over one million prints. In their own words these printmakers created about "three works of art" a week for over fifty years. These colorful works were never considered "high art"; but they were attractive and affordable to many Americans during that period. The business quite candidly advertised itself as "Publishers of Cheap and Popular Pictures." Many who bought these pictures decorated their homes with a vast variety of prints: city and rural scenes, hunting scenes, sports, humor, politics, portraits, ladies' fashion, disaster scenes, and memorial prints—virtually anything the firm could sell to the Victorian public in the United States. Religious, moral, and sentimental scenes were extremely popular as well.

One of the most popular of these prints was *The Drunkards* [sic] *Progress* (dated 1848) depicting the gaudy horror of the drunkard's fate. In a single picture, set on a staircase going up, across, and then down, we watch (and are instructed by) this moral and sentimental tale. We track the ruination of a dissolute young man 'from "the first glass to the grave," from a drink with a friend all the way to death by suicide. This cautionary tale clearly is a visual warning against the excesses of drink. The youth's besotted regress touched a chord in many hearts in its day, and it struck a resonant note with the growing temperance movement in the country.

Tapping into this same moral, religious, and didactic vein is this print from about 1850 published by Currier-without-Ives. *The Prodigal Son Wasting His Substance*, delicately but with a knowing wink, lifts the veil on a number of vices: drunkenness, sex, smoking, and squandering one's means in riotous living. Regarded, perhaps, as sentimental by many viewers today, this work nonetheless had some impact on spectators of the mid-nineteenth century.

Victorian morals and manners were taken seriously, even if not always seriously adhered to. An anonymous artist (perhaps someone like Fanny Palmer*) created this scene; it is a bit awkward, more than a little humorous, and it is intensely instructive.

In the tradition of William Hogarth's *Rake's Progress* from the early eighteenth century, this piece illustrates the action of its title. It is intended to represent the debauchery of the Prodigal Son—the quote from Luke 15:13 tells us as much. But each of the various characters disport themselves in a manner that is a mid-nineteenth-century gloss on the Lukan story. Looked at today, the scene seems to reflect the fevered action from some country inn or a college fraternity party. The central figure (who looks akin to the central figure in *The Drunkards Progress*) staggers awkwardly against a plush chair. He pours a stream of wine onto the green floor, widely missing the glass on the table. The liquid is red in the decanter, but it is colorless as it makes its way to the floor. His besotted expression says clearly that he is making a fool of himself.

A torpid and bleary-eyed companion watches the scene from the left. He too is obviously in his cups. A serving lady brings a tray of drink to a couple who seem to have more on their minds than drink. Their aroused expression and his roving hand bespeak some future intimacy. On the right a portly bald man blows a stream of smoke into a snoozing man's face. Each of the characters in this scene is somewhere on the road to degradation. Brothers and sisters, parents and friends, pay heed to the excesses pictured here. It happened to the Prodigal Son and his companions. It could happen to you!

The picture may look quaint, even contrived, to our eyes. The artistic style may be dated and the didacticism cloying. But this colored print from the shop of Nathaniel Currier does have a certain appeal. Many homes today have calendars or framed prints like this one on their walls. Though many of us have shed our Victorian tastes and sensibilities, the piety, the sentiment, the overt moralism have an abiding appeal. We may smile condescendingly at Currier's depiction. But our modern sensibilities tell us that there is health and moral value in watching how we pour our wine, blow our smoke, or waste our substance—or any of the gifts we have been given. This picture, like the parable, reminds us that supping with pigs comes next.

Fanny Bond Palmer (1812-1876), whose husband Edward preferred drink to work, supported her family by working as an artist for Currier from before 1850 until her death in 1876.

THE PRODIGAL SON WASTING HIS SUBSTANCE.

"He wasted his substance with rietous living."
Luke XV. 13

5

Nathaniel Currier

The Prodigal Son
Wasting His Substance
(undated)

Colored engraving
(9 x 12¾ ins.)

Wine, women, and song . . . the party's over. These themes form the moral frame of the two engravings by Crispin van de Passe (1565-1637). Each one derives from a series of works by Marten de Vos, the Elder (1532-1603), a highly regarded Flemish painter, draughtsman, and painter of altarpieces in Antwerp. During the late sixteenth century de Vos was considered to be the most important figure painter in Antwerp before Peter Paul Rubens. De Vos executed about sixteen hundred prints for publication. His drawings are appreciated for their lively, industrious, and generally vigorous character.

The latter qualities are illustrated in *The Prodigal Son Wasting His Fortune* from 1601. The engraved image is circular in form and is about the size of a jelly jar lid. Yet it is crammed with visual information that is both jolly and ominous. The scene centers on a party of merrymakers, three nubile music-making women and a youth whom we know to be the profligate Prodigal. The young man amorously grasps a fourth young lady under her breast, and she accepts his advance professionally. She is holding a generously proportioned drinking vessel in her left hand, an object which balances the two urns of wine behind the lutenist, thus establishing the theme of wine, women, and song.

It takes little imagination to perceive that the ladies are brothel workers who use music and spirits for profit if not for fun. Netherlandish art of the period often depicted brothel scenes; artistically they were closely associated with the subject of the Prodigal Son. While the central scene here portrays pleasure for hire, intimations of things to come are depicted in the hazy background. Through a leafy, shadowy arch, we see three scenes sketched in comic book fashion: the Prodigal being chased away, his sojourn among the pigs, and his reconciliation with the father. This sequence foreshadows events that will follow the party in the foreground.

These background scenes are used here to reinforce the moral injunction to the young profligate—and for us, the viewer, as well. The words are essayed on the circular border: "You have fallen into harmful pleasures! Turn back, my friend. Truly, it is not too late to choose the path to good character (Luke 15).

We know, of course, that the pleasure-seeking youth ignored that good advice. Rather, he continued to spend his time, seed, and fortune in the company of prostitutes. One of those background scenes sketched in the smaller work by de Passe (after de Vos) becomes the subject of a larger engraving, *The Prodigal Son Chased from the Inn.* That establishment is doubtless a tongue-in-cheek euphemism illustrating an old Dutch proverb: "Inn in front, brothel behind." The bawdy point is further illuminated by two avian images. The bird in the cage and the sign of the swan in this context are blatant erotic symbols. In the art of the time the caged bird was a common image illustrating brothel scenes, while the tumescent swan, the bird of love, was associated with Venus and Cupid.

Here, however, bought love has turned to active ire as four ladies chase the destitute and disheveled youth with broom and cudgel. As the Latin logo says: *Everything wasted, he was hastily driven out with passion.* Trying to fend off the blows, the shoeless and hapless youth narrowly misses being doused by a fulsome fall of fluid, possibly the contents of a chamberpot. It is a prodigious stream, for the liquid overflow seems to be more than would fit into the pot from which it is poured. In any event the combined action of anger, flight, and liquid brush-off announces good riddance, the party's over.

These two engravings visually interpret that part of the parable where it says the young man squandered his property in dissolute living. It is only later in Luke's story, when the older brother confronts the father, that we hear that the young son specifically wasted his property with prostitutes. Whether that is hyperbole or sexual sour grapes on the part of the older brother, such speculation has long intrigued readers of the story as well as artists. Artists like de Passe and de Vos told cautionary tales for those with eyes to see—stories that are sobering and worth pondering. Those who waste their inheritance carousing with wine, women, and song are advised to turn back, or some day, like the Prodigal, they will be obliged to flee the cudgel and dodge the spill when the party is over.

6 A–B

Crispin van de Passe, the Elder

Engravings after
Marten de Vos
(undated)

A (left)
*The Prodigal Son
Wasting His Fortune*

Engraving
(3¼ ins. diameter)

B (right)
*The Prodigal Son Chased
from the Inn*

Engraving
(7 x 9 ins.)

The devil stalks the Prodigal

Sometimes moral discourse teeters on the borderline between seriousness and drollery. With tongue in cheek, a cautionary tale can be told in a manner that evokes both serious thought and a knowing smile. In the visual arts, as in the case of this colored engraving by Martin Engelbrecht (1684-1756), word and image convey the paradox of earnestness and waggishness.

The captivating print, *Der verlohrne Sohn* (first half of the eighteenth century) both warns and amuses. The scene, an *al fresco* bordello, is rich in red, a color that is at once enlivening and suggestive. We perceive fourteen figures: eight partying humans, two serving satyrs, an overseeing devil, a snuffling dog, a howling statue, and a stuffed swan—the latter either for decoration or consumption.

In the foreground an amiable and corpulent young man engages in social interaction with an ample-bodied courtesan. They might be going to or coming from the table; they might be engaged in lusty conversation or song. The accompaniment for that song may be supplied by the lutenist in the balcony. It is possible that the lusty lad has left his own lute by the empty chair to engage in this other kind of duet.

Two members of the jolly company at the table are engaged in something like social intercourse, while two others seem to have been overcome by the effects of the grape. The leafy trellis and the classical architecture provide an agreeable setting for this party. Their conviviality is typical of many high-spirited gatherings at outdoor taverns, "spirited" picnics—or high class brothels. Everyone is having such fun that we might be tempted to step into the picture and join them.

What sends a cautionary chill up the spine in this scene, though, is the presence of some less benign figures. First there is the brace of satyrs acting as waiters for the party. The upper half of their bodies is human; the lower half is hooved. Satyrs were known as roguish lovers of wine, women, and men. They were also known to play tricks on human beings. It is appropriate that they lurk in the background about to serve what looks like burnt bird. This prank may be only the first of the tricks they plan to play on the carefree Prodigal.

The scene becomes more chilly by the presence of an elongated white statue immediately behind the buxom trollop. Instead of gracing the garden with a classical sculpture of Apollo or Aphrodite, Engelbrecht includes a diabolical figure with a bald head and Spock-like ears. The mouth of the statue is open, suggesting that it is either beginning to wail or joining the chorus elsewhere in progress. A vocalizing statue carries overtones of the Don Juan legend in which the statue in the cemetery warns the rogue of his approaching doom.

The icy feeling up and down our spine crystallizes when we finally take note of the sinister, sickly greenish figure lurking in the background behind the revelers. He appears to be pulling something taffy-like between his hands. We can't really tell what it is that he is stretching—perhaps it is the truth. The devil coolly oversees the merriment and casts a pall that the merrymakers cannot see—though we can. We also see what the artist intends us to see in this moral tale. The four-line German poem spells it out for us to read, mark, learn, and inwardly digest:

> With whores the Prodigal Son now drinks and lives in debauchery,
> Look how the devil is now busy with him.
> Oh, my! Young man, you should reflect on the times in bondage
> And see what the spirit of hell can accomplish.

The parable of the Prodigal Son is multivalent; that is, it has many things to teach those willing to listen and learn. When an artist like Engelbrecht translates the story into a visual experience, he uses symbolic means to underline the moral tale. Hence a stuffed swan evokes eroticism; a crooning statue warns of disaster; a lurking devil cautions the Prodigal—and the reader—about the spirit of hell. Will anyone take heed? Perhaps.

Veteran pastors are inclined to observe that pre-marital counseling is often a futile endeavor because, given the context, no one is really paying attention. In a similar way moral discourse, especially to the young, is a tricky business, for it is likely no one really hears the well-intended advice. Perhaps the only viable strategy is to do as Engelbrecht does, patiently mix the moral message with disarming humor—and hope that someone will look and pay attention.

24.

Omnia scorta vorant, luxus, convivia, potus
Et toruos famulos helluo plenus habet.
Temporibus nostris exemplum sume juventus,
Astus Luciferi maxima damna cave!
C. Priv. S.C Maj.

Filius deperditus inter
scorta. Lucæ cap. XV. v. 30.
Der verlohrne Sohn bey den
Huren. Lucä cap. XV. v. 30.

Mit Huren sauft und praßt nun das verlohrne Kind,
Sieh, wie die Teufel jetzt bey ihm geschäfftig sind;
Ach Jugend spiegle dich zu unsren Zeiten dran,
Und siehe, was der Geist der Höllen stiften kan.
Mart. Engelbrecht excud. A.V.

7

Martin Engelbrecht

Der verlohrne Sohn
(The Prodigal Son)
(Early eighteenth century)

Colored engraving.
(12 x 9 ins.)

The dissolute Prodigal

Ludwig van Beethoven (1770-1827) occupies a singular place in the history of western music. This composer is generally regarded as a transitional figure between the classical and romantic eras in music. That is—and this is a vast oversimplification—he bridges the gap between styles characterized by the structured and balanced on the one hand (the classical) and the passionate and emotional on the other (the romantic). Beethoven's early music is steeped in the classical style as seen (and heard) in such composers as Mozart and Haydn; his later muscular compositions might be said to prefigure the romantic music of Schubert and Brahms.

While these two anonymous, colored copper engravings (from about 1730-1740) antedate the music of Beethoven, they appear to illustrate something of the classical and presage something of the romantic in western art. Looking at *The Prodigal Son among the Prostitutes* we get a sense of order, elegance, and ornament. The formal dining hall, with its receding perspective, the rich finery throughout the room, the formal garden in the background: These reflect the influence of Versailles and anticipate the grand creations of Ludwig II of Bavaria somewhat later.

Somewhere in that picture, we know, the Prodigal is treating himself to the lush fruits this ordered landscape offers. But it is not easy to discern which figure he really is. He might be the amorous gentleman seen through the doorway on the left who is fondling the compliant courtesan; there is refreshment on the table behind her and implied pleasure in the canopied bed behind him. Or he could be the dandy on the right enjoying a game of cards with that attentive lady of easy virtue. Perhaps he is one of the male characters dancing in the vaulted open-air ballroom in the middle distance. Most observers identify the elegant wastrel with one of the red-coated party-goers at the table, most likely the one standing with a goblet in his right hand and a happy but slightly stupid expression on his face.

It is a grand scene in the classical mode, full of suggestive and carefully contrived details: the sinuous plaster ornamentation, the balanced bustle of busy servants coming and going, the brace of jeroboam-sized wine bottles in the foreground basket, even a little dog sedately going about his business near a richly laden side table. While we lack the outer scenes in this series of the Prodigal's story, this engraving gives us an elegant, not blowsy, picture of the high life which the son enjoyed before he descended into penury and subsequent renewal.

Refinement is replaced in the next scene, *The Prodigal Son with the Pigs*. Just as the later music of Beethoven became more emotive and exotic, the composition of this scene is in a different visual key. The Prodigal, clearly identified in the center of the scene, sits dishevelled on a gray blocky mass. He is surrounded by steely-eyed pigs going about their swinish business. In place of the orderly and elegant setting in which he basked previously, the young man here is placed before an emotive landscape, the kind often seen in romantic art.

Enframed by leaning trees and craggy cliffs, the prospect incorporates a meandering stream, rolling and verdant hills. We see a busy population as well, among which is a woman churning, another milking, a traveler crossing the bridge. Houses dot the countryside, and a mighty fortress is perched on a promontory. If it weren't for the scraggly pig keeper in the foreground, we might be tempted to take a ramble in this amiable rural landscape, perhaps to stop for a fresh glass of milk or to visit the steepled church in the distance.

But this is a scene of dissolution and disillusion: The blasted trees, the brutish pigs, the befouled son remind us of that. Something else may underscore this point as well. The well-dressed figure on the right is enigmatic in this context. He may be a gentleman who simply prefers not to get involved in the poor boy's plight, answering his outstretched gesture with a dismissive faux blessing. He could be internally pondering the platitude that often comforts the complacent: *There but for the grace of God am I.*

Another possiblity, perhaps fanciful, presents itself. This striding and confident young man could be one of those shadowy figures who sometimes shows up in German literature, a *Doppelganger*. This would be a ghostly double of a living person, especially one that haunts its fleshly counterpart. In this case, our romantic imagination surmises, he could be what the Prodigal was before his fall and what he might become in his rising up and going forth for reconcilitation. If so, then the figure and the gesture could represent something both reflective and proleptic. This ghostly double could be kindling both memory and hope in the pig-ridden Prodigal: *While folly has brought you to this place, grace will lead you home.*

Filius deperditus inter scorta.
Il figliuolo prodigo frà le puttane.
L'enfant prodigue entre les putains.
Der verlohrne Sohn bey den Hiren.

Filius deperditus Subulcus.
Il figliuolo prodigo porcaro.
L'enfant prodigue porcher.
Der verlohrne Sohn ein Schweinhirt.

8 A-B
Anonymous
German

Two colored copper
engravings from
a series published
by Georg Balthasar
[Bathasar] Probst
Optik print
(1730-1740)

A (left)
*Filius deperditus inter
scorta*
(The Prodigal Son
among the Prostitutes)

Copper engraving
(23 x 18¾ ins.)

B (right)
Filius deperditus subulcus
(The Prodigal Son and
the Swine)

Copper engraving
(23 x 18¾ ins.)

The Prodigal goes to live with the pigs

All art is contextual; but some art may be more contextual than others. When one looks at this version of *The Prodigal Son* and realizes that it was executed in the conflicted United States of 1967, the context declares itself. "Make love, not war." "Off the pigs." "All you need is love." "This is the dawning of the Age of Aquarius." Try humming a bit of this song from the hit musical of the 1960s, *Hair*. Then put the song and the aphorisms together with the wood engraving by Fritz Eichenberg (1901-1990). What emerges is a wry but haunting contextual interpretation of the parable.

The long-haired man, with LOVE tattooed on his left biceps, nestles amid a surround of pigs. The story from Luke says that the son was in need while he was in the fields feeding the pigs. But here, instead of reflective, the lad looks drowsy, vacant, maybe even spaced out. If so, then his condition is quite different from that of the son who "comes to himself" before rushing home. This somnolent fellow has not yet seen the light, though there may be early signs of that light reflected on his muscular shoulders.

This languid figure and the plump, pillowy pigs are at rest beneath a sprawling shade tree. In Christian art trees are often symbolic of good and evil, evoking the tree of life in the Garden. Yet here it is likely that the tree is merely providing shade for the lounging crowd beneath. Sometimes, to paraphrase Sigmund Freud, a tree is just a tree.

Likewise, there may be no intentional symbolism in the anchor tattooed on the triceps of the son's right arm. While an anchor has often been associated with hope and safe shelter, here it may just be a display of body art with only marginal symbolic meaning, like the German Cross suspended around the boy's neck. The scene is one of torpor, with the three pigs in the foreground showing more expression and sociability than the vacant, flaccid human.

The wry quality of the scene is consistent with Eichenberg's approach to his subject matter. This German-born illustrator left his native country for the United States in the 1930s when Adolf Hitler rose to power. Eichenberg's art career stretched from the early 1920s to the middle 1980s; he used wood blocks as his preferred medium for telling stories. Consciously taking his cue from his name (which means *Oak Mountain*), Eichenberg acknowledged that he approached wood like a duelist facing an opponent. Engraving in wood, he claimed, engaged his mind, heart, eyes, and most certainly his hand. Working in wood gave him sensual pleasure, a complete sense of release and satisfaction.

His pleasure has given satisfaction to many who have come in contact with his work. The artist illustrated a number of literary classics, like *Wuthering Heights* and *Gulliver's Travels*. He did many wood engravings of fables featuring animals as well as numerous biblical subjects, like *The Prodigal Son*. His haunting images are often wry and whimsical but always arresting. Like the characters from the Brothers Grimm, Eichenberg's bulky figures have an edgy quality, like dark but not particularly scary dreams. Overall, one might be inclined to describe Eichenberg as a fabulist, a teller of tales.

He tells one of his engaging tales here, setting a lethargic lad in the midst of pudgy and amiable pigs. As a commentary on the story set in the context of the 1960s, one could regard this woodcut as a vision of a hippie among the hippy. From our vantage point decades later we know that the context will eventually change and that the son will go home. But for a little while we wallow in an image from a time when many wanted to make love, not war, and thought all you needed was love. The storyteller suggests that while the son is embracing a plump pig, he may also be fostering in his own space a vision of a separate peace.

9

Fritz Eichenberg

The Prodigal Son
(1967)

Wood engraving
(9½ x 11 ins.)

The Prodigal trapped in the barnyard

Pigs in their customary habitat may be dirty and smelly as far as the general public is concerned. But they enjoy legendary status in literature. Most of us remember the lessons of foolishness and sagacity as displayed by *The Three Pigs*. And many of us have gleefully given vent to one of the great exhortations from that story: *Not by the hair of my chinny-chin-chin*. In another context, youthful toes were (and still are) counted and associated with pigs: *This little piggy went to market . . . and this little piggy cried, "Wee, wee, wee," all the way home*.

Likewise, many children—and adults—have admired the breathy and dotty exploits of Miss Piggy from the society of Muppets. And generations have doted on the stories of Freddy the Pig by Walter Brooks, who wrote twenty-six Freddy books between 1927 and 1958. During that same period a more serious cast of pigs (including Old Major, Snowball, Napoleon, and Squealer) fostered the revolution in George Orwell's 1945 allegorical novel, *Animal Farm*. These redoubtable pigs also gave birth to one of the most ironic sayings in the language: *All animals are created equal, but some animals are more equal than others*.

Another author and graphic artist, Arthur Geisert (b. 1941) has created noteworthy narratives populated by pigs. In 1986 he was recipient of an Illinois Arts Council Artist's Fellowship for *Pigs from A to Z*. The *New York Times* selected the work as one of the ten best illustrated children's books of that year. In 1991 Geisert followed that barnyard saga with a playful creation simply called *Oink*. That same year Geisert created this hand-colored etching, *The Prodigal Son*. It is a picture replete with pigs.

These pigs (nearly a score of them) are not fierce, steely eyed, dirty, or repugnant in any way. Rather, they are an amiable, sociable lot. This cordial barnyard community appears in the middle distance to be at rest or engaged in docile porcine discourse. One foreground pig pokes his snout and right foreleg through a slat in the fence gate, while another peers inquisitively at the viewer through an opening in the gate. They are curious pigs; but at the same time they seem to be scoping us out, wondering whether to invite us into the yard to join their company. Perhaps we *would* like to wander among them, for the yard is clean, the spacious farm buildings look appealing, and the ample grain stack looks like a suitable place for a snooze.

However inviting the attitude of the pigs may be, the demeanor of the bearded fellow with the tattered shirt is something else. He is doubtless the eponymous son, here depicted as an exhausted man in early middle age. His leathery face looks tired, his blue eyes are droopy, and his overall posture is slouchy, a figure of resigned discontent—in distinct contrast to the contented community of pigs.

His doleful demeanor is reflected in the gathering gloom of clouds and the trio of leafless trees. Now, it seems, is the approaching winter of his discontent. Unlike the pig who eyes us directly, the dispirited man gazes past us, possibly reflecting on his tedious, demeaning existence. We might be tempted to take a stroll among those contented farm creatures, but he appears to be a darkly discontented creature who would like to escape from their company.

His prison-like condition is signified by the confining strand of barbed wire. Only his left hand, holding a ragged ear of corn, is more or less free. He might be inclined to write a sad ballad of his existence with one of those pencils in his overalls, but he lacks paper and initiative. The stiff pod-like plant on our side of the fence underscores the dried-up quality of his dreary existence.

We look at him and wonder if he will ever find the gumption to get up and go home. We know from the parable that he does. Yet for the present moment he is trapped behind the fence in the company of pigs. In a sense his current situation reflects the condition and discontent of many farmers in the heartland of America. Forgotten by time and the economy they, like the son in this picture, are confined to the land with nowhere to go. On one level, Geisert suggests something of the difficulty of farm life, and we can see it in the man's eyes.

At the same time the artist from Illinois also shows us that farm life has an often-overlooked significance. We note that that spacious barn is both storage and shelter, a kind of agricultural womb that stores the nourishment for the larger population. We must acknowledge the fact that we are the ones who live off the produce from farms like this one. A long look at this scene stirs us into thinking about these matters. It is surprising how much we are able to see when we look at a tranquil gathering of pigs, some of which are at rest, some of which will go to market, and some of which, like the Prodigal Son, will go *all the way home*.

The original copper plate and five uncolored impressions are also in the Evenrud collection.

10

Arthur Geisert

The Prodigal Son
(1991)

Hand-colored etching
(23¾ x 17½ ins.)

The Prodigal enters the pig pen

In the Bible trees showed up on the third day of creation, and later they provided fruit for nourishment and temptation. Still later leaves of the fig tree supplied Adam and Eve with their first apparel. At the end of biblical narrative, in the book of Revelation, the narrator tells us that the tree of life grows in the midst of the new creation, and its profusion of leaves are for the healing of nations.

Single trees, groves of trees, forests of trees provide the context for myths, fairy tales, and works of art. Without trees to harbor elves and trolls, for example, the saga of *The Lord of the Rings* or Narnia would be shadowless space. Snow White, Hansel and Gretel, even the Three Bears are unthinkable without their forest setting. The landscapes of such artists as Nicolas Poussin and Thomas Cole would be featureless were it not for the abundance of trees flourishing in their landscape art.

Perhaps this arboreal passion is what prompted Auguste-Louis Lepere (1849-1918) to depict a magnificent, sprawling grove of trees in this etching of the Prodigal Son among the pigs. No trees are mentioned in the biblical story, but they dominate this print. Moving upward from low on the left, the canopy of trees rises and swells like the crest of a giant, leafy wave that ultimately breaks and hangs suspended over a smaller stand of trees on the right. The parable may tell us of the Prodigal among the pigs, but Lepere's print focuses our attention on the trees with their deep shadows and twisted, sinuous trunks.

We may be tempted to enter their inviting depth via a lumpy path in the lower center of the picture; once there in the cool depths, our minds would be free to wander and make various associations. Travelers might find solace and pleasure, though they might just as easily stumble on roots hidden in shadow. The dense forest also holds the possibility of menace or danger, even adventure. That is the way with leafy forests and twisty trees.

It is possible that the plodding Prodigal may have come from the depths of those trees, having left his boisturous but fortune-sucking company on the other side. Chastened and bent, his back echoing the diagonal slope of the tree behind him, the young man pushes his way through a gate and into a yard occupied by seven rooting, snuffling pigs. No longer the playful roué, this man shambles into the muddy yard like an exhausted mail carrier delivering his load. Rather than laying his burden down, however, the Prodigal is about to pick it up; the pigs will see to that!

By entering the enclosed yard, the lad turns his back on the evocative woods looming behind him. He enters a kind of fenced prison where the housing is rude and the fellow inmates ruder. The squalid reality of life among the pigs is not fully visualized, for Lepere, a master of print technique, only lightly sketches them in. For the moment the dense tonality of everything else in the etching—especially the leafy bulk of trees—is more palpable to the young man than are the pigs. But the pigs will grow on him.

The parable does not say how long the son sojourned among the pigs. It might have been a few days, weeks, or even months if he was a slow learner. Doubtless, the longer he stayed, the more real the pigs became. The spartan hut with its thatched roof, the irritating contributions from the insect-rich pond across the way, and especially the growing reality of his pig mates eventually made him come to his senses. When he did, he might have begun the journey home by opening the gate and walking along the road.

We might speculate about what his journey would have been like had he entered that tangled density of trees. On that shady way he might have found solace or he might have met menace. He might have encountered a grumpy bear or a hostile troll, for one never knows what will happen upon entering the woods. In any event, the unknown road is preferable to the known pig yard prison. Whatever he encountered along the way, the Prodigal eventually made his way home to his welcoming father. There, in a different kind of yard, he found the father's open heart, and he fed on fatted calf rather than feeding fattening pigs.

11
Auguste-Louis Lepere

The Prodigal Son Entering the Pig Pen (1913)

Etching
(12¾ x 9½ ins.)

The son turns toward home

Ablazing sun, its rays splitting the sky, beats down upon a figure leaning heavily on a staff. His face and shoulder are illuminated by that light, so the picture radiates intense heat. At the same time, the arching canopy of trees provides a measure of cool and comfort for this figure whose body is composed in the rough shape of an X. The lower part of his figure, not to mention the congress of pigs, are bathed in that shade, so the picture also contains a welcome degree of relief. The Prodigal Son in this small woodcut by the American artist Benjamin Miller (1877-1964) is transfixed, worn, and warm. Bent and still, he is illuminated by light, but he is also lost in shadow.

That contrast and that stillness capture the Prodigal at what seems to be the crucial moment of the story. He stands in the shade and in the light. We can see that he is about to leave his dissolute life behind and turn toward what one hopes will be a brighter future. He has turned his back on his shady past where he squandered his property in dissolute living in a distant country. That part of his life is now over, symbolized, discreetly, by the fading shape of a woman on the downward slope of a hill in the distance.

Now, it appears, the son's direction is to be forward. His body and staff lean toward the right, and if we follow the meander of the stream and the rise of the hills we can see his hoped-for destination. Strategically looming on the top of the highest slope is the solid shape of a secure villa or a mighty fortress. It is a stirring moment, but one pervaded with stillness and quiet. The son stands at a major, life-altering juncture. He is about to set aside the wasted past and opt for a new deal. With him, if we lift our eyes unto the hill, we can see that this moment proffers the glimpse of home and reconciliation.

Benjamin Miller was one of the preeminent woodblock printers working in America during the first half of the twentieth century. He spent most of his career in Cincinnati, Ohio, and was known for distinctive work which was frequently filled with biblical imagery. His art was inspired, as he admitted, by a passionate love of the Bible stories which in early youth he used to read to his mother. From 1924 to 1935 he created a large body of work, which also included social subjects, literature, and abstractions.

Known as an Expressionist, Miller was influenced by such noted artists as Paul Gauguin, Emil Nolde, and Christian Rohlfs (who also created an impressive *Return of the Prodigal Son* in 1916. See page 91.) Miller's virile, imaginative, and inspirational woodblock art appealed to a large audience. While his large volume of print work was widely heralded and won many awards in his day, he is, for many viewers, relatively or totally unknown today.

As we look at this woodcut of a young man who caresses his staff at the crossroad, we get an appreciative glimpse of this printmaker's powerful hand. In a relatively small space (the work is shown approximately actual size), Miller creates the impression of heat and shade; he delineates stasis and change; he invokes past and future. At the same time, he does not skimp on the pigs. Six of them—some with illuminated features, all in deep shade—congregate around the brooding son. While he is ruminating on his past and contemplating his future, the surround of pigs constitutes his present. In this telling moment, next to the son's right leg, one of those pigs looks out at the viewer with down-slanted eyes and mouth. "Here we are, and there you are," he seems to grunt pigishly. "We know who we are and where we are going. How about you?"

12

Benjamin Miller

The Prodigal Son
(1924)

Woodblock print
(7 x 6¾ ins.)

The
Swedish
son goes
astray and
then comes
home

Before cinema, large wall hangings and panorama paintings augmented people's view of reality. Such eye-filling works afforded viewers an experience of other places and people without their actually "being there." Panorama paintings were a form of education and faux travel, colorful windows through which people could glimpse the wider world. Fortunate patrons of this art form were able to revel in the Battle of Gettysburg, stand in reverent awe before a cyclorama of Jerusalem, or take a virtual river boat ride down the Mississippi, all in realistic and colorfully painted scenes.

A comparable experience greets the viewer of *The Story of the Prodigal Son* by Johannes Nilsson (1757-1827). The parable is told in seven colorful scenes extending over fourteen and a half feet. We watch the cocky son as he bids a hat-waving farewell to his father. We join him in revelry in four subsequent party scenes. Then we observe him in quiet discourse with pigs before he humbly returns home to his father. We do not merely observe the story as it unfolds; we imaginatively participate in the panorama of parable from beginning to end. (The work in its entirety is illustrated on pages 66-67.)

Nilsson was a Swedish artist who painted wall hangings in a style called *bonader*, a Scandinavian folk art form prominent in the late eighteenth and early nineteenth centuries. These paintings drew their subject matter from Scandinavian mythology and Bible stories, often portrayed in sequential scenes. In a flat folk art style, brightly colored figures from the middle class were painted as fashionable men and women acting the part of biblical characters. Exotic and imaginative trees, plants, and animals abounded. *Bonader* were, in effect, imaginative and stylized biblical paintings in the guise of folk tales. More than 200 such wall paintings by Nilsson still exist.

These wall hangings decorated people's houses; at the same time, however, they were edifying devices that reflected and encouraged Lutheran piety. *Bonader* paintings, while pleasant to look at, were intended for preaching and edification. Such pictures were created to inspire people to live faithful lives, to foster deep spirituality, and to prepare for eternal life.

The opening and closing panels (pages 65 and 69) of this *bonader* may be regarded as an *inclusio*, an artistic device that places similar material at the beginning and end of a work. The visual bracketing here consists of the white stucco house with red roof tiles and blue stars, with the father standing under a red arch. The action gets under way on the left as the son sets off on his high-stepping horse.

In the next scene (page 66) four hospitable hostesses appear to serve good—and doubtless strong—Swedish coffee. Baked goods that look like pretzels and waffles supplement the brew. If this is debauchery, it is very sedate—as it is in the next panel (page 67) where the son demurely dances with two companions in a setting of violin music and a riot of flowers.

The actors in this drama get down to business in the following scene (page 68) where the lad, now wearing a red stocking cap, reclines under a striped blanket. More coffee is served from a big pot. Next (page 68) we see the wigless youth with tousled hair; he is being stripped of his coat. It seems, in the way of nature, that all the coffee (and other visible drink) have caught up with the lusty lad.

The next scene (page 69) contains an alert and open-mouthed quintet of pigs (one of them with large blue spots) standing attentively before the young man. Now wearing a dark blue robe and a watch cap, he kneels before the gathering. Stick in hand, he looks as if he is conducting a vocal group with a baton. In the background, the fecund shapes of trees, plants, and floating blue bubbles witness the musicale. In the final panel (page 69) the repentant son, hat in hand, kneels before his stalwart father. Smoke billows from the star-studded house, and it looks as if the horned calf is being dragged inside for slaughter, roasting, and consumption. The journey out and back has clearly affected the young man, for now his clothes are simple, and he sports a fringe of beard. Moreover, in these last two panels his hair has turned from black to blond.

Standing before this panoramic wall hanging, we may experience some change too. Gazing from left to right but pausing to look, we might have the happy impression that we have traveled through a biblical fairyland. Watching the son travel on his journey (and drinking all that presumptive coffee), we might likewise be moved. Finally, if we stop to think about the import of the story as Nilsson has told it, we may sense a tingling in our spirit. It is possible that the wide window of this *bonader* might tickle our imagination and deepen our piety.

13 A–G

Johannes Nilsson

Story of the Prodigal Son
(1750)

Seven scenes, painted
on linen
(Total length: 175½ x
24 ins.)

13 A Scene 1: The son
leaves home.

13 B

Scene 2: The son drinks coffee and eats with fancy ladies.

13 C
Scene 3: The son
dances with fancy
ladies.

The entire *bonader*—
more than fourteen
feet long— is painted
on two pieces of linen.
It was designed to be
viewed as a continuous
narrative, as shown
in this composite
photo. The collector
has mounted it on
a mustard-colored
burlap background as
shown to the left.

13 D
Scene 4: The son goes
to bed.

13 E
Scene 5: He loses his
fancy jacket.

13 F
Scene 6: The son tends pigs.

13 G
Scene 7: He goes home to his father.

The story of the Prodigal told as a moral tale

In the sixteenth and seventeenth centuries—and later—artists produced many multi-part Prodigal Son narratives. These narratives often came in a sequence of four or more pictures. Ostensibly intended to inspire devotion or evoke a pious response, they nonetheless gave emphasis to the erotic pleasures of the tavern or the brothel. After all, the parable did refer to the younger son's carousing with prostitutes, so it seemed legitimate, even justifiable, to include a scene of boisterous merrymaking. Such a biblical plot device gave artists license to make frank, even erotic depictions of the pleasures of the flesh.

At the same time refinements of morals and manners dictated that subsequent scenes show regret and repentance on the part of the son, preferably with a convincing display of anguish and suffering. An obvious example of this phenomenon of "having your cake and eating it too" took place in Hollywood during the 1930s. Because many films of that period were long on sex and short on morals, the Hayes Office was created. This watchdog agency saw to it that some kind of moral uplift and corrective balanced flash and flesh. That is, vice, no matter how attractive, had to give way to virtue in the end. Rectitude and righteousness had to triumph in order to keep the perceived moral universe in balance.

We see a similar trajectory in this four-panel work by Pietro Testa (1611-1650). As in most sequence pictures, the updraft of pleasure on the one hand and the uplift of morals on the other come to life in the way the artist portrays the story. Testa chose to use classical forms and shapes. The characters and architecture seem to derive from the art of ancient Greece and Rome. This legacy is apparent in scene two where the seminude son, his elegantly curved back echoing that of the satyr, reflects balanced classical forms.

At the same time there are details in this risqué (but carefully controlled) scene that are both intriguing and suggestive. The chained monkey views the refined orgy with an air of sadness, implying that the son is every bit as captive as he is. As in much of Christian art the monkey is emblematic of degraded humanity. The animal symbolizes humans distorted by the sins of greed and lust; they are subject to spiritual blindness—sinners ensnared and blinded by the devil. The simian features on the face of the woman gesturing with her right arm emphasize this theme. We are not sure whether she is pointing to further pleasures in the space beyond or if she is making a gesture for the son to get up and leave, his luck having run out.

In the scene that follows, the son appears to be paying the price for his wasted ways. He repents in a lush landscape composed of shade trees, a beckoning lake, and towering mountains. He compresses his hands tightly in anguished prayer, though his attitude is not shared by seven somnolent pigs, one of which doubles as a footstool for the son's left leg. As if in compliance with some seventeenth-century Hayes Office, Pietro Testa balances the books: high living is offset by deep repentance.

The opening and closing scenes in this sequence of etchings, the Departure and the Return, are full of anecdote as well. The father who looks decrepit in the first scene seems to have regained a measure of dignified robustness in the last. The well-groomed horse and the stylized camel of the Departure are replaced in the Return by a compliant calf about to have his brains knocked out. Further, the docile dog in the first scene gazes with canine curiosity at a horse turd deposited at the base of the steps. Later the dog sniffs with much interest at the foot of the kneeling son, perhaps detecting the odor of left-behind pig.

As with many such sequence pictures, the whole is greater than the sum of its parts. A deep lesson lies at the heart of these well-designed etchings. Viewers are invited into the journey of the son from departure to return. Along the way we share in the debauch, symbolically informed that there is a price to be paid; then, amid the genteel squalor of pigs and lush shade trees, we come to our senses. In Testa's work, we take the trip in style, for the animals are companionable, the architecture is solid, and the landscape is gorgeous.

In the end, though, we are moved at the deep emotion etched in the facial features of the sturdy father and the limp son. While we anticipate the coming banquet, we also remain concerned about the stolid figure of the older brother hovering behind the father. At the same time we can come to appreciate the earthy humor of a dung-gazing and pig-sniffing dog. In these four etchings Testa reaches for high drama and low humor. By these means he intelligently draws us into the history of the Prodigal Son, and that history becomes our own.

14 A-D

Pietro Testa

*The History of the
Prodigal Son*
(c. 1745)

Set of four etchings
(each 11½ x 8 ins.)

14 A
The Prodigal leaves
home.

14 B

The Prodigal among
the prostitutes

14 C
The Prodigal in misery
among the pigs

The Prodigal returns
to his home and his
father.

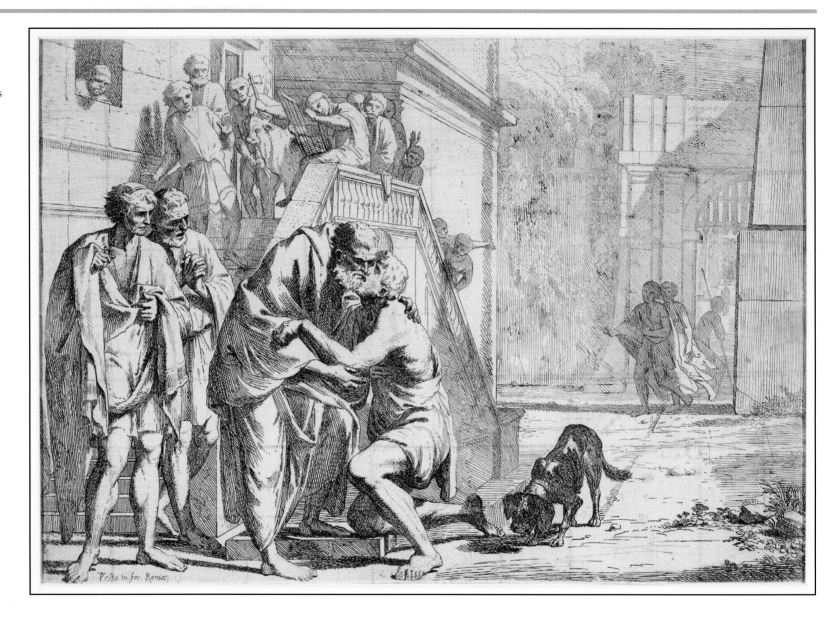

Of what great blessings in my wretchedness have I deprived myself! From what a kingdom in my misery have I fallen! I have wasted the riches that were given to me, I have transgressed the commandment. Alas, unhappy soul! Thou art henceforth condemned to the eternal fire. Therefore before the end cry out to Christ our God: Receive me as the Prodigal Son, O God, and have mercy upon me.…

As the Prodigal I come to Thee, merciful Lord. I have wasted my whole life in a foreign land; I have scattered the wealth which Thou gavest me, O Father. Receive me in repentance, O God, and have mercy upon me.

Tone Two and Tone Four for The Sunday of the Prodigal Son
Mother Mary & Kallistos Ware, *The Lenten Triodion*
(London: Faber & Faber, 1978)

Facing page: Ben Earl Looney, *Prodigal's Return* (See also pages 86-87.)

Return

The son comes home to an empty house

In the parable Jesus indicated that the father joyfully received the wayward son and robustly welcomed him back unto his household. In this lithograph Thomas Hart Benton (1889-1975) intimates that the father is absent and the household is in ruins. Instead of a show of reconciliation or a demonstration of compassion as in the work of other artists, Benton depicts abandonment, ruination, even alienation. The son has come home, but no one is there. Indeed, there is no home.

Benton, in many of his other works, presented scenes of the Midwest as a bountiful breadbasket, and in particular he portrayed the farmer's toil as noble, even epic. However, caught up in the throes of the Great Depression of the 1930s, the artist also saw, as in this work, those scenes turning sour. Here the American Dream has evaporated, crisped by a harsh light and raked by deep shadows. The land is fallow, and the house is ramshackle. No older brother hovers in the margin to ask: Where have you been? Even the vaunted fatted calf lies bleached in the grass, skeletal remains signifying a feast that is not to come.

American art of the nineteenth century often portrayed the landscape as bountiful and blessed, though paradoxically many artists used the device of a "blasted" or broken tree in the foreground to symbolize a vanishing wilderness or the encroachment of civilized decay. At the foot of the beard-stroking son in Benton's lithograph a dead limb protrudes, an image that drives home the reality of barren waste. It is a not-so-subtle reminder of how much had really vanished in the American scene. That limb and the son himself perch on the edge of a featureless, suggestive blot. Perhaps it is a muddy shadow or an open pit—a black hole that has sucked the life out of the hope and dream of return.

The son fingers his beard and gazes upward, inviting speculation on the part of the viewer. Ask a number of people to interpret the expression on his face, and they will likely give a variety of responses: surprise, puzzlement, disappointment, disbelief, dismay. Knowing the context of the art work—

the pervasive Great Depression—helps to explain, even amplify, those reactions. Reflected in this scene of homecoming thwarted is a prevailing sense of melancholy and pathos. What has happened? Where has everyone gone? What will happen next? If the son had stayed at home, would this scene of desolation have been forestalled?

The sheen of dust is reflected on various surfaces, while sullen fingers of cloud stretch over the land. The encroaching gloom looms over baffled son, ruined house, and bleached bone. Looking at this grim lithograph one might be inclined to be offended, for it turns the parable of the Prodigal Son on its head. The message of hope and homecoming is eclipsed by a vision of darkness and uncertainty. Of course, that message reflects something of the context in which the work was created. The somber reality that confronted Benton's Prodigal was shared by millions of Americans at the time.

While the picture offers no immediate comfort, it nonetheless sets before us a prickly series of questions and challenges: Is it possible to find signs of life in a seemingly barren landscape? In what ways might we be able to accept the implicit lament of this scene and still find a fruitful affirmation for the future? Is decay, whether brought on by nature or greed, inevitable or avoidable?

The broken and abandoned scene that greeted the bewildered son has not necessarily been patched and replaced with unalloyed bounty in our day. In many parts of the Midwest the land lies fallow and has been left behind. In many cities throughout our nation and the world, scenes of corruption and dereliction confront us. These realities cause us to stop dead in our tracks and scratch our chin like the figure in Benton's picture. The parable as reinterpreted by the artist afflicts our conscience and causes disquiet. Further, it provokes us to think about what has been done and what needs to be done in our ravished world. If we believe that God, the Father and Creator, is somewhere in the midst of that broken world, then we are obliged to unpack that neatly roped suitcase, take out our belongings, and figure out what to do next.

15

Thomas Hart Benton

Prodigal Son
(1939)

Lithograph
(13 x 10 ins.)

A kneeling posture is frequently associated with praying. Sometimes people also think of kneeling in terms of gardening, washing the kitchen floor, and proposing marriage. Artists seem to favor kneeling as the appropriate body language in scenes that depict the returning Prodigal Son. In this mezzotint by Louis Charles Gautier d'Agoty (1740-after 1787) the Prodigal *really* kneels. For one thing, his hands are clasped tightly in supplication and for balance. This pious gesture complements the dirty soles of his feet which, perhaps uncomfortably, we notice near his discarded staff.

But mostly we notice how his knees press deeply into the worn concavity of the step. Sculpted by countless footsteps over many years, this step may have been the son's departure point. Now, as if hollowed to fit his kneeling knee, the step is the platform for this highly emotional reunion. The father, for his part, leans forward, his curiously armored feet poised on two steps. His arms are widely stretched in a pre-embracing gesture of helpless wonder or, better, wondrous helplessness.

The velvety, rich red garment covering his shoulders contrasts with the son's mangy red rag wrap. As involved viewers we cannot avoid sharing an embarrassed peek at the son's buttock through a torn slit in his soiled covering. His condition is all the more touching when we compare his shabby sash with the velvety richness of the father's. The son is definitely down on his luck as well as his knees.

We might assume it is a servant who stands behind the father holding a garment which will soon change the sartorial condition of the penitent. His disengaged, diffident expression contrasts with the warm, endearing look on the face of the aging patriarch. Together the three figures are positioned in a step-like shape that is echoed in the blocky, dirty gray architecture behind them. These architectural shapes effectively divide the picture, on one side of which is this tender scene of homecoming.

On the other side are two visual vignettes that provide a counterbalance to the highly charged scene we've been looking at. One of these scenes involves two figures striding toward the homecoming. Having arrived by horse (whose head we glimpse against the trees), one of these figures poses somewhat

foppishly. He may be the older brother who has not yet heard the news of his brother's return; he is in for quite a surprise once he mounts those stairs.

The other diversion is the musical activity enacted by five characters high up on a balcony. Two of them are playing instruments, lute and violin; and the others look as if they are singing or observing. Together they provide a musical background for the dramas, one unfolding and the other about to take place. We might surmise that the musicians are offering a sonata by Morizio Cazzati (1620-1677), the musical father of the school of Bologna in the mid-seventeenth century. That would be an appropriate conceit, for Cazzati was active in Bologna about the time the original painting (of which this is a mezzotint print) was created by Guercino (1591-1666). Guercino, who painted the subject of the Prodigal seven times, lived in Bologna from 1642 until his death in 1666. It is possible that Guercino could have had the music of Cazzati in his ears as he painted.

Guercino included some visual quotes from the influential artist Michelangelo Merisi da Caravaggio (1573-1610). Caravaggio was known for realistic down-to-earth touches such as we see here in the son's torn wrap, his begrimed feet, and the coiled dramatic gesture of the father.

The emotional tableau of the central characters and the counterpoint diversions provided by others in Guercino's original painting are preserved in d'Agoty's mezzotint. (Mezzotint, by the way, is a method of engraving a copper plate to produce effects of light and shadow, especially when coloration is added. This method of reproduction is particularly significant since much of Caravaggio's work, and by extension that of his followers, depends on the play of light and shadow.)

As we look we might imagine sweet music floating from the balcony; and we can certainly anticipate the surprise about to be sprung on the dandy. Especially we witness the dynamic wonder of reconciliation, even if the artist(s) are presenting an uncomfortable truth: Repentance can be hard on the knees.

L'Enfant Prodigue
Grave d'après le Tableau Original ... de Guercino D'Acento
Dedié à sa Majesté ... le Roi de Sardaigne
Tiré de ses Galeries, par son très humble ... et très soumis Serviteur, Louis Dagoty

16

Louis Charles Gautier (or Gauthier) D'Agoty

L'Enfant Prodigue
(ca.1770)

Color mezzotint after Guercino (Giovanni Francesco Barbieri)
(23 x 24½ ins.)

A hard welcome

Scenes of reunion, homecoming, reconciliation—scenes we associate with the return of the Prodigal Son—are often permeated with visual signs of tenderness, happiness, gentleness, a sense of relief or tranquility. In this rendition of *The Prodigal Son* by Leon Golub (1922-2004) other reactions may come to mind: a perception of rawness, brutality, raggedness, even a sense of the macabre. It is because of images of this kind that one critic observed that no one has ever accused Leon Golub of "painting pretty."

We look at this early and not-so-pretty lithograph (from 1948) and come away with a mixture of confusion and fascination. It is not what we expect when we consider the son's homecoming, and it is not executed in a fashion with which we are familiar. The lines, shadows, and shapes in this print border on abstraction, something we associate with the art of the late 1940s in the United States. Emerging fom the horrors of World War II, artists like Franz Kline, Phillip Guston, Mark Tobey, and Lee Krasner shunned representational art in favor of a more free-flowing and personal, even idiosyncratic, expression.

This expression was achieved through non-representation, the free use of form and color (or the absence of color). Abstract expressionism as a style in the arts was rebellious, highly personal, and often anarchic. To a certain extent Golub's art from the 1940s and early 1950s participates in this dynamic condition in the visual arts. Looking at this print of the Prodigal Son, we can recognize the energy and tubulence that arises out of a highly personal style of expression. It is not a pretty picture; rather it is, consciously, disquieting.

Just because this work is familiar with the neighborhood of abstract expressionism, however, does not mean it has taken residence in that territory. Golub never fully embraced abstraction. He was a leader in Chicago's figurative movement, and he challenged the dominant style of abstract expressionism in many ways. For one thing, he never lost his interest in the depiction of the figure, though he did stretch the boundaries of realism, as he does in this picture.

We clearly make out two heads in this print, one in profile and one full-face. Presumably, the leonine head on the left is that of the father, strangely contained, who is receiving his returning son. This head is a suggestive mass of shadow, shape, and line that challenges us to perceive hair, nose, eye, ear, and throat. The more we look, the more we see a kind of lion king who is not altogether approachable.

Yet the other figure, in all likelihood the son, does presume to approach. We see his two eyes wide open, suggesting fear and trembling but also evincing a hesitant temerity. Not knowing what kind of response he will receive, this figure nonetheless draws near, willing to take his chances. The more we look, the more we perceive a suppliant son, one who may be ignored or dismissed—though not easily.

In many of his works, Leon Golub essays the human condition in a semi-abstract but nonetheless forcefully representational manner. Often he comments on power and abuse; other times he evokes brutality and political corruption. His is an art of confrontation and revelation. From his Jewish background he depicts civilization's victims of savagery. "I'm sort of political, sort of metaphyscial, sort of wiseacre," Golub once said in summarizing his art.

We may or may not see any of that in this early work, which is neither a wholly realistic nor a fully abstract portrayal of father and son. Because we know the subject matter and the story, though, we are open to seeing a remote father who has been injured by his son's defection. If he sees the son at all it is only out of the corner of his eye. Otherwise, he scowls and growls, but he also stares and cares. He allows the son, whose owl-eyed expression is scared and bared, to approach. Both figures implicitly seem to understand, each in his way, that there is an element of judgment even on the cusp of reconciliation. We know this is true, because we know how to stare imperiously into the distance even as we know what it is to gape in hope. While this is not a pretty picture, it is a promising one.

17
Leon Golub
Prodigal Son I
(1948)
Lithograph
(14¼ x 11½ ins.)

An unsettling return

When, on Easter Sunday, 1984, the British artist Edwina Sandys unveiled her bronze sculpture *Christa*, she created quite a stir in the religious community. The disquiet was understandable, for the four-foot tall work was a crucifix on which hung the figure of a nude woman. Such a gender inversion in the telling of a religious story may have been disturbing, but it was not necessarily new, for the Bohemian artist Alfred Kubin (1877-1969) released his lithograph *Prodigal Daughter* over sixty years earlier in 1921. Envisioning (and re-imaging) the scene of the return from Luke 15:20-24, this dark work pictures a nude woman groveling on the ground before a hulking figure.

This re-imaging of the story has the capacity to shock and offend just as the Sandys work did many years later. Here we see a nude woman, with steeply curved back and ample buttocks, prostrate before a sinister troll-like figure in a hooded cape. This latter figure seems to represent the father in the parable, as the "daughter" does the son. However, the gender of the caped one is not apparent and the gesture is disturbingly ambiguous. The hands could be extended in blessing; but they could also be reaching in rejection, groping, or something even more ominous. The shadowy, pinched expression of the face suggests something rather more malign than conciliatory.

The imploring woman writhes on a ground that could be barren or muddy earth, suggestive of the life—and the pigs—that the son/daughter had left behind. Her hands, clasped imploringly, are raised over her head so that we see none of her facial features. Embarrassed, we gaze at her nakedness while pitying her condition. We stare, but we also want to look away, wishing we could supply a covering for her nakedness. In her exposed state she is not only beggarly, she is also extremely vulnerable. Helpless and humiliated, she is exposed not only to the elements, but also to the gaze of viewers. Which of us—male or female—would want to be in that state or assume that position?

The darkly sensual nature of this scene invests it with an aura of the grotesque and the surreal. In looking at this lithograph we might be reminded of a threatening fairy tale, one inhabited by hobbits, crones, witches, and evil stepparents. The hatched cave-like space from which the cowled figure emerges exudes an air of mystery and unease. That dark space provides the kind of visual narrative that taps into the dark recesses of unconscious reality. It is a scary and unsettling scene!

Kubin's work in general gives a disturbing view of reality. Forces of the dark side frequently emerge in his art. His pictures—even his religious works—do not so much comfort as confront the viewer with the kind of grotesqueness often found in the visual field of such artists as Bosch and Goya. His lithographs and drawings are psychic and spiritual studies informed and shaped by personal trauma, by the horrors of World War 1, and by personal illness and obsessions. We are gripped rather than soothed, confronted not so much by beauty as by the horrific.

In these visual nightmares—one of which we see here—we are obliged to reflect on the turmoil of our lives and the transitoriness of earthly and unearthly things. We come to see the necessity of either submitting to or rising up against forces over which we have little control. Like works that have emerged from the hands of other tortured artists (Beethoven and Dostoyevsky come to mind), Kubin's work functions as a kind of *memento mori*, reminders of our mortality and the challenge to side with life rather than death. Kubin, a survivor of more than one suicide attempt, bore witness to these ongoing options in his life as well as in his work.

Kubin informs us through his art that human beings are surrounded and under attack by monstrous forces. Yet we must dare to find ways of coping, sometimes by resistance and rising up, sometimes by pleading in the muck as the exposed woman in this picture. Ten years before he executed *Prodigal Daughter*, Kubin had articulated convictions that are readily apparent in this work. "How did I come to create such things?"he wrote in 1911. "It was one and the same power that led me to dreams and silly pranks in childhood, later to sickness, and finally to art . . . Fantasy has put its hallmark on my existence; it is fantasy that makes me happy and makes me sad. I recognize it constantly inside and outside me."

By depicting both the fantasy and the fantastic, the vulnerable and the mysterious, Kubin has squeezed something disturbing but provocative out of the parable. We are gripped rather than soothed by the return of the child, a pleading daughter at the foot of a menacing being, a sinner under the hands of what might be judgment or acceptance. We need to look long and hard to figure out what is really going on here and what might happen next. What kind of dawn lies on the other side of nightmare?

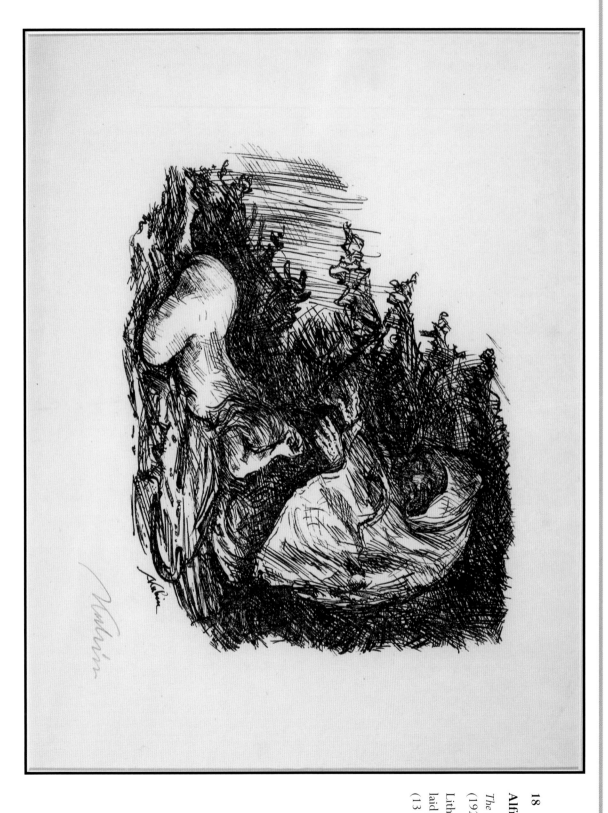

18
Alfred Kubin
The Prodigal Daughter
(1921)
Lithograph on heavy
laid paper
(13 x 10 ins.)

Home is where they have to take you in

Nobody knows the trouble I've seen,
Nobody knows but Jesus . . . .
Sometimes I'm up, sometimes I'm down,
Sometimes I'm almost to the ground . . . .
Oh, yes, Lord.

One can imagine this old spiritual being sung as the drunken son staggers home, upright only because of the support of a woman and a man. The woman may be the mother; she looks old and concerned enough. The man may be the father, though he looks young enough to be the older brother. His anxious look, particularly around the eyes and mouth, may contain just a touch of disapproval. After all, this limp, returning Prodigal is in a stupor. He has the vacant expression of the inebriated, and his left hand holds the cause, an empty whiskey bottle.

Rumpled, and with one pant leg cut off at the knee, this returning Prodigal is in a sad state, an object of trouble and care. Nonetheless, one person stands on tiptoe with excitement. A young girl on the left treats the drunkard as if he were a returning hero. She reaches up over the mother and stretches a branch with leaves (a victor's laurel?) over the son's head. She appears to be the one member of this family who is overtly glad to see him, though the bucket-holding boy standing slightly apart from the rest stares agape at the scene. This is something to behold!

The characters are bunched together, solidly curved like a mound; one of them, a grandmotherly type, sternly looks and gestures at a boy who with arms upraised, is bending over a steaming kettle. She seems to be admonishing him to get busy and stir the steaming pot. But what is in that vessel? Is it fatted-calf gumbo, the "banquet" for the returning son? Or is it a boiling mass of laundry that might contain some kind of robe, for such is promised in the parable. Overall, this scene of return is not so much joyous or forgiving as it is one of relief and concern. This particular homecoming

is ambiguous, seeming to imply that home is where you go when you have nowhere else to go, a place where they are obliged to take you in — or at least not throw you out.

Ben Earl Looney (1904-1981) was on the first faculty of the Ringling Brothers School of Art at Sarasota, Florida. This print is a slice-of-life scene that fits in with his overall artistic output. His obituary noted that he was an artist known throughout the state of Louisiana for his watercolor drawings of southern life. Further, he was a great painter of rural landscapes and murals. As a southern regional artist (influenced by such midwestern regionalist artists as Thomas Hart Benton and John Stewart Curry), Looney is said to have painted every plantation in the Pelican State. There is an added dimension of poignancy as we look at this scene with post-Katrina eyes.

This scene of a returning Prodigal is definitely rural, but it is not obviously situated on a plantation. The modest house and the even more modest outhouse in the background along with an empty can and bottle in the left foreground bespeak rural poverty. We surmise that this is an African-American family who do not live off the fat of the land — there is no fatted calf here. Instead, this group is knit and bound together, subsisting modestly on the scrambled earth. In such straitened circumstances it is not surprising that they display more concern than joy in receiving and upholding the soused son.

Yet, because they are family — implicitly a loving and caring family — they take him in. Having the son home drunk is better than not having him home at all. In the end, we may fancy, the initial spiritual changes tune and key, and the mood shifts from weary lament to a tired, but confident, prayer:

Precious Lord, take my hand, lead me on, let me stand,
I am tired, I am weak, I am worn.
Through the storm, through the night, lead me on to the light,
Take my hand, precious Lord, lead me home.

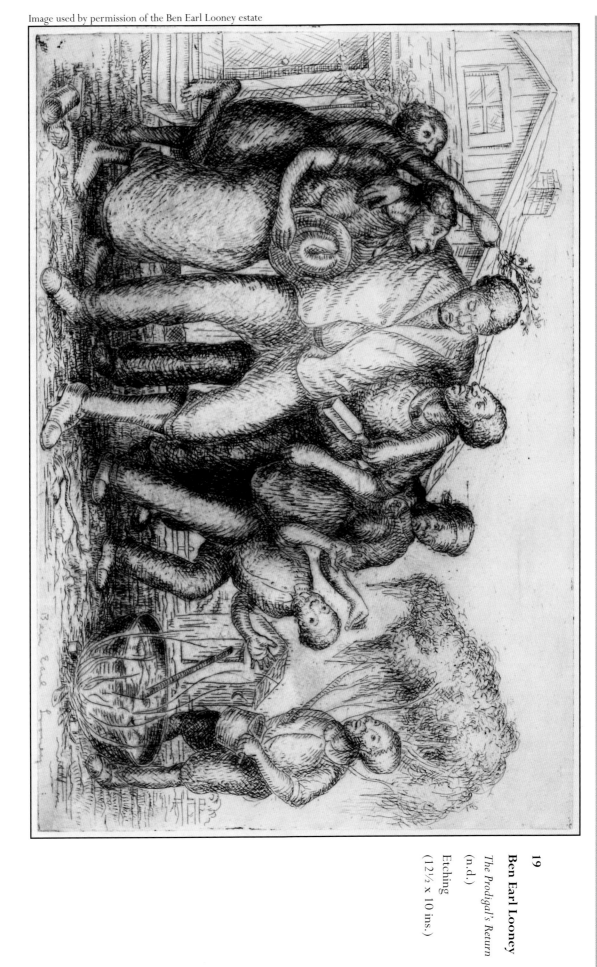

19
Ben Earl Looney
The Prodigal's Return
(n.d.)
Etching
(12½ x 10 ins.)

The grieving son comes home too late

The fragmented and frenzied pace of life in the early twenty-first century contrasts with the seemingly more coherent and measured style of the late nineteenth century. What we experience today contains many benefits, to be sure, though it tends to leave us with little patience for the leisure and propriety which (perhaps wrongly) we associate with the Victorian era. We linger little and rush much; ours is not a gentle world or a romantic time. The angular, vibrant, and often abstract art of our day presents a different picture of reality from that of Victorian artists. Because of the chasm that exists between the times, many find pictorial art of the nineteenth century, particularly Salon art, to be embarrassing, even meretricious; and we relegate it to the attic of our aesthetic.

Yet, for those whose taste and sensibilities permit, there can be a certain charm and appeal in the pictorial style and sentimental narrative that was popular over a century ago. Henry Mosler (1841-1920), an artist virtually unknown today, was an acclaimed and successful American painter in his day. His paintings often won international prizes, and his *The Prodigal's Return* was reported to be the only painting by an American in the Luxembourg Gallery in Paris. (As if to illustrate the change in aesthetics, it should be noted that the prestigious museum which once proudly housed nineteenth-century sculpture and painting collections is now a gallery dedicated to promoting temporary exhibits.)

An emotional and sentimental atmosphere permeates this photogravure of Mosler's 1879 painting of a prostrate Prodigal who has returned too late to greet his now dead mother. She lies in a candlelit cabinet bed, while he kneels in abject grief before the highly polished, though worn and scratched piece of furniture. There is no father with whom to be reconciled, though the photogravure does contain a "father" in the person of a pensive priest who strokes his chin while holding a prayer book in his left hand. Perhaps, unlike the son, this thoughtful cleric was there in time to perform the last rites. His respectable sash and soutane contrast with the son's disreputable clothing and dirty bare feet. The vagabond life of the son is seen in his discarded hat and sack, the kind of traveling kit associated with knights of the open road. This attire is contrasted with the cavalier (presumably the son at his departure) in the tiny picture above the enclosed bier.

This retelling of the parable is charged with emotion and sentiment that stretches modern artistic sensibilities. Raging grief, absorbed reverie, and an air of melancholy pervade this scene. The work requires that we make an intentional move to enter into this distant scene from the late 1870s, especially when we recall that the art world of the time was scintillating with the light, color, and vibration of the Impressionists.

Still, there are rewards for those willing to make that jump. It is possible, for example, to be moved by the reality of grief and missed opportunity. The comforts of religion in such cases are sympathetically portrayed in this scene, something not always present in depictions of the clergy. The tender, even romantic (thought perhaps also moralistic) interpretation of the parable can arguably have a place in the constellation of our sensibilities.

One way to approach Mosler's rendition of the Prodigal might be to regard it as a visual realization of the hymnody of the period, for the two forms of expression have similar emotional appeal. Two hymns come to mind: "Jesus Calls Us; O'er the Tumult," a hymn written in 1852 by Cecil Frances Alexander, evokes the anguish of one tossed about by life's wild, tempestuous sea. "What a Friend We Have in Jesus" from 1855 has a textual pertinence because the author, Joseph Medlicott Scriven, wrote the hymn and sent it to his mother to comfort her in a time of sorrow. One might try humming or singing these hymns while looking at Mosler's picture. It would be like briefly entering a lost world, a world that had many now unfamiliar modes of expression that attempted to address the human condition in a poignant and affecting manner.

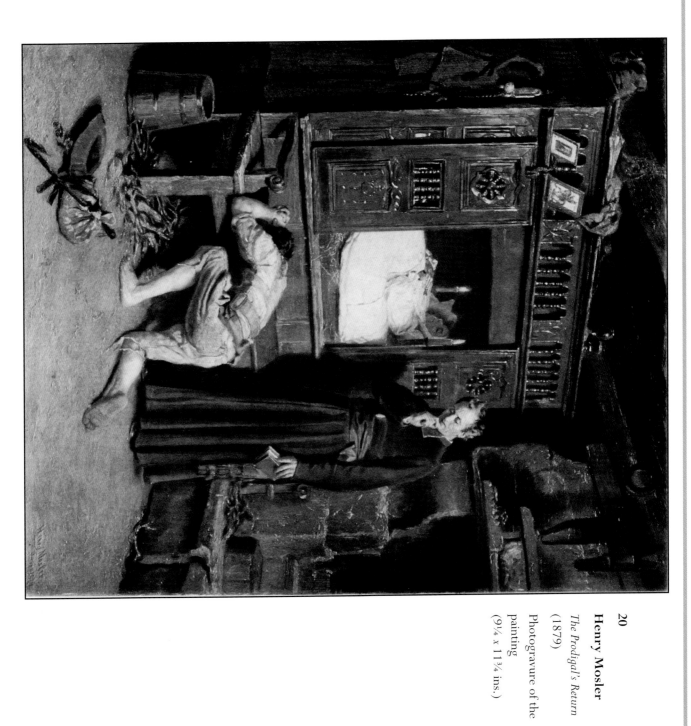

20
Henry Mosler
The Prodigal's Return
(1879)
Photogravure of the
painting
(9¼ x 11¾ ins.)

Works of art often reflect or grow out of the context in which they are created. Knowing that this woodcut by Christian Rohlfs (1849-1938) was executed in 1916 at the height of World War I helps to interpret what is going on in the picture. During that "war to end all wars" Rohlfs created a number of religious and symbolic works which were meditations on the madness of war and the undeniability of death. For him death, like war, was not so much an evil to be actively resisted as it was an inescapable inevitability.

The subject of the Prodigal Son occupied Rohlfs' mind during this horrific period in Germany, and he executed a number of differing realizations of the subject. For Germany the war was lost, even though the carnage continued. In his artistic creations the artist tried to gain some respite and freedom from the distressing events of the time. Over and over, in successive renditions, this Prodigal scene became a reflection on return to a loving, understanding, forgiving father. In this particular version, however, there seems to be a certain intensity and ambiguity as the father puts his hand on the son's head.

Viewers will never be of one mind in interpreting artistic expressions, especially when asked to interpret facial features. Looking closely at the face of the father here, one may be inclined to ask what the old man is feeling as he bends and clasps his son. Is it relief and joy or is it, perhaps, exhaustion and sadness? The eyes are uneven, one eyeball more prominent than the other. The lips bend downward as if frowning or grieving.

Overall, the face could be seen as expressing a mournful world-weariness which knows that even though the son has been found, something else may have been irretrievably lost. The relationship between father and son, after all, has been altered, and there is no return to the way things used to be. One might see a contrast between the son's expression of youthful expectation (*I'm back—think of that!*) and the strained expression of the mature father (*Yes, you're back, and I don't exactly know what to think of that!*).

The ambiguous nature of the reunion is enhanced by other elements in this picture. The monochromatic sienna of the surface reminds one of rust. While light shines through windows to the right and left, the center of the picture is in deep shadow. The reach of the father with his tent-like shape almost absorbs the scrawny figure of the son. Hand and beard look like the tines of a rake, and the overall pyramidal shape of the scene gives it an air of solidity and gravity. Even allowing for perspective, one senses a puzzling aspect of proportion. If the naked son were to stand, he would be half again as tall as the robed father, and he would, in fact, be bowed by the upper frame of the picture.

The somber overcast in what should otherwise be a joyful scene may indeed reflect Rohlfs' war-weariness. It may even mirror something of his personal past. Born of peasant stock, Rohlfs was sickly as a youth. As a result of lingering effects of rheumatic fever he lost his right leg in 1874 when he was twenty-five years old. Out of physical necessity and as part of his therapy he decided to create works of art. Influenced by the art of Edvard Munch, Vincent van Gogh, and Paul Gauguin, the independent Rohlfs was also in touch with, though never closely allied with, the art movements of his day like *Die Brücke* and *Der blaue Reiter*.

He was less interested in prevailing fashions in art than he was in following a vision that conveyed his own personal depths of meaning. This commitment brought him to create works (like this *Return of the Prodigal Son*) that had an inner resonance with direct and expressive forms. The artist once said of his work: "Creating art grows from an inner instinct, and who would undertake to explain this?"

Ironically, while this work reflects his inner instinct about return during a time of war, Rohlfs was about to set out on the most creative period of his life. In 1919, at age seventy, he married, and his subsequent works became more and more vigorous until his death at the age of eighty-eight. Sadly, for him and for the world of art, he was banned by the Nazis in 1937 as one who created "Degenerate Art." As a result, four hundred twelve of his works from various museums and collections were confiscated; and he died not long after, forbidden to paint or exhibit.

Fortunately, many of his works survived the ban and seizure. In particular we are fortunate to see and be in the presence of a lanky Prodigal as he is welcomed by a world-weary father. In their reunion we perceive some of the ambiguities that are conveyed by color, expression, shape, and artistic vision. On the other side of those windows there may be the rattle of war, but at the heart of the picture there is return and grace.

21
Christian Rohlfs

Return of the
Prodigal Son
(1916)

Woodcut printed
in reddish brown
in the manner of a
monotype's unique
proof
(13½ x 19 ins.)

Political scandal forces a prodigal son to resign

Political cartoons in the daily newspaper possess both relevance and currency for us. Because they deal with current events, we recognize the relevant characters and situations that are being satirized. But when we look at a political cartoon from an earlier age, we may find that the wit has been dulled and obscured by the passage of time. If we want to find out what the fuss was once all about, we will need to brush aside the dust of time and clarify the context.

Such is the case with this witty engraving by Thomas Rowlandson (1756-1827). It was in its day a timely and popular commentary on a British scandal that rocked king and country in 1809. Frederick, Duke of York, was the second son of George III, the king who had "lost" the American colonies a few decades earlier. Frederick was commander-in-chief of the army, and among his nonmilitary activities was a dalliance with his mistress, Mary Clarke. Clarke, on her part, had ambitions beyond her common sense, for she parlayed her favored position with Frederick as a go-between for military commissions and promotions, something we might regard as insider trading today.

When word of her power-brokering got out, a public scandal erupted. Chancellor of the Exchequer Spencer Percival rose up in most high dudgeon and delivered a caustic three-hour speech in Parliament calling for Frederick's resignation. The speech found such favor in the court of public opinion that Frederick was forced to resign his post in 1809, an event which prompted this hand-colored engraving by Rowlandson.

In it Frederick, a somewhat porcine figure, kneels before his kingly father, blubbering into a large white handkerchief. Appropriate to the situation and befitting the tradition of political cartoons, he utters a compressed quotation from Luke 15:20-21: "And he arose and went to his Father, and said Father I have sinned before thee, and I am no longer worthy to be called thy Son." The groveling figure is stripped of his uniform coat, hat, and sword; and before him is a document with the word "Resignation" written on it.

The father, the king, is seated half-hidden by his right hand, a yellow pillar, and the purplish curtain of a royal baldachin. Out of his mouth spills his aggrieved but not very angry response: "Very Naughty Boy! Very naughty Boy indeed! However, I forgive you but don't do so any more."

This print, a scene that doubtless never took place, at least not in this form, is clear political commentary. Yet its form and punch derive from the Lukan parable. Visually and verbally the character of Frederick parallels the son in the story, and the quotation ballooning from his mouth reflects the biblical source. But the father is something else. He doesn't accept or embrace the son as in the parable. Instead, he is distant and embarrassed, offering a rebuke-filled word of forgiveness, though not from Luke. It is, rather, a subtly pointed paraphrase of John 8:11, from the story of the woman caught in adultery. This is political satire with a biblical bite!

Rowlandson knew what he was doing. Like his friend and rival James Gillray (who also invoked the subject and text of the Prodigal [page 115] in a satirical foray called *Reconciliation*), Rowlandson was an astute observer of the current scene, as in this work entitled *Resignation*. He was a prolific illustrator, and his commentaries pilloried all walks of society: servants and scholars, soldiers and politicians, clergy and tradesmen, flirts and fops. He worked so quickly and hastily that his pictures often lacked finesse and polish. He was often accused of being coarse and indelicate, although his drawings were not nearly as exaggerated as those of his more outrageous contemporary, Gillray.

Nonetheless, Rowlandson hit his mark over and over again. So numerous were his works that Princeton University has more than nine hundred volumes with his illustrations as well as about two thousand individual prints.

Rowlandson was a true and refined humorist. As such he held up a mirror to current fads and foibles. In this commentary on one of the royal scandals of his day he reshaped the parable of the Prodigal from Luke to fit the circumstances of his day. When clever and skilled artists like Rowlandson invoke biblical images, we must be prepared to be stretched and to make connections. Sometimes we may be provoked by a new slant on interpreted truth, and sometimes, as here, we may be prompted to smile at truth that is colored by context.

Works of art are constructions that shape and challenge our vision. Sometimes, they help us discover how naughty we have been. Pilloried, we might then be pressed to listen to the king speak, and be resolved to mend our ways.

THE PRODIGAL SONS RESIGNATION.

22

Thomas Rowlandson

The Prodigal Son's Resignation
(2 March 1809)
Hand-colored
engraving
(12½ x 8¾ ins.)

The surly elder brother skulks away

The parable in Luke 15 is most often referred to as *The Prodigal Son*. That is perfectly understandable, because the wastrel son appears to be the main focus of narrative attention. He took his share of the property and left home. He squandered that largesse and spent time among the pigs and other lowlife. Eventually he came to his senses and, repentant, returned home. There, contrary to all expectations, he was lavishly received by his enthusiastic father.

Most people, when they read the story all the way to the end, come to realize that it has no tidy moral or conclusion. Because of the complex dynamics at work in this open-ended story, some readers, commentators, preachers, and artists have alternatively focused their attention on the warm and enthusiastic response of the father. Instead of regarding the story as the *Prodigal Son*, these interpreters prefer to see it as the parable of the *Profligate Father*.

Others who are familiar with the parable see yet another dynamic at work in the narrative, and they have chosen to attend to the role of the elder brother, the one who churlishly challenged the father for his unreasonable and extravagant reception of the wayward younger son. These exponents regard the story not so much as that of a prodigal son or a profligate father. Rather, they see it as a story of a *Begrudging Brother*. And there is some justification for this view, for if anyone ponders the account that takes place in verses 25-32, *begrudging* is not too strong a word to describe the elder brother's attitude.

Jan Shoger, who taught printmaking for twenty years at St. Olaf College in Northfield, Minnesota, and is now professor emeritus of art, is one of those visual interpreters who has focused on the older sibling. However, when we look closely at her sensitive print, we see something more—even other—than the anger and resentment usually associated with the titular figure in the parable. Shoger offers a nuanced psychological study of a man who appears conflicted. The brother may be surly, as the story says; but here he also displays an inward looking, distant, even sad expression.

That he is the focus of attention is apparent, for the receiving father and the kneeling younger son occupy less than half the neatly divided pictorial space.

The two of them are outside on what might be a flagstone path with a tree and a (bluish) grassy knoll in the background. The boy has an open-eyed, vacant expression, dazed and dumb. The father has a snowy white beard and an open mouth, as if he is solemnly saying, "Oooh . . . you have come back." This pair occupies the middle distance of this domestic outdoor scene, and, as we can see, their combined visual mass—including the boy's discarded pack—takes up less visual space than the brooding elder brother on the right.

This figure—the elder brother—is a consciously separate entity. He is partitioned off from the rest of his family by some kind of vertical earth-colored curtain. This screen frames his body and separates it from the action of repentance and homecoming outside. It looks as if the curtain may have just been drawn aside, for a small strip of it is seen on the left. Being closer to the viewer's visual plane, this elder brother bulks large and, with capped head bent forward, is caught in mid-stride. His beard is fuller than his brother's, yet it is less grizzled than his father's. He is a member of the family; but with his back turned, he is also separate from them. He represents the broken side of an otherwise happy story.

His clenched left hand, with extended thumb, underscores his determined self-distancing. He is striding away both physically and psychologically into his own separate space. The expression on his face is both arresting and suggestive. As already noted, it is distant and inward looking. Even more, it is the face of someone who has wearily concluded that his place has been taken, whose secure dreams have been scattered.

Now he feels compelled to reconfigure his place in the universe; his life has been changed by what is going on outside on the path beneath that leafy tree, and he doesn't like it. When we look at him, we recognize his look. It is one we have doubtless worn ourselves on occasion. After all, events in life—even bittersweet ones like reunions—have a way of shifting the ground under our feet. And, like the elder brother, we are inclined to shut down, go inside, and brood on what it all means.

Image used by permission of the artist

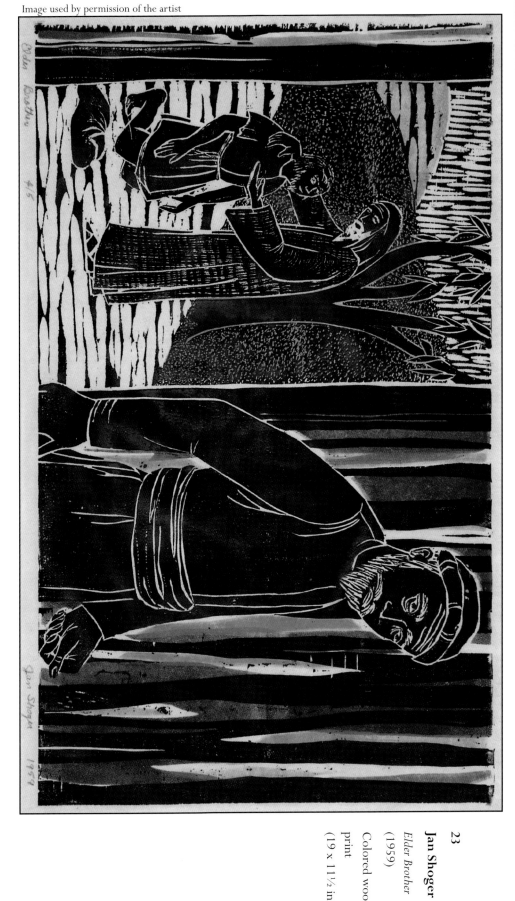

23
Jan Shoger
Elder Brother
(1959)
Colored woodblock
print
(19 x 11½ ins.)

The Prodigal on the Midway

Taking a long look at Joseph Smith's silkscreen print is a little like taking a stroll around a state fair. Fairs, as we all know, are for educating and entertaining. They appeal to a variety of tastes and conditions, even our vanity. Fairs offer a colorful array of sights that are dazzling and bewildering, familiar and fun. Slowly strolling around the golden circle of Smith's print with our eyes (the circle is not even seven-and-a-half inches in diameter), we come across a compressed, bizarre midway of "delights." The fancy is not so far-fetched, for the artist himself likens the colors and images in this work to Hieronymus Bosch's sixteenth-century grotesque painting, *Garden of Earthly Delights.*

While Smith's work is more contained and focused than the sprawling exaggerations of Bosch, it shares some features with the offbeat world of grotesque art where images are distorted and exaggerated. In that world landscape and figures confront us in an intentionally strange and disordered way, for the grotesque is a weird place where things are turned upside down and inside out. In that sense Smith's work evokes that shivery range of feeling, causing us at once to laugh with amusement while being struck with confusion and foreboding.

Here in our meander we notice a flat, fleshy pig, one who might be a contender for a blue ribbon, the ideal of porcine excellence. Oddly, a stack of coins extends the pig's snout, linking ham with lucre—from pork to pork barrel. Floating behind and next to the pig is another midway wonder, a woman twirling in a dance, though her right foot possesses only four toes. Her red dress is hiked up suggestively high, the vivid color reflected in her come-hither lips. Staring straight ahead with an eye heavy with mascara, she seems to be trying to seduce the viewer. But her head and arms are teasingly positioned in what appears to be the son's midsection. As if to accentuate his weakness, her toes are like the point of an arrow directed at his Achille's tendon. The action of this whirling seductress is a not very subtle reference to the son's dissolute living.

Another sign of that dissipation is the upturned bottle, only a drop left—indicating that the wine is gone. If one proverb cautions against giving your strength to women (Proverbs 31:3), then another warns that wine is a mocker, and whoever is led astray by it is not wise (Proverbs 20:1). Wine . . . women: that leaves song, which in this context is not so benign. Gross music is represented by a curved brass instrument attached to the son's navel, another touch of the grotesque. Whatever tune emerges from this twisted horn, it is likely to echo the caution of the Teacher in Ecclesiastes (7:5): It is better to hear the rebuke of the wise, than to hear the song of fools.

There is some indication that, even though the song has been played by the dissolute fool, he may have heard the rebuke through the hearing aid in his ear. The title of this work, after all, is *Prodigal Repentant.* We have seen that the stretched and encircling body of the son has been the grotesque theater of debauchery. Yet that shape, like the floating fetus in the closing scenes of *2001: A Space Odyssey,* also suggests rebirth. The artist says as much: "[U]nlike a fetus waiting to be born with eyes closed, the Prodigal's eyes are wide open. He knows what he has done, and repents of his wrong, hoping that his father will extend some form of forgiveness. His realization is none too soon, for his arm and hand are already taking on the form of a pig's leg and hoof."

And that brings us full circle to where we started, with the prize-winning pig at the state fair. Yet, at the same time we seem to have moved beyond the grotesqueries depicted in this scene. These bent emblems of commerce, wine, women, and song are about to be left behind in favor of rebirth and return. Having been to the fair, notably vanity fair, the son directs himself to a new reality. It is salutary and sobering to make the move from vanity to sanity.

Image used by permission of the artist

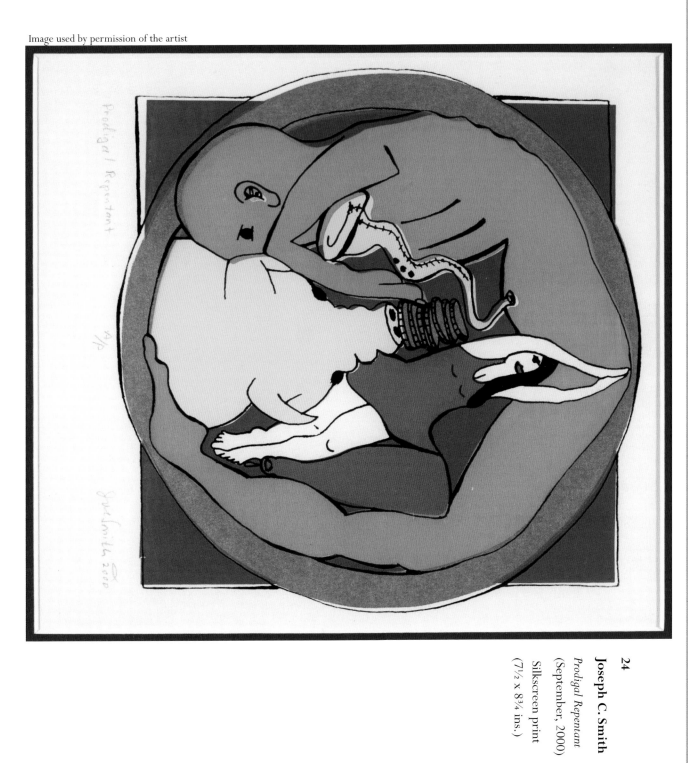

24

Joseph C. Smith

Prodigal Repentant
(September, 2000)

Silkscreen print
(7½ x 8¾ ins.)

A painful and angry return

A young man with a high forehead, wearing a purple T-shirt, looks over his right shoulder at the viewer. With a truculent expression on his face, he points at a wreck of a house perched atop a dirt mound. His twisted mouth might be confronting us with an expression that both accuses and excuses. "See that mess out there?" he snarls. "That's not my fault. I'm in no way responsible for that. The old man's gone and life's tough, but don't blame me."

We might be justified in regarding this rebel with or without a cause as an urban episode of blight and abandonment. It takes a conscious act of exegesis to understand this scene as the (not so joyous) return of the Prodigal Son. For one thing, there *is* no father. Neither is there an older brother, a fatted calf, or the comfortable trappings of home life. Instead, we see the skeletal hulk of a house that, judging by the dentate trim at roof level, might once have been elegant. Now, however, the boxy structure with black, vacant, and charred windows conveys emptiness and dereliction.

There is a Kafkaesque quality to this landscape. The son stands excluded behind a chain link fence, one of several fences that restrict access to the house. Further, there are no steps. A surrounding railing further bars entrance. What is that rocky board-strewn mound of dirt anyway? Who builds houses that way? And what about those barren and blasted trees on that sere hill behind the house? Are they signs of blasted hope, an arid prospect masked by the son's aggressive expression?

These questions possess a kind of legitimacy in light of the artist's own observations about his work. An art professor at Mount Saint Mary's University in Emmitsburg, Maryland, Tim Vermeulen admits that this version

of the Prodigal Son comes from his own spiritual and emotional quest to find home. "As a Christian," he says, "I have found it difficult to accept or recover the loving arms of the father. I experienced my father most powerfully as punisher, and I think for many people the experience of our father mirrors our impression of God. So, much of my work seems to be about recovering a sense of God as caring and nurturing."

Perhaps, then, the surly son is not so much challenging as he is questing, evincing more anguish than anger. He gestures over the weed- and flower-filled stretch of "lawn," which also contains a chained and emaciated dog. The young man looks and blurts over his shoulder. By his bearing he might well be inviting us into his pained frame of mind. "See that mess out there? I wish it weren't so. I keep looking, but I am not finding. I finally come home only to see that dad and everybody else are gone. It really hurts, and I am both mad and sad."

This picture of anger and pain, exclusion and abandonment confronts us with paradoxical possibilities. The son may be a self-excusing hothead with an attitude. But alternately he may be a deeply conflicted young man on a quest, looking for but not finding the home he desires. Either way, this Prodigal scene deserves to be interpreted on its own terms: a grim context with signs of a disturbed consciousness. The son's look and his gesture force us to ponder a difficult prospect, one that both irks and confronts. The landscape may be bleak and not especially promising. But we can still take a long look over the fence and regard the one who points, each of us in our own way trying to recover a sense of a hidden God who, we hope, is caring and nurturing.

Image used by permission of the artist

25

Tim Vermeulen

*Return of the Prodigal
Son*
(1999)

Oil on panel, Pamar
varnish
(7 x 11 ins.)

The son brings home a fox

For much of the history of western Christian art, biblical images have conformed to conventions developed during the Renaissance. That visual conformity has begun to change because of such artists as Sadao Watanabe (1913-1996). Schooled in the tradition of traditional Japanese folk art, Watanabe, soon after World War II, addressed a very basic question: Is it possible for Asian artists to interpret the Christian story out of their Asian imagination and still express that Christian faith in a way that makes both a visual and spiritual impact?

In a body of work almost entirely done in the technique of stencil dyeing called *katazome*, Watanabe's answer to this question was a convincing yes. Creating more than three hundred sixty stencil prints dealing with both Old and New Testament scenes, the artist became a pioneer in expressing the biblical faith through scenes and images deriving from Japanese traditional culture. In the process he become internationally famous. His works have been acquired by museums throughout the world, and his scenes have become familiar to many in the form of expressive calendars which are often prized, framed, and saved as both popular and fine art.

Most important of all, however, has been the way Watanabe's art opened our eyes to see the Christian story in other than western art terms. We instantly know—and are moved by—his depiction of the Last Supper, for example, even though the visual grammar is as un-Renaissance-like as the sushi and saki on the table. As a result we are privileged to see the familiar in a fresh way, and we are enabled to appreciate the transcultural validity of the Christian message. Over time Watanbe has become representative of many artists from other than European cultures who have enriched our perception of the bible story.

Watanabe repeated, in varied form, certain biblical stories. For example, he executed something like twenty versions of the Last Supper and fifteen of the Wise Men. He did at least three renditions of the Prodigal Son: in 1973, 1976, and this one from 1983. While this version is typical of his work as a whole, it is also singular. It displays the sinuous line and Asian features normative in Watanabe's work. Yet, while most of his stencil prints contain solid color backgrounds in red, orange, or even blue, this work lacks that feature. The sheer background gives the figures a kind of delicacy we sometimes see in the tracery of certain stained glass. On the whole, the color here is minimal: just a splash of red in the figure on the right and in the flowers of the father's robe, and a few strokes of blue in the son's garment and in the images at the top of the picture.

The scene is at once a picture of stillness and motion. The father is frozen in a gesture of blessing, while the son, his body built of curvy slabs, kneels, lost more in thought than contrition. All motion comes from a single winding line that that runs and rises through the center of the picture. This line links the father and the son and moves our eye upward to the right. A curious cloud-like or tree-shaped black, blue, and white mass hovers over the scene, suggesting the possibility of cool shade in an otherwise open landscape.

The august gesture of the father is contrasted to the animal figure next to the son. Is that a dog? Or is it perhaps a fox, a folk symbol in Japan of slyness and play? The latter is surely possible because it seems to be wearing a red scarf, and we know that foxes do not usually wear red scarves. It is, perhaps, a touch of the *fabulous* in the midst of the biblical. We notice also that this standing animal looks back at the father, its paw extended in a gesture of blessing that echoes the latter. It is something Saint Francis might have enjoyed. The fox is a bit of visual and interpretive play, a note of humor, something of the kind that often appears in the works of Watanabe. This scene of homecoming contains serenity and motion; it is also pensive and perplexing, gentle and droll.

While the stencil scenes created by Watanabe are by now familiar to most viewers—they are still very popular—it is important to remember that artists like him have only relatively recently taught us to see "with new eyes." This expansion of vision is part of Watanabe's legacy; thankfully, artists throughout the world are continually widening the horizon. We can be very glad that this Japanese artist found his vocation by addressing himself to that central question about the largeness of the Christian Story. He has clearly expanded the narrative for us by a body of work that illustrates what he once said: "I have always aspired to portray stories and episodes from the Bible. In this disturbed world, I would like to be able to heed the voice of Heaven." Happily, that voice speaks in many languages, and in our still disturbed world it tells the old, old story of unseen things above.

26

Sadao Watanabe

The Prodigal Son
(1983)

Katazome, pattern-
drying process
(8½ x 9 ins.)

The son comes home through fire and tears

For most people a mystery is a particular type of light reading, something by Agatha Christie or Rex Stout. For others a mystery is something inexplicable, like the incomprehensible workings of a computer or a teenager's whim. To acknowledge the mystery of the living God, however, is to admit a mystery of a different magnitude. This mystery is not understood by fact or data alone. Rather, the mystery of God is one that lurks, works, blossoms, and bursts all over the place: in liturgy and worship, in contemplation and devotion, in music and the arts.

This understanding of mystery resonates with the thought and art of the Romanian artist Marian Zidaru (b. 1956). In an artist's statement Zidaru acknowledges that "the inspiration of an artist always comes from the Father, through the Holy Ghost; that is why my art does not belong to me: It comes from God and serves him . . . My art is not art; my art is a message for 'those that have ears to hear and eyes to see.'"

If we open our eyes to look at his *Intoarcerea Fiului Risipitor*, we might see something of the mystery of Orthodox icons. We gaze on the figure of Christ enthroned, for he dominates this work. He is the white-robed, kingly yet gentle figure who sits on a plush throne, surrounded by geometric figures. This vision of glory floats on a heavenly golden background.

This striking image is clearly a visual reference to the Orthodox icon of *Christ in Glory*, a figure of the Christ-Pantocrator, one who is ruler of the universe, the one who will come to judge the living and the dead. Usually pictured with a book on his lap (instead of a chalice as here), the model for this icon may be traced to a fifteenth-century prototype by Andrei Rublev, the great Russian iconographer. This icon is a figural and geometric composition that portrays the divinity of the transfigured Christ. The effect here is enhanced by a trio of wing-covered angels whose eyes peer in wonder at the enthroned Christ.

According to an interview the collector had with the artist, we should interpret this icon rather literally in terms of the coming Rapture. A snake at the edge of the icon, a howling woman in hell, and the word FOC (Romanian for *fire*) tell us where hell is. With hell at his back and through the images of many tears, the son is returning to a loving father. An arrow points the way.

Still the son does not immediately encounter his waiting father. Rather he bows down, following the movement of a second arrow. But instead of bowing to his father, as in the biblical story, he is gesturing in wonder and obeisance to the figure of Christ enthroned. This Christ, in the mystery of the triune faith, is one with the Father and the Holy Spirit. As the second person of the Trinity, the Son of God was said to be the perfect image and likeness of the Father. Enthroned in glory, he is the one who, in this iconic telling of the story, accepts and forgives the returning Prodigal. The three angels in heaven on the right dance the hora.

Our eye ranges from the right to left, from the dancing angels to the thrusting figure of the son. There is no doubt that the enthroned Christ is the pivot where our gaze comes to rest. This dazzling figure reaches out in blessing with his right hand; he offers the means of grace, the cup of salvation, with his other hand. All prodigal sons and daughters are invited to look and see, to come and bow down before the throne of grace. In Zidaru's vision the icon is a means by which we may discern the mystery of repentance and redemption.

In the end Zidaru is right: his art is not art, at least not in the traditional sense. Icons are not religious pictures; they are not realistic representations of some religious scene or personality. Rather, icons are windows that open onto a different, spiritual reality. In the company of *Christ Pantocrator* we might encounter a simple interpretive poem that could help us see (if we have eyes to see) what the icon is all about.

The Icon*

A holy Bible
for the simple and unlettered.
A visual theology
for the contemplatives and connoisseurs.
One of the mysteries
of the personal Theanthropic**
Presence of the Word.
Medium of grace
toward sanctifying virtue.
Doxology to the absolute Beauty.
A single ray of the "Eighth Day's" light!

*from *What Do You Know About Icons? An Aesthetic, Historical and Theological Approach to the Icons of the Orthodox Church in the Form of Questions and Answers* (Attiki, Greece: Etoimasia Publications, 2001)
**Theanthropic=the God-man

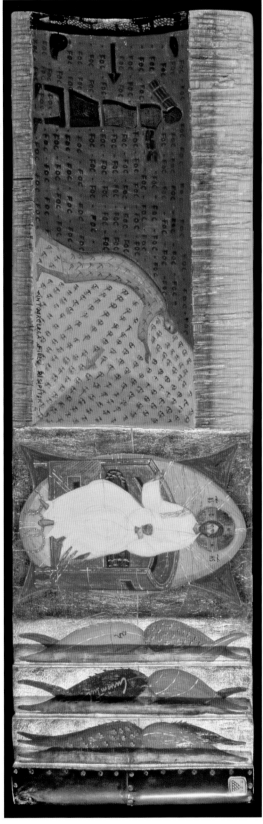

27

Marian Zidaru

Intoarcerea Fiului
Risipitor
[The Return—or the
Way Back—of the
Prodigal Son]
(2004)

Egg tempera and ink
on wood
(8 x 20½ ins.)

Prodigal son who art in heaven:
Son who saved yourself by trusting,
serving since as an example
to millions of prodigals,
son who knew the horror of absence,
the emptiness of sin
and yearning for his father's house,
help me to pray, this agonizing night,
for prodigal parents
whose sin consists
in turning Christ's parable upside down
by erasing the Father's image in themselves.

15 May 1951

I pray incessantly
for the conversion
of the prodigal son's
brother.
Ever in my ear
rings the dread warning:
"The one has awoken
from his life of sin.
When will the other
awaken
from his virtue?"

29 August 1962

Dom Helder Camara, *A Thousand Reasons for Living*
(Philadelphia: Fortress Press, 1981)

Facing page: Adolphe Beaufrère, *Return of the Prodigal* (See also pages 108-109.)

Section 3

Reconciliation

The father seeks the son

The first impression one gets from looking at Sybil Andrews' work is the eye-catching series of lines that curve and dance over the surface of the picture. They circle and swirl; they are spiky. The line leaps from father to son, from the solid but curvilinear hill to the background waves (of foliage?) that claw the air. At the same time, having acknowledged all the coiled motion, one also gets the feeling of stillness, restfulness, even tenderness. The figures relate to one another peacefully, and an autumnal quality pervades the surrounding landscape. In this balance between action and stillness one is held suspended and moved by the image of compassion.

This paradoxical visual and emotional effect is doubtless intentional on the part of the English-Canadian artist, Sybil Andrews (1898-1993). She liked to talk about the "sweet line" in the picture—and there are a lot of sweet lines in this work. Moreover, Andrews, who worked as an aircraft welder during World War I, knew how things were dynamically constructed and related.

Images in her work, including this one, suggest that what something looks like is not so important as its "felt" quality. She once wrote: "If I ask you to draw a stool, or a car, or a house, or the view outside, I am asking you to draw an object—a material object. But if I ask you to draw a picture entitled "Compassion," what are you going to do? Compassion is not a thing. It is not an object to be picked up and handled. Compassion is an emotion you experience in your mind, your soul, your spirit, your imagination. . . ."

The spirit and the imagination—and perhaps the mind and soul—can be moved by looking deeply at her linocut version of the *Prodigal Son*, done in England in 1939 at the outbreak of World War II. The graceful yet powerful quality of this work emerges in a number of ways. The curve of the father's bent body echoes the line of the kneeling son. The father's right hand in shadow seems to be pressing down in blessing while his left hand (the brightest colored object in the picture) simultaneously reaches to lift the son up. Both figures, while flat (as figures are in linocuts), seem to imply dimensionality. They stand or kneel in contrast with the lightly colored sky, enframed by those circular curves which may be trees or rays of light or, as someone suggested, the hint of angel wings.

The artist is known to have inveighed against the notion that emotion is expressed only through facial features like tears or smiles. For her, emotion

resided in and was expressed by the whole figure from head to toe, in every line and curve of the body. That sense of compassion, given and received, radiates even though there are no detailed features on the face of the father or the son.

Both figures perch on a brown, round mound composed of sharp chunks and furrows. It is not unreasonable to suggest that this hill may echo Job's dung heap. That effect is heightened (or lowered) by an octet of pigs cavorting on the slope. Their presence is not only a reminder of the son's former, debased occupation, but those pigs also suggest something else. Either they followed the son home, or the father in this interpretation of the parable has journeyed to the heap where the son and his swinish comrades were living. In this manner the artist has interpreted the story in an earthy, imaginative way.

Many people of a certain age may recall the grade school experience of "doing linoleum blocks." It was an exercise both simple and complex. It was fun to slice away with the blade; but it was not easy to remember which part of the carved line would stand out or be empty space. Sybil Andrews did most of her artistic work in the medium of linocut. She claimed that it was a wonderful medium that forced her to simplify and learn the great lesson of balance. While her work reflects such modern art movements as Futurism, and while her work bears certain stylistic resemblance to the whippy lines of her American contemporary, Charles Burchfield, Andrews speaks in her own voice.

She tells us that compassion counts. With her sharp tools and equally sharp insights she beckons us to relish motion and stasis. She invites us to look at the lines and where they take us, to trace them with the eye or the finger and see where they lead. In this picture they focus our attention and that of the bent father, of curved nature—even of the eight little pigs—on the bowed head of the son. It is he, kneeling on the heap, who is approached and touched, blessed and lifted. The son is the one who is the object of line and compassion. Follow the line, in both picture and story, and allow yourself to be likewise blessed and lifted up, the object of the Father's compassion.

28
Sybil Andrews
The Prodigal Son
(1939)
Color linoleum cut
on paper, 54/60
(8 x 11¾ ins.)

The father hurries to greet his returning son

While some versions of the encounter between the accepting father and the Prodigal Son possess a certain stillness and gravity, this one by Adolphe Marie Timothée Beaufrère (1876-1960) evinces a discernible degree of energy. The propulsive movement of the father, seen in his stretching forward and in the flutter of his trailing robe, suggests uncorked excitement. A sensitive viewer might readily express concern for the health of this elderly running figure. He might trip or he might have a heart attack. His throwing caution to the winds is understandable, however, for it is likely that any one of us, upon the return of someone who was lost, would run with our skirts flapping, too.

The rush of the father is contrasted with the stasis of the son who kneels and leans like a compact lump in the road. The father is action, aching to embrace; the son is stillness, waiting to be embraced. We know, of course, that the story in Luke does not indicate that the son kneels before the father. Rather, the implication is that the son is in motion, for the text says he set off and went to the father. By this account, we would more readily expect some kind of standing embrace. Kneeling, as if in contrition, is a created gesture, a bit of poetic license; that posture is what artists—and we —might envision for the returning penitent.

In this scene by Beaufrère we see more than a stop-action etching. The racing father and the still son have not yet touched, yet it is possible to anticipate their union in the reverse S-curve in the tree limb above the old man. That sinuous limb echoes and unites the curved backs of father and son. We see them still apart, but the landscape implies that they are symbolically one, as they physically will be in just a moment.

Other details add to the visual delight of this scene. For instance, an implement that looks like a curved cane rests on the road beside the kneeling son. That is an anomalous inclusion, for we know that the lad had recently been spending time among pigs. Pigs, notoriously hard to herd (the Romans used Rottweilers to herd them), might be poked with a stick to send them along. But we would not expect a pig herder to use a shepherd's staff for

the purpose. Yet there it is. We can see the curve of that crook reflected in the bend of the road in the lower right of the picture. It veers away from the principle characters, and on that part of the road we observe a man in a horse-drawn wagon loping into a copse of trees. Horse and wagon appear to be heading toward the splendid villa on the other side of the trees and lake, most likely the home from which the father had been hustling.

Beaufrère composed this etching with a spacious amount of cloud and sky occupying fully half of the picture space. The celestial space lends an open quality to the scene which is a counterpoint to the coiled tension of father rushing to son. The loose handling of space and line may be something Beaufrère learned from his teacher, Gustave Moreau, a late nineteenth-century Symbolist artist noted for academic works that evoked a fantasy dream world. Interestingly, the mystical Moreau was also the teacher of the great Fauvist painter, Henri Matisse.

As we see in this work, Beaufrère, essentially a landscape artist, was attracted to religious subjects. Although he is virtually unknown today, he had an international reputation in the early years of the twentieth century, winning many medals and prizes for his paintings and etchings. This particular etching was executed in 1921 in the shadow of World War I. Its bucolic atmosphere, though, shows virtually none of the abiding anxiety in the aftermath of that conflict that we often find in the works of other artists of the time.

What this picture does show, however, is a graphic evocation of sorrow and acceptance. In its own way, Beaufrère's work is a pictorial metaphor for grace. The son doesn't seek the gift; it races toward him. Knowing himself to be unworthy, he hunkers down on the road, soon to be scooped up in a rushing wind of embrace. Energy and stasis, curves and clouds, limbs that embrace: These features are all visible in the picture. But the greater significance lies in the assurance that the son will soon be lifted up and ushered beyond the bend in the road where he will at last be in his father's house, safely at home.

The Evenrud collection includes another work by Beaufrère, *L'enfant prodigue dans les bras de son père*, in which the father embraces the son.

29

**Adolphe Marie
Timothée
Beaufrère**

*Return of the
Prodigal Son*
(1921)

Etching and dry point,
46/60
(7¾ x 5 ins.)

Return with sphinx

In this engraving by Marten deVos (1532-1603) the Prodigal Son is pictured four times. In three of these depictions circumstances cause his upper body to lean backwards. Dominant in the foreground we see that the rushing father causes the son to lean backward, the recipient of an extraordinarily emotional embrace. Behind and to the right we perceive the son in the company of snuffling pigs leaning backward on his staff. His body language suggests that he is just now coming to his senses.

Different senses are aroused in the background banquet scene where a discernibly stout son leans back in a chair, this time with a woman of loose virtue on his lap. He is portrayed yet once more in the deep distance, framed by an arch; this time he leans forward, running from a female figure who is chasing him with a stick. These background scenes evoke the engravings after de Vos by Crispin de Passe titled *The Prodigal Son Wasting His Fortune* (1601) and *The Prodigal Son Chased from the Inn* (n.d.). See the essay on de Passe/de Vos on page 51.

While much of the story of the Prodigal Son is illustrated in this engraving, we see no depiction of the departure from home, the scene that began the drama. Speculatively, we note that de Vos included a water-spouting sphinx on the left and a dead tree stump on the right. These stone and wood objects may merely be decorative enframing devices, but the sphinx could denote something else. The sphinx, a figure originally from Egyptian mythology, frequently appeared in sixteenth-century European art as a recumbent lion with an erect human head (usually female), often wearing eardrops and pearls.

In Greek drama Oedipus consulted the sphinx and learned that he would one day kill his father, something which tragically and unknowingly he did. In Luke's parable, according to village society in the Middle East, when the son demanded his share of the property, that request was tantamount to expressing impatience for his father's death. Thus, the presence of the sphinx here might be a stony echo of that deadly request and, therefore, an oblique allusion to the son's departure. If so, then all the major scenes of the story (the elder brother excepted) are directly or indirectly represented. On the other hand, it must be stated that sometimes a sphinx is only a sphinx and not necessarily a symbol of departure and death.

What *is* clear, however, is that the central focus of de Vos's engraving is the reunion of father and son. This act dominates everything else in the picture, including the architecture. The father grips the son in such a fierce embrace that the latter, as noted, is forced backward. The apparel of each figure ripples with deeply-shaped folds. The father wears a rich robe with a scarf that streams from his horn-capped head. He overwhelms the kneeling figure who does not appear much wasted by his adventures. He looks physically fit and trim; he still wears his ruffled collar.

Sartorial concerns drop away as we look closely at the faces of these two figures. The elder has a stately beard, and his face contains a noble and passionate expression. He may have been "dead" according to the village custom of the day, but he is acutely alive in this print as he grasps his lost son with a rib-crushing grip of acceptance.

For his part the son appears to be on the verge of tears, for he could hardly have expected such a reception. He utters his protestation: "*Pater, peccavi ni celum et coram te, iam non sum dignus vocari filius tuus.*" ("Father, I have sinned against heaven and before you; I am no longer worthy to be called your son" Luke 15:21.) His left hand tentatively reaches up to the father as he is unequivocally received and restored. We know that *he*, not the father, was the one who was dead and is alive, the one who was lost and is found.

He was indeed lost. That we see in the small background scenes: his sojourn with pigs; his feasting with fools (with musical accompaniment); his expulsion from the brothel, an echo of the primal expulsion from the garden. But now he is found. That we see in the hints of excitement: the shadowed figures expectantly gesturing in the doorway, the servants stunning a compliant calf in the distance beyond the well.

We are moved by the passionate act of reconciliation. We also ponder the sobering back-story and the signs of what will happen next. From the corner of our eye we observe the sphinx, the unique demon that symbolizes destruction and bad luck. We note, however, that from its mouth there springs a strong stream of water. And water, in Christian terms, is also symbolic. It signifies cleansing and life. By water, believers are made members of a community, one that proclaims liberation from sin and death. It is wondrous to ponder the reconciliation, but it is also worth watching the sphinx.

30
Marten de Vos

*Father, I have sinned
before heaven and before
you; I am no longer
worthy to be called your
son.*

(1585)

Engraving
(9 x 8¾ ins.)

The father goes out to meet the son

The focus of this work by Jean-Louis Forain (1852-1931), that which immediately draws our attention, is the reconciliation of father and son. Their embrace is a tender and timeless expression of contrition and pardon. The son, who had been far, far from home, is here unconditionally welcomed. The visual effect of this reunion is achieved by the massing of the figures and the calligraphic line that shapes them. Forain executed several versions of this scene before deciding on the perspective he achieved in this composition. He said that he wanted to get the true expression of his feeling, the appropriate sentiment.

The work achieves its impact by the low horizon line and the strong diagonal of the road. No wider than a finger's width on the left, the road broadens and curves to more than a hand's span on the right where the towering figures meet in mutual embrace. Such a visual device seems to have satisfied Forain's desire to depict the appropriate sentiment. For us, as viewers, the widening road gives visual form to the story when we recall that the son had "traveled to a distant country" and that the father first sighted his son "while he was still far off."

From one point of view the parable is about distance and propinquity: The one who was once far off is now near. The notion of coming home from afar is a motif that occurs elsewhere in the biblical narrative, as in the story of Jacob's journey in Genesis. The sending of the seventy and their return in Luke 10 also illustrates this phenomenon of leaving and returning. Hymns often express a sense of separation and the desire to return. Martin Luther captures this awareness of "going home from afar" in one of his hymns:

> To God the Holy Spirit let us pray
> Most of all for faith upon our way.
> That he may defend us when life is ending
> And from exile home we are wending.
> Lord, have mercy!

In this etching Forain has captured the moment when the Prodigal comes home from his self-imposed exile. Under a wide expanse of sky we see a flat landscape with a spare tree and a few diminutive buildings. At the bend in the road, however, distance has been annihilated. The son has come down the long, dusty road, his clothes in shreds. Tossing aside his hat and walking stick, he kneels in contrition. The father, with thinning hair and furrowed expression, has seen his son while he is still far off. Tossing aside grief and

dignity, the father bends forward and places his hands on the son's shoulder in blessing and pardon. Forain achieves this deeply emotional effect simply by letting line and perspective have their way.

Forain was a moderately successful artist in the late nineteenth and early twentieth century. As a young painter he achieved some recognition; he exhibited numerous works in four of the eight Impressionist group exhibitions between 1872 and 1886. However, critics at the time noted that he was "an uneven artist, slipping often on the slope of anecdotal illustration." He was accused of following "Degas with one foot and the caricaturist Grevin with the other." Today, we can see that his paintings did owe much to the style and subject matter of Degas who was his friend and mentor.

Perhaps because his overall work was somewhat derivative, he never achieved first rank status in the art world. We see in his engravings, as here, a visual debt to Rembrandt. Elsewhere his work invokes—and even imitates—the quality and subject matter of Daumier, the major caricaturist from the golden age of French graphic arts in the mid-nineteenth century.

It was as a satirist that Forain achieved the greatest success and recognition during his lifetime. For over thirty-five years he was a cartoonist whose penetrating comments appeared in daily and weekly Parisian newspapers. He prided himself in being an inflexible character and a person of opinion. His social commentary, therefore, possessed a strong, satirical bite. His deft line and social wit exercised such power and attraction that a whole generation of French men and women greeted one another with the question, "Have you read the latest Forain?"

In this engraving of the Prodigal Son's return, however, Forain strikes a different graphic chord. He achieves a remarkable spatial and emotional effect. The effect is sentimental, to be sure, but not in the sense of being mawkish or saccharine. Rather, Forain creates a union of emotion and idea that draws the viewer into the picture. This fusion emanates from the monumental embrace at the bend in the road. It is heightened by the manner in which space is treated, especially in the delineation of distance. It culminates in the joyous explosion of emotion at arrival and homecoming. This dramatic depiction of reunion may be read as a summary of the parable for anyone who from exile returns home and receives embrace.

Fourain did five versions of this scene; two are in the Evenrud collection.

31
Jean-Louis Forain
*Le Retour de l'Enfant
Prodigue*
(The Return of the
Prodigal Son)
(ca. 1900)
Etching
(16¾ x 11¼ ins.)

The parable becomes a political allegory

A richly appareled father embraces his raggedly clothed son. The text along the bottom of this print pinpoints the gesture: *And he arose and came to his Father, and his Father saw him, & had compassion, & he ran &fell on his Neck, & kissed him—Read the Parable, Verse 16th to 24th.* This ennobling scene is aptly entitled *Reconciliation*, one of the themes that readily emerges from the parable in the eyes of artists. The lad is in tatters, with scraggly wig, torn and tattered clothes. A garter dangles from his left leg, while a bit of his bare belly shows above his scrofulous trousers.

As if carried on the wind, a line of text drifts, barely legible, from the son's backside, "Heaven and before thee, and am not worthy." This is part of the speech (Luke 15:18 and 21) that the son sobs to the properly gartered father before the latter orders a change of clothes and lays on a banquet for the now reconciled lad. The touching domestic scene is reinforced by an open-armed, generously bosomed, and flatfooted woman (presumably the mother, who is not mentioned in the parable). She is backed up by a pair of ovaloid maidens and a brace of lanky red-coated gentlemen. The parable, while spoken in Jesus' time, is here depicted in early nineteenth-century Great Britain. Visually this is a story of homecoming and reconciliation.

But, because the work was executed by James Gillray (1756-1815), who was perhaps the greatest satirist of his day, we can infer that there is more going on beneath the surface. Gillray possessed an extraordinary talent for caricature, and his works always have bite and underlying layers of meaning. He mercilessly and often scatologically skewered the foibles and hypocrisies of his contemporaries in all walks and classes of life: politics, society, the military, and the church. In this instance of family reunion Gillray seems to be inflicting one of his more gentle satires. One of the men in the background (who might be mistaken for the cherry-cheeked older brother) is holding a rolled document with the words "New Union Act. Britain's best Hope."

The controversial Act of Union was passed by Parliament in 1800, an attempt by Prime Minister William Pitt the Younger to link England and Ireland into a single kingdom. The Act was intended to establish free trade between the two countries and offered many concessions to Roman Catholics (though the official religion of Ireland was to be the Anglican Church). If one were to

look at the figure of the sharp-nosed man holding the Act and compare his features with Gainsborough's portrait of William Pitt the Younger (including the rosy cheeks), the viewer might see a strong resemblance.

Knowing that Gillray employed satire the way political cartoonists of our day do, we might reasonably surmise that there are at least two stories in this hand-colored etching. The outer story shows the father welcoming the son as it says in Luke's parable; in the implied narrative England embraces Ireland in accord with the Act of Union. One is the Gospel, the other is Gillray. Who or what the amply endowed and welcoming woman is, is a matter of speculation. Knowing Gillray's penchant for satire and caricature, however, it may not be too far-fetched to envision her as the open arms of Mother Church, for she too was caught in the Act. One way or the other, we are treated to more than one depiction of reconciliation.

For the last five years of his life Gillray was incurably insane. Throughout his life he gnawed on the bone of discontent because his "lowly" art, while wildly popular with the public, kept him from being recognized as a true artist by the artistic establishment. He was not admitted to the Royal Academy because his engravings were considered to be only a set of "ingenious mechaniks." Still, he seems to have had the last laugh, for his legacy lives on in the works of political cartoonists who daily focus our sight and enrich our imagination. Moreover, Gillray's works, warts and all, have come to be recognized by the art establishment. His numerous etchings have been the subject of major exhibitions at the Tate in London (2001) and at the New York Public Library (2005).

Gillray's art cautions us not to be satisfied with easy answers to complex events. He calls us not only to look, but also to reflect upon what lies beneath the surface of perceived reality. His sense of humor and style of moralizing may be out of date, but the chop of humor and the bite of morality are not. Whether his characters illustrate the Gospel or are merely caught in the Act—or both—the goal and hope of reconciliation between family members, social groups, and even nations reach from the page into the real world. All of God's errant children stand or lean in need of embrace.

THE RECONCILIATION. — { *And he arose and came to his Father, and his Father saw him, & had compassion, & ran, & fell on his Neck, & Kiss'd him.* —
—*Read the Parable Verse 16th to 24th* —

32
James Gillray
The Reconciliation
(1804)
Hand-colored etching
(13¾ x 9¾ ins.)

The Prodigal comes floating home

Certain gift shops offer potpourri to their customers. A combination of flower petals and spices, potpourris sweetly scent the air, an alluring temptation for the buyer. Potpourris, however, are more than petals and spices to sweeten a room. They are any combination of incongruous things, a miscellaneous collection of objects like an anthology of short stories and humorous verse or a great assortment of cars. Anyone who has ever been to a smorgasbord has tasted a potpourri of food.

When we look at this pen and ink drawing by Carl Grupp (b. 1940), we are confronted with a potpourri, a visual smorgasbord of images. On one level, the work is confusing and amusing, something between a surrealist exercise and a flash panel for a comic strip. On another level, it is an explosive interpretation of the parable of the Prodigal Son composed of a medley of disparate but highly suggestive elements.

The picture contains no fewer than thirteen human (or human-like) figures, seven animals, and a farrago of objects: a basketball, a series of light bulbs, and a skeleton lying in the foreground with its bony arm reaching into the abyss (an arrow with the word *abyss* says as much). A horned (and presumably fatted) calf noses a cornucopia brimming with food and drink. He is suggestively ridden by a figure that looks like a crash dummy.

We also can pick out a steaming cup of coffee next to a potted plant, a floating platter of roast fowl pierced by a carving knife, and a noble cactus standing stiffly at attention on the right behind the light bulbs. It is a work populated by saints and sinners; it skirts the boundary between fantasy and reason. And it contains elements of apocalypse and trinitarian doctrine. How do these disparate ingredients fit together and convey the return of the Prodigal? The enigmatic and galvanic title may suggest a way: *Electricity! That's the Curse What Done It.* *

It is more likely that the fertile wit and imagination of Carl Grupp are "what done it." As a long-time professor of art at Augustana College, Sioux Falls, South Dakota, Grupp is an artist with roots in the classical approach to drawing. He was also schooled in Abstract Expressionism, and he admits a debt to the cartoon world. He has confessed an admiration for cartoonists like Charles Schultz (the creator of *Peanuts*) and Gary Larson (*The Far Side*).

In one way or another all these influences play into this visual potpourri. "I love drawing," he has said in an artist's statement. "Drawing is like going

on an adventure, sometimes peaceful and pleasant and at other times rough and scary [sic]. Drawing is like fighting a war. Drawing is like making love. Drawing is like praying. Drawing is life itself."

This ink drawing is full of life. The bearded figure in the center is Grupp himself. In a wistful autobiographical act, he extends his right arm to his own prodigal son. The young man, who is either dropping or dribbling the basketball, is flanked by a company of figures, some of whom look like ecclesiastical personalities. Two semi-nude women occupy prominent positions near the lad; they doubtless reference his wastrel days. To recall his humiliation, three pigs glare piggishly behind the son (though one of the pigs, in cartoon fashion, says "Quack Quack").

A more ominous figure surges to the right, riding a cadaverous and uni-horned horse. This figure, trailing tongues of flame, recalls one of the four Horsemen of the Apocalypse from Revelation 6, the pale green horse whose rider's name was Death. This *memento mori*, this reminder of mortality, is perhaps moderated by the singular floating platter with a bird ready for carving. This could be a roasted turkey, since that fowl is most frequently associated with Thanksgiving—and the return of the son is certainly a cause for giving thanks. On the other hand, as if to add symbolic weight to the robotic, skeletal horse, it could be a sign that someone's goose is cooked.

Elsewhere, a boy rides on the back of a dog. In the sky a thick bank of clouds glowers over the whole scene. But there is something else. Rising from the potpourri of images is a figure that resembles an open-armed Christ. Suggesting both the crucified and the resurrected Christ, this figure extends his arms over everything in a gesture of blessing. His featureless face glows; and the faint triangle in the radiant circle recalls the Trinity. If electricity was the curse "what done it" in the first place, then it would seem that the electrifying power of grace is what does it in the end.

*An alternate explanation for the title is contained in a story the artist tells about an old lady of his acquaintance. Frustrated, she blamed all the troubles of the modern world on electricity. It is possible that the light bulbs in front of the cactus and behind the Horseman of the Apocalypse illustrate this idea.

Image used by permission of the artist

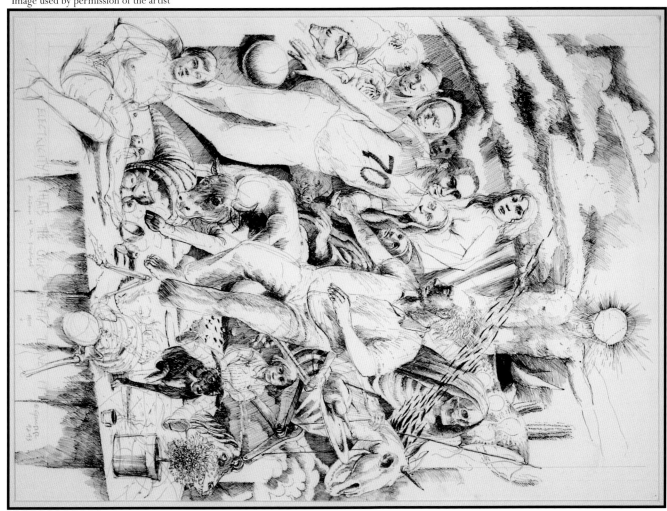

33
Carl Grupp

Electricity! That's the
Curse What Done It or
Return of the Prodigal
(1992-1993)
Ink drawing
(20¾ x 29 ins.)

A peaceful reunion

It is said that in its time medieval stained glass was the Gospel for the illiterate. Looking at the flat surface of light-infused glass, believers learned the Christian story from creation to apocalypse. Even today one can be similarly informed and educated. Yet there is another dimension to this art form. Whatever information it may communicate, stained glass also conveys a sense of calm and serenity. Many people who intentionally look at stained glass find a sense of peace and stillness in the full play of color and line.

Something of that sensation is present in the richly colorful works of He Qi (b. 1948) who is regarded as one of China's ranking contemporary Christian artists. He was the first Mainland Chinese to receive a Ph.D. in religious art after the cultural revolution. He wrote his dissertation while studying in Germany where he pursued research in medieval art. It is likely that his studies influenced the way he views color, for he transcribes color in a manner that reflects stained glass. To stop and look intentionally at a painting by He Qi is to experience a sense of calm and serenity.

At the same time other, more modern, influences permeate his art. Some of his figures float in the air like those of Chagall; some figures possess the flat perspective we associate with the art of Picasso and Matisse. Yet He Qi's pictorial program arises out of Chinese cultural types. In this way he visually westernizes the Christian story and opens our eyes to the global reach of the biblical narrative.

In He Qi's *Return of the Prodigal Son* we experience a rich range of color and a dramatic sense of calm. Motion arrested, the white-bearded father sits in his chair. He displays authority and compassion as he bends forward over his kneeling son. The young lad does not lean into the father as in many representations of return and reconciliation. Instead, his head is bent backward at an uncomfortable angle. He grabs his father's arm, but he appears to be gazing upward at the figure behind a striped wall.

This green-coated man bears a yoke on his shoulder while urging a full grown beast—a bull or an ox, certainly not a calf—forward. The delicious round moon shines both behind and on top of the beast, making the hump of its shoulder look like a mountain in the moonlight. The expression in the eye of this stolid beast of burden suggests dour resentment as he is prodded onward to eventual slaughter.

On the other side of an archway stands a woman, framed in red. She peers out of the window, and her gaze is on a line with the father and son below. One could inscribe an inverted triangle by tracing the line of her look down to the eye of the kneeling lad, up to the arm of the man in green, and back again to her eyes. It is a subtle compositional device that lends stability and stillness to the scene.

The picture is sprayed with circles: the yellow moon, the gray and black receptacle on the left, the stylized snowflakes on the father's robe, the bowl under the chair. The son's knee seems to slice into this bowl, and his discarded staff points toward a pair of alert chickens on the floor—their presence in this domestic scene suggests that the pigs have definitely been left behind.

Overall, this work conveys an autumnal sense of stillness, one that invites rest and contemplation, the way a stained glass panel does. He Qi intends for his art to suggest peace in the midst of worldly turmoil. "I want people to hear my peaceful message, the Gospel message," he has said in an artist's statement. "The peaceful message is very important today. We need to listen to the voice of heaven." He Qi's art suggests that when people open themselves to experience reconciliation, they are in a position to hear the still, small voice of heaven speaking of a peace that passes human understanding.

Artist's sketch for *The Prodigal Son*.
Acrylic and ink
(5¼ x 8¼ ins.)

34

He Qi

*Return of the
Prodigal Son*
(1996)

Ink and color on paper
(27½ x 27½ ins.)

An ordinary, yet extraordinary embrace

When people come home, having spent time away, it is often an occasion for rejoicing and embracing. That outpouring surely happens when someone safely returns from college or the military. The expressive sense of homecoming is warmly apparent during the holidays when family and friends gather from far and wide to affirm and celebrate their connectedness. In the visual arts there are few images of homecoming more heartwarming and haunting than those inspired by the return of the Prodigal Son.

Sister Marion Honors (b. ca. 1937), an artist who has created art in a convent in Rural Latham, New York, captures the spirit of homecoming in this eponymous woodcut print. In this small work we see two figures huddled in warm embrace. One of the figures—who could be male or female—leans into the other with apparent tenderness and affection. The smile conveys a quiet sense of peace and joy, as if there is nowhere else he or she would rather be.

Because of the way the woodblock was cut, a vertical streak beneath the right eye could be read as the track of a happy tear. In like fashion, the slight smudge on the left cheek might, given the circumstance, be a blush denoting a kind of self-consciousness or even a shy sense of embarrassment. If this is the return of the Prodigal, then we would likely expect these emotions to register on the face of one who has come home.

The print exists in open space, with no horizon line or background detail. These two people might be greeting one another in a living room, an open field, or an airport where people do meet and embrace after a journey. We do not see the face of the figure in a floral robe—which likewise could be male or female. But there is no mistaking the affection in the body language and the gesture of embrace. If the one figure expresses a tearful joy at being home, the other, even though faceless, clearly reciprocates. We can't help but notice how the extended hands of the two figures intensify the embrace. In terms of visual volume each hand is about as large as each head, which lends a kind of uplift to the scene, a manual sign of affection that further connects the two figures.

Connectedness is an admitted theme in the art of Sister Marion. She has spoken of the need to address the disruptions between one another and the earth. The role of humans, she avers, is to give praise, to respect and care for the earth, and to heal our connections. Healing and restoration are apparent in the parable of the Prodigal, as they are here in this print which echoes the story. The reconciliation that we witness is the extraordinary outcome of an ordinary though generous embrace.

Seeing and capturing the extraordinary in the midst of the ordinary is also an avowed aim of Sister Marion's art. In an artist's statement she affirms: "I like to think that my art is about that light-dark, fire-filled, close-at-hand, blessed, common stuff that we call THE ORDINARY [sic], where we are used to the fit of its daily realities. As surely as anything, THE ORDINARY [sic] is where we meet the Divine, where we are at home with the whole community of life, here, on Earth."

People leave home all the time: to go to school, to serve in the armed forces, to work at a distance, to travel to new and far away places. Departure means disruption. In the fullness of time, however, we hope there will be homecoming and re-connection. In that ordinary, yet extraordinary, event, people tend to greet one another with a big-handed embrace. That enfolding may be accompanied with tears of joy, a leaning together, maybe even a shy smile of welcome to mark the connectedness of those who were once afar but now are near.

These elements, common to our experience, are surely evident in Sister Marion's woodcut of homecoming. We like to think that these same dynamics were at work in the story of the return of the Prodigal, the template for this work. In that biblical homecoming we learn that the one who was lost had been found; we also discern that the homecoming was the beginning of celebration. We know from sight and touch that there are fewer things in life more satisfying than safely coming home; we also know there are fewer blessings more cherished than being warmly welcomed.

"Homecoming" copyright 1991 by Marion C. Honors, CSJ

35
Sister Marion C. Honors, CSJ

Homecoming
(1983)
Woodcut
(10 x 14 ins.)

The father cradles the son

In the twenty-first century people of faith are becoming increasingly aware that the biblical story transcends cultural barriers. The unity of the church is realized and enriched when hymns, art, and other elements of worship from different parts of the world are shared. An artist who embodies this awareness in her work is one of Sri Lanka's most famous contemporary artists, Nalini Jayasuriya (b. 1926).

In her paintings, sculpture, pottery, stained glass, and enamels this self-taught Christian artist reflects both South Asian images and the influence of Buddhist forms. In an artist's statement Nalini Jayasuriya says about her work: "I come from a land of rich, ancient, and diverse cultures and traditions. While I carry the enriching influences of both West and East, I express myself through an Asian and Christian consciousness with respect for all confessions of religious faith."

In her *Return* (1999) one can readily identify the climactic scene of Luke's parable of the Prodigal Son. A young-looking father holds his son, who is curled in a fetal position, on his lap. It would seem that paternal love and acceptance contain a nascent maternal aspect. The father, however, looks not at the son whom he clasps in an endearing, passionate bear hug; rather, with hooded eye and open mouth, he gazes at a third figure. This third figure is perhaps the older brother who stares vacantly at the father, wondering whether his place has been usurped. But the third figure could just as likely be a dazed servant whom the father tells to bring a robe, a ring, and sandals, and then to slaughter the fatted calf and prepare for the feast.

The flaccid, scraggly son wears a dirty white garment. His head is bowed, and he stares dumbly downward. It looks as if he is about to take the father's left thumb into his mouth. His exhausted state is further revealed in his limp hands with which he is idly or nervously fiddling. The fingers of his right hand are bent in a peculiarly double-jointed way that parallels the father's left hand. That is, the fingers of both figures curve outward, a gesture that catches the eye and tempts the observer to try to do the same. Chances are that few viewers will be able to duplicate the gesture.

After giving up this exercise, our eyes are free to move from the hands and faces of the figures and roam around the background. It is featureless—no trees or buildings there, just swirling streaks of blue giving way to gray and black. Slashing through this acrylic gloom, however, are vibrant streaks of red, which pick up the color of the son-or-servant's headpiece as well as a smear on the returning son's leg. Perhaps our eyes are looking at an abstract expression of coursing blood or the fiery red of the dawning of a new day. Both of these elements are implied in the story.

But our gaze returns again and again to the father's intimate embrace of the son's limp body. In outline they form a kind of oval. It is possible this shape reflects Nalini Jayasuriya's conscious respect for other confessions of religious faith. In her writing she talks about the *Mandala*, the squared Circle, the ancient visual diagram that unfolds the hiddenness of wonder and the wonder of Wonder itself. If there is nothing else in the father's embrace there *is* wonder.

This Christian artist tells the biblical story in a way that is both familiar and unfamiliar to western eyes. She presents the scene of return, which is instantly recognizable to anyone familiar with the story from Luke. Yet she subtly shows how the love of the parent contains elements of both the paternal and maternal. Moreover, from her Asian background, she mixes into the visual narrative a consciousness of a larger religious faith and a sensitivity that transcends cultural barriers.

There is at least one more thing to look for. Nalini Jayasuriya's use of color and abstraction in *Return* suggests an interpretation of the story that is both sanguinary and sanguine. That is, the return is not complete until there is some form of bloodshed. The artist suggests that complexity in her painting: bloodshed and hope, elements which are reflected in the death and life of Jesus of Nazareth, the original teller of the story.

Permission requested

36
Nalini Jayasuriya

Return
(1999)

Acrylic on fabric
(23¾ x 28¼ ins.)

When I was a child, I spoke like a child, I thought like a child, I reasoned like a child; when I became an adult, I put an end to childish ways.

The father sweeps the son into his arms

This autobiographical reflection was penned by St. Paul in 1 Corinthians 13 in reference to his own misguided youth. But it might well summarize the sense of what we see in this depiction of *The Return of the Prodigal Son* by Ed Knippers (b. 1946). In this emotional vision of welcome home it is plausible to assume that the son has put an end to his childish ways and begun the painful process of becoming an adult.

With a rich blue sky in the background we see a robed father embracing his nude, kneeling son. The tearful tableau is a summary of past sorrow and present joy, deep regret and future promise, ritualized repentance and physical forgiveness. We cannot see the face or the emotions of the returning son; but we note his muscular upper body as his arms fiercely embrace his father. In turn, the father, with tearful, compressed eyes, enfolds his son in a manner that reflects Jesus' words when he declared his desire (in Luke 13: 34) to gather the children together as a hen gathers her brood under her wings.

The physicality of this painting is not incidental to Knippers' artistic output. As an intentional Christian artist, Knippers often portrays biblical characters (including Jesus) nude. He does this to emphasize the full humanity of these characters—especially the humanity of Jesus. Knippers is committed to creating a visual effect that is different from standard, what he calls Sunday School, art. Intending to create a visually compelling narrative, the artist does not aim so much to be anatomically accurate as physically dramatic.

He acknowledges that physicality is a gift of God and must be appreciated but never worshiped. This painterly physicality makes some viewers uncomfortable, and in certain religious circles there has been a hesitant, even negative reaction. Others see in his art a healthy acknowledgement of our bodily state in this world. Bold nude figures, as may be seen here, are Knippers' way of affirming the human body in creation; it is a way of fleshing out the Christian tradition.

In the early 1980s Knippers saw a production of George Balanchine's *The Prodigal Son* in Paris. The production included the original sets painted by the French Expressionist painter Georges Rouault (1871-1958). This experience inspired Knippers to do a series of paintings based on the parable of the Prodigal Son. This particular version, painted in 1999, exhibits the artist's ongoing fascination with that moving story. The return of the penitent son is good news.

However, as Knippers views the story, it is not unmitigated good news. Off to the left and leaning into the painted frame, stands the other son. Also nude, he stands with his arms folded in a posture that telegraphs resentment. We cannot see the Prodigal's tearful face, though we can presume he is crying. Neither can we see the facial features of the older brother, though we can posit his pique. His body language suggests a state of vexation caused by the younger son's warm reception. This perceived slight leads to a show of wounded pride and causes the brother to turn his back and sulk. Clearly he has some emotional business that will have to be taken up with the father (and perhaps with his brother) at a later time.

While we take note of this son's posture of resentment, we are nonetheless swept up in the painted mass of forgiveness. The landscape is featureless, but the welcome is eloquent. As viewers we are drawn to the inviting oval of arms and heads that enframes the upper bodies of father and son. But as participants in the larger narrative we might imagine ourselves being swept into that forgiving space. In the parable Jesus said that the father put his arms around his son and kissed him. This painting shows that scene. It is also possible to envision a wider embrace that gathers the children together (even the resentful ones) as a hen gathers her brood under wing.

37
Ed Knippers

The Return of the Prodigal Son
(1999)

Oil painting on wood panel
(24 x 36 ins.)

Is it really my son?

In film, camera setups determine the way we see the picture. A long shot, for example, shows a lot of scenery, while individual characters may occupy a relatively small visual space on the screen. A medium shot focuses on the actors, though scenery may still be in the picture. A close-up shot, however, brings the camera in tight, filling the screen with the actor's head or face. Where the director places the camera is important. The setup determines what we see and how we interpret the action on the screen.

Artists employ many similar techniques in creating their visual effects. Some artists create an imposing landscape and depict human subjects in a diminutive way. Alternately, artists may bring the focus in closer, employing a medium view; this practice allows us to concentrate on human figures. If the artist chooses a close-up, we can concentrate on facial and emotional expression. In scenes of the Prodigal Son story an artist like Jerem. [sic] Wachsmout (page 165) favors the long shot, depicting landscape with small figures. Someone like Sybil Andrews (page 107) focuses more on the characters while still creating a sense of place.

A picture that is much like a close-up is *The Legend of the Prodigal Son*, an engraving by the Belgian artist Maurice Langaskens (1884-1946).* This scene allows us to see the intensity in the father's eyes as if a camera had moved in expressly for that purpose. His eyes bore into the son's eyes like hot lasers exorcising a demon. Those expressive eyes contain affection and gratitude as well as surprise and disbelief. Coupled with compressed lips, furrowed brow, and pressing hands, the father's gaze seems to be saying, "I see my son before me, but I can hardly believe my eyes."

The close-up view of this reunion also permits us to see the son's languid eyes as he virtually melts in his father's embrace. His long lashes and gelled comb-around hair give the lad a passive, almost feminine, quality. His open mouth could suggest amazement, or it could mean that he is in the process of giving his set speech. Or he might be about to offer his father a tender kiss. Their relationship as father and son is obvious from their respective aquiline noses. Their mutual affection is apparent in the way the balding father holds his son's head and in the son's tentative grasp of the father's wrist. The son's demeanor seems to say, "I have sinned, and I am not worthy; but, gosh, I am really glad to be home."

While the close-up sizzles with present emotion, a distant view reminds us of past separation. The son's former condition among the pigs is depicted in the background. His back is to us, head bent, as if in dejection or prayer—or both. While the clothes of this half-naked penitent are shabby, he wears a pair of sturdy wooden clogs. Beyond the pigs, and echoing their curved rumps, the road curves over a rise in the land. The youth, it seems, is about to take the long road home.

The prominent close-up of father and son assures us that he made it, there to be welcomed and embraced. Langaskens focuses on the intimacy of the reunion by bringing us in close. He reinforces the tender but intense dynamic by bathing the surface of the engraving in a sepia tone. This thin coffee-colored wash deepens the furrows and shadows and softens the lines while heightening the emotional effect. The father's penetrating gaze and the son's expectant expression interpret the legend of the Prodigal Son in a way that invites us to share the warmth and affection. It might also cause us to reflect on the nature of return: "Safe at last, we can now begin anew."

---

* Sometimes the artist's name appears as Langaskins with a birth date of 1876.

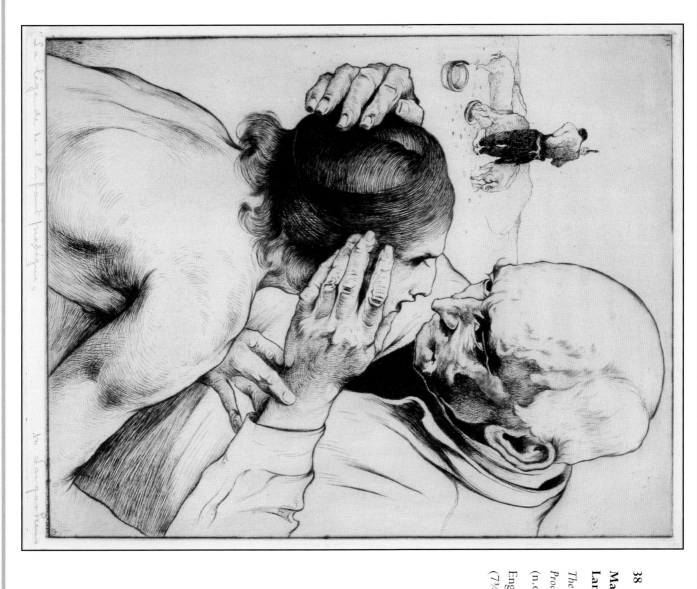

38
**Maurice
Langaskens**

*The Legend of the
Prodigal Son*
(n.d.)

Engraving
(7¾ x 10⅛ ins.)

A blind father receives his son

To be blind is to be cut off from seeing the sights, shapes, and colors of the world. A persistent theme in the Bible is care and concern for the blind, and one of the most heart-warming miracles is the restoration of sight. When Jesus began his ministry in Luke 4 he declared, quoting the prophet Isaiah, that the Spirit had anointed him, among other things, to proclaim recovery of sight to the blind. Appropriately, the last miracle Jesus performed before entering Jerusalem to die was to restore sight to a blind beggar (Luke 18:35-43).

The artist Rembrandt van Rijn (1606-1669), like many other artists, was haunted by the thought of blindness. That is understandable, for an artist lives by seeing and creating. Depictions of blindness pervade many of Rembrandt's most moving works, as we see in his etchings and paintings of the story of Tobit, of Jacob blessing the children of Joseph, and images of the blind poet Homer. While it is not certain, some commentators like Simon Schama and Henri Nouwen suggest that Rembrandt portrays the elderly father as blind when he receives the Prodigal Son. That thought is intriguing, for in this print from 1636 (as in his majestic painting of 1669, now housed in the Hermitage) Rembrandt may be suggesting that the father, with eyes shut tight, has become blind in his old age.

The bedraggled and emaciated son, for his part, has his eyes shut fast as well, blinded, perhaps, by his tears or the awful realization of what he had done. In this intensely emotional scene we see anguish and agitation on the faces of both father and son. It is not a pretty sight, but it is truly moving. The two are locked in an embrace so fierce that the father's forward motion lifts his right foot from his shoe. The son, in return, presses into his father's chest cavity with the ferocity of a train racing into a tunnel.

This drama of reconciliation takes place on a raised platform, the two figures solidly occupying the center of the picture. Their combined mass dominates

the space like a living pyramid. The son has apparently come through the stone arch on the left. That part of the picture glows, and features are suggested rather than defined, though we can discern sketchy outlines of buildings, shrubbery, and rocks, as well as human and animal figures. Because definition is lacking we are free to imagine that the son has turned his back on his hazy past. His staff, lying diagonally on the stone platform, is like a direction marker, pointing away from the shimmering expanse behind him and toward the rock solid area ahead. The son, in effect, has come from nowhere and has finally arrived somewhere. Once lost, he is now found! He is home.

In contrast to the hooded eyes of the two central figures a maid servant above them stares wide-eyed. She leans out a window, holding the shutter open so she can see what's going on. Coming from the right side of the house two servants bring robe and shoes. Moving discreetly down the steps, they have anticipated the father's command for clothes. The servants, though ancillary figures, are important. Like supernumeraries elsewhere in life, they remind us that the quotidian will continue once high drama has past.

While we know life will go on, we are stopped in our tracks whenever we look at this expressive moment of reconciliation. We see that Rembrandt has created a blinding scene of pity, forgiveness, and compassion. As in many of his works, he has created a complex vision of sin and sight, blindness and light, and the gripping dynamic of costly grace. In the midst of this heartbreaking and eye-opening scene we sense the robed father declaring his blind joy: "This son of mine was dead and is alive again; he was lost and is found!" At the same time we perceive the ravaged son who has safely arrived. On his behalf we may be moved to hymn a grateful response: *I once was lost, but now am found; was blind but now I see.*

39

**Rembrandt
Harmenszoon
van Rijn**

*The Return of the
Prodigal Son*
(1636)

Etching
(5¼ x 6 ins.)

The son comes back to the farm

Wheat does not appear anywhere in the parable of the Prodigal Son, though it shows up several times in Luke's gospel. When wheat is mentioned in these texts, however (3:17; 16:7; and 22:31), the surrounding context is judgment, dishonesty, or denial. Therefore, imagination delights in seeing the golden plenitude of wheat that appears in this version of the Prodigal Son by John August Swanson (b. 1938).

Wheat is the pronounced image in the large central panel of harvest; it figures as a repeated signature in fifty small surrounding panels, each one about the size of a postage stamp. Even though the Lukan references to wheat are cautionary, the grain is a salutary symbol in Christian art where wheat is regarded as the staff of life. It symbolizes the bread of the Eucharist. And it suggests the bounty of the earth. We cannot escape seeing that latter suggestion made manifest in this version of the story of the Prodigal Son, one which Swanson executed between his first realization in 1970 and the most recent one from 2004 (pages 155 and 157).

The shape and format of this work differ from the others; and the pictorial influences on the artist are perhaps more readily apparent here. In an artist's statement from 1998, Swanson admits that he owes a debt to Medieval and Persian miniatures, to Byzantine art and Russian icons, and to the work of the great Mexican muralists like Rivera and Orazco. In this work the scale and detail of the smallest panels, the flatness of the figures, and the sun-drenched coloration of the whole work are evidence of these influences. The overall effect is dazzling to the eye, extending an invitation to look closely and ponder the five parts of the story.

A young man rides off like a troubadour, a proud feather stuck in his hat. A brightly colored crowd of people and animals gather to bid him farewell and wish him well. The lad leaves with his inheritance to seek his fortune in a distant, walled city. Perhaps he once had it in mind to develop a sound investment portfolio, a hedge against inflation. But we later see him gambling and drinking his money away. He still sports his proud feather, but we sense a downturn in his luck and life style. We surmise this change in his wincing expression and by the fact that he is a loser at cards; after all, two ones do not beat three crowns.

So he becomes poor, hungry, and ashamed. He sits stationary, surrounded by pigs under a leafless tree in which gather a flock of sinister black birds (a murder of crows?). His feather and fine clothes are gone, and his distant expression conveys the vacancy of his situation. A scene in the lower border where the youth drives his herd of pigs to their evening meal underscores his miserable condition. It looks as if the pigs will, in their way, enjoy a more savory meal than the youth.

Then years pass, according to the artist's reckoning, though that amount of elapsed time is not explicitly expressed in Luke's account. The Prodigal Son returns, and the central panel explodes with action, color, enthusiasm, and welcome. We are back to the wheat, the dominant feature in the landscape, though a green strip of front yard also teems with life: women washing and hanging clothes; a man sawing firewood; sheep, goats, chickens and chicks, all busily coming and going. We might be looking at a prosperous hacienda bursting with vigor. The wheat field itself is alive with activity: a man cuts a vagrant stand of wheat, a women is running or dancing, workers are cutting and stacking wheat, a couple are picking apples. The scene is one of abundance pressed down and overflowing.

And the abundance is most apparent in the father's eager stride as he rushes to embrace his son. Visually the father is the largest figure in the picture. By actual measure he is as tall as any of the four surrounding panels. He and his son wear similar hats; both have their arms open in immanent embrace. Attentive dogs and flapping geese join the jubilation. Even the earth, with its springing wheat and ample apples, bursts forth in fruitful celebration.

The scene is rimmed with more than thirty rectangular vignettes. Some of these recapitulate the journey of the son, including a thwarted trip to a bakery; some are farm or domestic scenes, like a woman milking a cow; some are serigraph snapshots of animals, like a squirrel, a rabbit, even an incongruous fish. They all enframe and embellish the basic scene of welcome, homecoming, reconciliation, and bountiful harvest.

With a slight exercise of imagination, we can see how this ebullient work by John Swanson from 1984 reflects the equally high-spirited gospel song and words by Knowles Shaw from 1874:

Sowing in the sunshine, sowing in the shadows,
Fearing neither clouds nor winter's chilling breeze;
By and by the harvest, and the labor ended,
We shall come rejoicing, bringing in the sheaves.

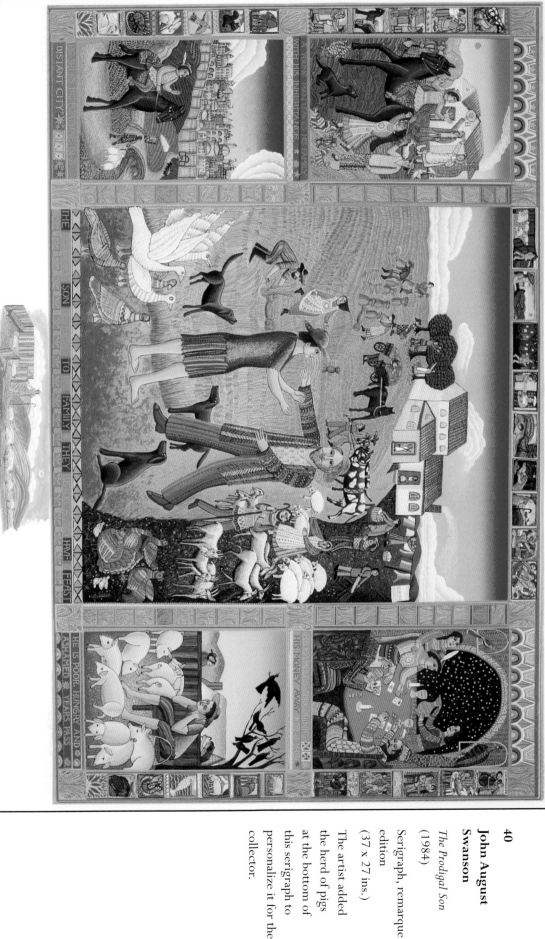

Image used by permission of the artist

40
John August Swanson

The Prodigal Son
(1984)

Serigraph, remarque
edition
(37 x 27 ins.)

The artist added
the herd of pigs
at the bottom of
this serigraph to
personalize it for the
collector.

Even a stone would weep!

Much of the visual impact of these pictures by James Mesplé (b. 1948) depends on the artist's use of the *Authorized King James Version* of the Bible. Modern translations, like the *New Revised Standard Version*, render the pertinent part of Luke 15:20 this way: "he ran and put his arms around him and kissed him." The picture's title phrase, "fell on his neck," which is closer to the original Greek, derives from the older version. And that is important in Mesplé's monoprint, for the son's neck is very prominent, rising like a pillar from the fabric of his harlequin-like collar. Further, a strong neck also emerges out of the russet, gray, and blue beard of the father.

The gray strands of the father's beard commingle with the streaming strands of the son's collar piece. The effect created is one of floating in air, for we see nothing more of the son's body than his statuesque neck and head. That prominent head with its multicolored, calligraphic curls is tilted slightly forward on the column of the neck, and, if we were to look at a statue such as *Hermes* by Praxiteles (330-320 B.C.E.) we might be inclined to infer a Greek sculptural derivation for Mesplé's figure.

Mesplé, an artist prominent in the Chicago art scene of the late twentieth and early twenty-first centuries, accepts the role of the artist as mythmaker. "Myths, which are certainly a part of the foundation of contemporary American culture," he said in 1996, "are stories full of wonder and mystery—two ingredients which often appear to be missing in modern life." That conviction is certainly reflected in the sculptural head of the son which does evoke an aura of wonder.

That classical clarity is contrasted with the emotional depiction of the father. He presses forward to kiss the son's neck with such force that his own facial features are compressed by the action. Two marble white tears flow from his sea-blue eye. Those tear drops are reflections of the son's own bluish-white coloration. At the same time two tears stream down the son's cheeks, also from deep blue eyes. These tears, appropriately, are tinged with the coloration of the father's face. Thus the two figures are contrasted yet bonded by style and color as well as by gesture and deep emotion.

The embracing pair are set against a background of midnight black and vibrant autumn leaves. It is not likely that maple and oak leaves flourished in first-century Israel. But they create a colorful context for this picture; and they provide a means by which we might see the story in contemporary terms.

Three smaller works (page 134) by Mesplé complement this tender scene; two of them contain pointed references to our time, making the story both time-bound and timeless. The first is a depiction of the naked son with long brown hair. He is lying upside down (from the viewer's point of view) in the mud next to an overturned bucket of scattered corn seed. A pair of aggressive pigs race toward him intent on wresting several scattered ears of corn from him. The lad lies passively with a dazed, almost drugged look; his brown eyes stare vacantly at the charging pigs.

This vignette is contrasted to a bordello scene in which the son lies with a bejeweled floozy who grabs him in embrace. At the moment, though, the son is intent on playing cards with an elf-like figure, something that might have emerged from the dark side of *Alice in Wonderland*. The son, in playing the ace of hearts while lying with a loose woman, seems to be trying to "turn two tricks" at the same time. The contemporary reference in this scene can be spied by looking through the leaves of the scrawny plant in the window. Way in the distance stands the Sears Tower in Chicago, hometown of the artist and contemporary locus of those who would (to reference the *King James Bible*) waste their substance with riotous living.

In 2005, sensing that his telling of the story was incomplete, Mesplé painted the parable's opening scene in which the wrong-headed son claims his inheritance. Dressed in Roman garb (with his boots fringed like those of a jester) the son bows in mock humility. The father, who would tower like a giant if he stood, is dressed like an oriental potentate. He dispenses the inheritance in the form of 25-cent pieces, which spill from bags—three dollars in quarters—and float in the air. With Chicago, again, in the background an ironic Statue of Liberty stands on a window ledge—ironic because the floating loan taken out by the son betokens bondage not liberty.

Taken together, these four works by Mesplé provide a colorful and thoughtful interpretation of the story from Luke. We are caught up in the mystery and emotion of an intense reunion. We can contemplate the timeliness and timelessness of the story that ranges pictorially from sculpture to skyscraper, from scattered seed and coin to autumn leaves, from the darkside of fantasy to the warmth of a kiss so intense that it flattens the features of the giver. It is a scene of welcome so tender that it might bring even a statue to tears.

Image used by permission of the artist

41 A–D
James McNeill
Mesplé

Four scenes in the life of
the Prodigal Son
Various dates
Various media

The pictures were not
painted in story order.

41 A
..."and ran, and fell on
his neck and kissed him."
(Luke 15:20)
(1990)

Mixed-media/
monoprint

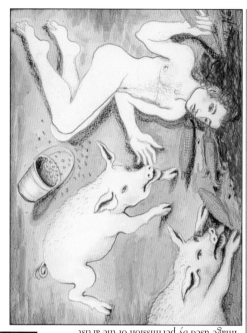

41 B (top)

The son asks for his inheritance

(2005)

Colored pencil, pencil, watercolor (12 x 8 ins.)

41 C (center)

The Far Country: Chicago

(1998)

Colored pencil, pencil, watercolor (12 x 8 ins.)

41 D (right)

Pigs, Pigcorn, and the Prodigal

(1997)

Colored pencil, pencil, watercolor (12 x 8 ins.)

The ultimate theme of this story, therefore, is not the prodigal son, but the Father who finds us. The ultimate theme is not the faithfulness of men, but the faithfulness of God.

And this is also the reason why the joyful sound of festivity rings out from this story. Wherever forgiveness is proclaimed there is joy and festive garments. We must read and hear this gospel story as it was really meant to be: good news! News so good that we should never have imagined it. News that would stagger us if we were able to hear it for the first time as a message that everything about God is so completely different from what we thought or feared. News that he has sent his Son to us and is inviting us to share in an unspeakable joy.

The ultimate secret of this story is this: There is a homecoming for us all because there is a home.

Helmut Thielicke, *The Waiting Father*
(New York: Harper, 1959) p. 29.

Facing page: J. Wachsmout, *After Vernet* (See also pages 164-165.)

Section 4

Celebration

A very British welcome

The final years of the eighteenth century in England were bursting with cultural energy. King George III, who had recently lost the American colonies in their War of Independence, had but a few years left in his reign. In truth the country was already on the cusp of the culturally rich Regency Period—Jane Austen, born in 1785, was already gathering material for her great literary venture. In the late 1790s William Pitt the Younger, was holding on as prime minister; the sharp pens of Thomas Rowlandson and James Gillray (page 93; page 115) were satirically active; the American ex-patriot painter Benjamin West was president of the Royal Academy; and in 1797 the proto-feminist author Mary Wollenstonecraft breathed her last.

Abroad, that same year was notable as well. Franz Joseph Haydn was at work composing his great oratorio, *The Creation*, in Vienna. Napoleon was setting the world on fire, having conquered Venice in May. John Adams succeeded George Washington as president of the United States. On September 20, 1797, the U.S. frigate *Constitution* ("Old Ironsides") was launched in Boston.

One day earlier (back in England on September 19), Haines and Son, from Fetter Lane, London, issued this set of six hand-colored engravings of *The Prodigal Son*. While the original artist is unknown, this series of prints clearly—though more soberly—stands in the tradition of the series of engravings of William Hogarth (1697-1764). Hogarth's *Rake's Progress* first appeared in 1735; and this set, released by Haines more than a half-century later, echoes that rakish commentary on folly.

The Haines prints recount the drama of the Prodigal Son in three acts, each containing two scenes. The first act shows two domestic scenes in which the son receives his patrimony and then takes his leave. Initially it looks as if the world is his oyster: there is an impressive array of currency before him, and two globes beckon at his back. On the face of it his future seems to contain great expectations, further hope of which is suggested in the second scene. Nattily attired and well supplied with horsepower, the son shakes his plump father's hand. This optimistic scene is only slightly dampened by the mother's tearful expression at the base of a curved staircase.

She has good cause to weep, for the second act in this prodigal drama reveals a mother's deepest fears: debauchery and then misery. In scene one the son sits on a couch having a merry time. Wine is in abundance and women as well, one of whom seems to be performing a late eighteenth-century form of lap dance. The picture above this merry-making displays a naked and supine woman, an intimation of what might come later in the evening. The crone on the right who is sweeping up the son's cash, the apparent loss from a dice game that preceded the present revelry, intimates something altogether different.

In the following scene that suggestion of loss is fulfilled as we view the son in the dirty depths. While the surrounding countryside is pleasant to look at, the son's condition is not. He is ragged and befouled; his high living company has been replaced by a herd of snuffling, poking pigs. He looks directly out at us with a baleful, hung-over expression. The contrast between him and the bucolic landscape on the one hand and his present and previous condition on the other, is telling. It would appear that this is the centerpiece of the drama. Here we witness the experience of loss and the moment of self-discovery, and we realize that if the story has a moral, this is it.

That moment of discovery leads to repentance, as the first scene in Act III reveals. On bended knee before a now much slimmer father, the ragged son kisses the offered hand, hoping he may find some place in the home he so incautiously left behind. The signs for acceptance are good: the mother gestures welcome (a little sourly, perhaps); a servant holds a fresh garment; and another servant is, appropriately, butchering a fatted calf in the background.

A happy ending to this British biblical drama is enacted in the final print. Ten robust members of the gentry sit around a table about to feast on what looks like a roast goose, though it may be (it should be) a cut of calf. A string ensemble plays—perhaps music by Haydn—from a balcony. It is possible that one of the figures seen through the door on the left may be the older brother, though that sibling may well be the heavy-set fellow at table warily waiting to be served his portion. In effect, all's well that ends well. We have witnessed the six-part drama, and we have learned what the anonymous English artist wants us to know: Don't waste your patrimony, for you may not be so fortunate as the son in the story. You may live it up for a while, but you are likely to land—and remain—in the mud with the pigs.

The PRODIGAL SON receiving his PATRIMONY.

42 A-F
Anonymous
English

The Prodigal Son
Set of six hand-
colored lithographs
published by Haines
and Son, London
(19 September 1797)

The PRODIGAL SON taking leave of his FATHER.

42 A (top)
*The Prodigal Son
receiving his Patrimony*
(10 x 6½ ins.)

42 B (bottom)
*The Prodigal Son taking
leave of his Father*
(10 x 6½ ins.)

42 C (top)

*The Prodigal Son
revelling with Harlots*

(10 x 6½ ins.)

The PRODIGAL SON revelling with HARLOTS.

42 D (bottom)

*The Prodigal Son in
Misery*

(10 x 6½ ins.)

The PRODIGAL SON in MISERY

The PRODIGAL SON returned to his FATHER.

42 E (top)

*The Prodigal Son
returned to his Father*

(10 x 6½ ins.)

The PRODIGAL SON Feasted on his RETURN.

42 F (bottom)

*The Prodigal Son feasted
on his Return*

(10 x 6½ ins.)

Let the party begin!

In this engraving by the Flemish artist Nicolaes de Bruyn (1571-1656) we are clearly expected to focus our eyes on the impressive mass of the bowed father and the kneeling son. And initially we do. But the restless eye inexorably slants off to the right and takes note of the three proximate women. Since this trio are well-dressed and gaze raptly at the principle figures, they are not likely servant girls. Our imagination suggests that one of them may be the son's mother, the other two being aunts or perhaps sisters. The elder brother is absent from the scene.

This grouping of the principal figures and the women creates a diagonal that echoes the slope of the staircase off to the left, and our eye wanders in that direction to study the party in progress. The son has barely returned, and the revelry is already underway! Halfway up the stairs a bearded man turns and extends his right hand in greeting to a well-dressed woman. It is as if he were giving her a sixteenth-century "high five," a gesture that underscores the merriment of the occasion.

Farther up the stairs a servant approaches a group of revelers with a salver of food. Ahead of him on the balcony more than a dozen guests are eating and drinking. Another servant enters from the right holding high a tray of food while two other servers pour wine from flagons. These appear to be very accomplished pourers, for the lengthy arcs of liquid clearly require accuracy in order to get the wine into the cups of the guests and not onto their heads.

The jollification seems to be lubricated by the abundant food and free-flowing wine, but it may equally be enlivened by the trio of trumpet players farther along on the balcony. With puffed cheeks they are obviously blowing up a brass musical storm. They may be trumpeting a fanfare in honor of the returning son, perhaps a scaled down version of a work by Giovanni Gabrieli (1557-1612). Or they might be launching some sprightly *Instrumentalmusik* by the earlier Flemish composer, Heinrich Isaac (1450-1517). Whatever the tune, the air is alive with the sound of music.

The players on the balcony are providing the frisky melody for the party, but off to the left and under an arch it seems that an ax-wielding servant is accompanying them with a gory percussion. He is hammering a resistant calf into submission prior to its becoming further provender for the guests. Between these two musical offerings the son is acclaimed by trill of trumpet and by the thump of slaughter. The music and butchery are each, in their own way, visible and audible signs of the father's great gratitude at the Prodigal's return.

The father's joy is most visibly manifest by his warm embrace. Clothed in a fine flowing garment, he leans forward like a furry mound. The plush undercover at the father's exposed left foot suggests that many animals gave their life for this rich garment. The shadowy nap of the robe contrasts with the smooth surface of his tight-fitting skullcap.

The father's finery is in stark contrast to his son's poverty. The son's muscular limbs emerge from threadbare garments. His thick hair and scraggly beard (and perhaps a ripe body odor) also contribute to the sensation that he is not far-removed from the pig sty—something the excited dog to his rear may also sense. Neither sight nor scent deters the father, however, as he clasps both of his hands around the son's neck. More, he looks deeply and with feeling into the face of his wide-eyed and open-mouthed son who was once lost but is now home.

Deep in the background of this New Testament story are the penetrating observations of the Teacher of the Old Testament book of Ecclesiastes, that sobering series of sayings that focus on the limits and contradictions of life. In chapter 3, verse 3, the sage observes that there is "a time to weep, and a time to laugh; a time to mourn, and a time to dance."

In this depiction of the son's return we see that the time of weeping and mourning is over, at least for the time being. Now it is time to eat, drink, and be merry; it is time to raise the sounding trumpet and wield the culinary ax. It is a time for the father to embrace the son and for the women—and all of us—to look on with wonder and approval. On this occasion all the senses are engaged: sight, touch, smell, hearing, and speech. Together in this sensible scene of reconciliation everything proclaims, "Welcome home; let's have a party."

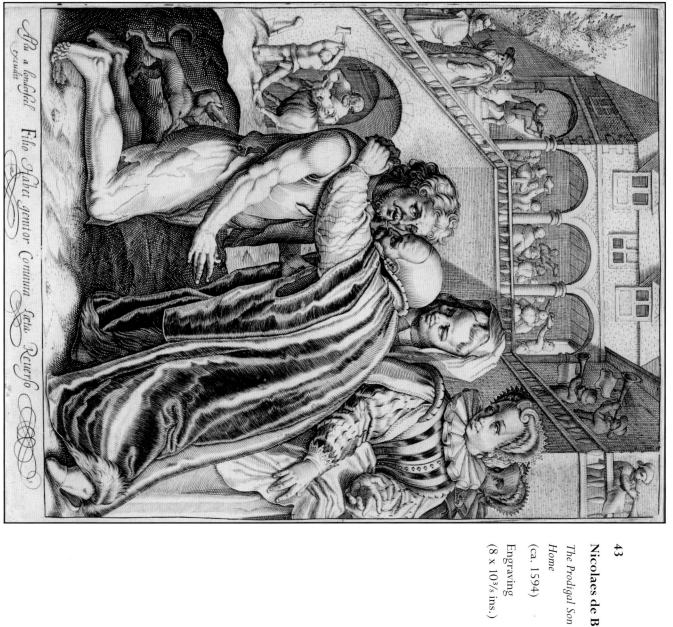

43

Nicolaes de Bruyn

The Prodigal Son Returns Home

(ca. 1594)

Engraving

(8 x 10³⁄₈ ins.)

Home in the heart of Texas

Texas, in the American imagination, looms large. Many of us have thrilled to tales of the Texas Rangers. Most of us will always "Remember the Alamo." And some of us will recall the vocal forces of Mitch Miller's musical gang singing, "The stars at night, are big and bright (*clap, clap, clap*) deep in the heart of Texas." Some of that cultural memory survives in the triptych called *Two Sons* by James Janknegt (b. 1953).

Like Texas, it is a large work (85 inches by 24 inches); in the wide central panel we can see the stars at night, big and bright, as well as the prairie sky, wide and high. The triptych is peopled with sunburned figures from the south Texas culture. The panel is charged with motion and excitement, while the flanking panels radiate a discernible discontent on the part of each primary figure.

One of the two sons sits and sulks on the left, a partially eaten Big Mac in his hand. Surrounded by ground beef instead of ground pork, he is, perhaps, the dissatisfied trash man for this drive-in emporium. An overturned garbage can, with the detritus of fast food dining, echoes his mood. The young man wears the McDonald's logo on his green shirt and hat. The arched golden M in the upper left echoes the red neon M in MEN. The latter is a tantalizing invitation to satisfy men's hunger not with hamburgers but with sex. The blue movie-like screen above the diner reveals a strip dance of naked ladies, a scene which strangely does not seem to capture the young man's attention.

The expression on his leathery face registers despond and discontent. Yet something else in the panel sparks a different tone. In a disk the color of the rising sun the face of the father appears, as if he is calling the son to come to his senses. The disk "bleeds" into the central panel and is the target for three airplanes zooming through the star-filled Texas night. (When the son left home, he literally took flight.) At the bottom of the panel we see a parallel strip containing a bus station, a bus, a brace of automobiles, a pickup truck, a track shoe, and a bare foot all pointing in the opposite direction. This transportation system suggests that, by hook or by crook, on wheels or on foot, the son will soon be on his way home.

His arrival does not seem to be unalloyed good news, for in the panel on the right we see the other son, most unhappy. He sits on a tree stump with the skull of a steer near his right foot (perhaps the skeletal remains of the fatted calf?). That this young man is not happy is most readily apparent by his scowling expression and his violent action of breaking a guitar on his left knee. He won't be singing "The Yellow Rose of Texas" at the barbecue.

He has his back to a musical ensemble standing under a tree who *are* singing and making music, however. They play for those who are preparing and consuming the provender on the table. This backyard barbecue is reminiscent of those boisterous shindigs that President Lyndon Johnson used to throw on his Texas ranch. While those events were big and brawly, they did demonstrate the vastness of Texas hospitality—something the surly, guitar-breaking son refuses to entertain. Meanwhile, suspended over the ranch house, like a mirror image from the left panel, a disk glows in the sky. In it we see the father looking down on the older son with an expression that both invites and disapproves.

The main action, of course, takes place in the central panel. Emerging from a city that the artist says contains memories of Austin, the son walks toward home. Minus his McDonald's uniform, he walks barefoot, paying little heed to the spiney thicket of cactus along the path. The father fairly flies toward him with flailing arms, followed by a trio of field hands. The field hands bring a coat, a ring, and boots. They all seem happy to see the son, and they appear ready to get to the barbeque and the music. With the rising sun and scudding clouds in the prairie sky, we get the impression that this is a great moment deep in the heart of Texas.

While James Janknegt enjoys painting a variety of subjects, he especially favors creating works that illumine the biblical narrative. He reads the biblical story closely and then places it in the context of his own time and place—in this case, south Texas. Reflecting a theme that often appears in the Bible, the artist wants the viewer not just to look, but also, as he has said, "to see what the shadows of this world are disclosing about the Government of the Promised Son. . . . Truly, artists and art can bring hope to the world."

Anticipating the Promised Son by reflecting on the Prodigal Son—actually, Two Sons—Janknegt acknowledges the dark and the light, the frustration and joy, the flight out and the walk home. The seductions of fast food and lightning sex prove to be considerably less filling than the satisfactions of home cooking. The artist calls on us to do more than just look. He wants us to *see* and sense the richness of the story where the sage in bloom is like perfume (and) reminds us of the one we love (*clap, clap, clap*) deep in the heart of Texas.

44
James Janknegt
Two Sons
(2002)
Triptych, oil on canvas
(85 x 24 ins.)

The son comes home to an elegant French feast

It takes about three minutes to read the parable of the Prodigal Son from Luke 15 aloud. Some observers have suggested that is only a fraction of the time it may have taken Jesus to tell it. Oral teachers like Jesus often embellished a story at some length to maximize its effect and involve the listener. The author of Luke's gospel, in editing the story, was probably the one who compressed it into its present form of twenty-two verses.

Artists, like good storytellers, frequently embellish the story of the Prodigal Son by visually uncoiling the narrative. They create a number of scenes that embroider Luke's account. Such artistic invention invites the viewer to experience a fresh, though not unfaithful, retelling of the story. Inventive retellings artfully challenge viewers to consider novel interpretations. Such a challenge is issued in a series of six eighteenth-century hand-colored etchings, *Parable of the Prodigal Son*, based on the earlier painted works of Jean LeClerc (1587-1633).

Whereas the parable simply states that the younger son demanded his share of the property that belonged to him, the first colorful print shows an impatient son cajoling his father before a table laden with currency. Behind the red-coated son we see the bent-over backside of a servant who is likely scooping from a chest even more lucre for the demanding youth. Foreshadowing misfortune for the impulsive young man, the omniscient narrator, who speaks in rhymed quatrains in the French captions (not shown in the reproductions), informs us that "this gold, this precious metal, will be quite dangerous for this young fool."

The narrator expands the moralistic commentary in the next scene where the son takes his departure with an entourage of four horsemen. A woman (the mother?) watches and waves from a parapet while, according to the text, a good and tender father flows with tears. "What impudence you have, ungrateful son." The text further suggests that the young man on the right with his hand in his coat may be the older (and wicked) brother.

The story steams up with a scene of overindulgence. With detritus from gaming behind, spilled wine underfoot, and sexual prodigality ahead, the dissipated son probes the depths while groping a breast. The commentator remarks soulfully: "These three graces will become three furies who will deliver your heart to the most cruel regrets."

In the next scene five pigs replace the three temptresses. The youth disconsolately ponders his fate in a scene the commentator describes as *The Prodigal Child in His Greatest Misery*. Not counting the sleek gray pigs, the son stands alone, the pitiful curve of his body echoed by the twisted tree behind him. All the other scenes in the series contain from four to thirteen characters. Here, the solitary son "feels the pain of his lamentable condition."

Fifth scene: Seeking forgiveness in the bosom of his father, the son evinces *sincere repentance which is worth more than any virtue that we will experience*. Surrounded by exultant family, compliant servants, and solid architecture, the son (in a green coat for the only time in this sequence of prints) is home at last. A frisky dog and the distant slaughtered calf denote a fitting familial feast—a righteous contrast to the earlier debauch.

The festivity unfolds in the final alfresco scene with meat and drink, music and merriment—a family reunited. The rejoicing father signals for more wine; the servants spring to comply. Those at the teeming table seem to be content: the text affirms, *In this new feast one tastes pure joy*. However, a discordant note is struck by the presence of a blue-coated figure kneeling behind and distracting the returned Prodigal. This might be the disgruntled (and possibly drunken) older brother; he is a mysterious someone either blowing a raspberry or hoisting a flask. The disconcerting quality of this presence is underscored by the commentator: "A jealous person is shooting bitter looks at you, making your happiness more sweet."

The storyteller—the artist as well as the commentator—concludes with this open and ambiguous ending. In Luke's gospel, as well, Jesus left the parable open-ended. After all, narration and nuance, interpretation and embellishment are what tellers of tales do to inspire and challenge the imagination. In artful retellings of this parable we hear about the journey out, the travails along the way, and the way home. Along the way we observe the dynamics of pride, waste, repentance, resentment, homecoming, forgiveness, and—ultimately—grace.

45 A-F

Anonymous French (after Jean LeClerc)

The Prodigal Son (ca. 1770)

Set of six hand-colored etchings published by A. Ragona

45 A (left)

L'enfant prodigue exigeant sa legitime (The Prodigal demands his legacy)

(10¼ x 9¾ ins.)

45 B (right)

Le départ de l'enfant prodigue (The departure of the Prodigal)

(10¼ x 9¾ ins.)

45 C (left)
Vie debauchée de l'enfant prodigue
(The debauched life of the Prodigal)
(10¼ x 9¾ ins.)

45 D (right)
L'enfant prodigue dans la plus grande misère
(The Prodigal in the greatest misery)
(10¼ x 9¾ ins.)

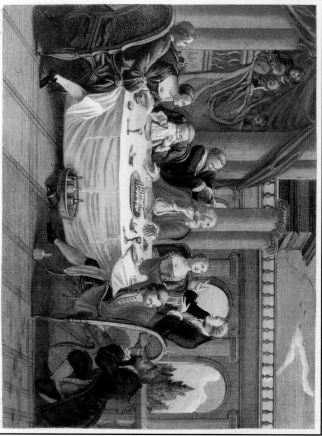

45 E (left)
*L'enfant prodigue
reclamant le bonté de
son père*
(The Prodigal
reclaiming his father's
good will)
(10¼ x 9¾ ins.)

45 F (right)
*Rejouissance pour
le retour de l'enfant
prodigue*
(Rejoicing at the
return of the Prodigal)

The story of the Prodigal Son with illustrative captions

Instruction manuals often include drawings that contain a corresponding sequence of letters (A, B, C, etc.). Brief narrative captions accompany these letters to describe what part A is and how it relates to part B, etc. If one follows the pictures and the captions, everything should make sense. A picture may be worth a thousand words, as the saying goes; but a crisp caption is an indispensable complement to a complicated picture.

The Spanish Jesuit Hieronymus Natalis (1507-1580)—also known as Jerome Nadel—had something like this process in mind when he undertook a work urged upon him by Ignatius Loyola. In 1595, fifteen years after Nadel's death, his complex project was published. A book of one hundred fifty-three engravings, it was called *Adnotationes et Meditationes in Evangelia* (*Notes and Meditations on the Gospels*). This extensive work, intended to be an illustrated guide for prayerful meditation on the Gospels in the tradition of Loyola's *Spiritual Exercises* (ca. 1541), was in truth like a manual of instruction, complete with lettered captions.

Notes and Meditations was a very important visual tool in the Counter Reformation, for it illustrated the life and teaching of Jesus for the common person. The lithographs were arranged according to the order of readings used in the liturgical year as prescribed by the *Roman Missal. Notes and Meditations* was very popular and quite influential, for visualization of the Gospel was every bit as important for the Catholic Church as preaching the Gospel was for the Protestants. The tension between visual and verbal expressions of Gospel truth, as illustrated in this sixteenth-century work, is a matter that persists to this day.

These perspective drawings, almost like theatrical set pieces, proved to be very effective as aids for evangelization and meditation. Nadel, one of the first ten monks of the Society of Jesus, selected the biblical scenes. He commissioned and directed the layout of the book, and he composed the caption notes for each scene. This set of four engravings of the Prodigal Son is visually rich, and the story is greatly enhanced for the believer by the accompanying Latin narrative.

The four scenes which comprise the Prodigal's story were intended to be considered on the Saturday after the Second Sunday of Lent (*Sabbatho post Domin. II. Quadrag. and Eodem Sabbatho*). We see at the top of each scene *Anno*

xxxiij [sic], which tells us that this story supposedly took place when Jesus was thirty-three years old, not too long before his death. The first caption in the first scene informs us that (A) Jesus at Bethany, following the dedication (the cleansing?) of the temple, teaches, and that (B) he did so against the uncivil Pharisees. The story unspools in text and picture from there.

The prints are full of visual delights. For instance, a swaggering youth, looking like a gladiator, calmly views the inheritance transaction. Is he a member of the family, or is he symbolic of the temptations soon to come? Those temptations seem fairly calm in the next scene when caption A tells us that the youth indulges in profligate or lavish living. The banquet in the alcove actually looks fairly sedate, even though it takes place under erotic symbols of birds fully plumed and fairly plucked. The figure of the jester adds a note of burlesque to the expulsion scene, as does the large slug-like staff crawling on the ground.

Having been chased by a shoe-wielding wench, the youth next becomes a swineherd and A, kneels beseechingly at the feet of a stern oriental master. But B, the adolescent comes to his senses in a clarifying shaft of light in the middle distance before he C, takes the road back to his father. In the fourth and most complex engraving A, the father embraces the son; B, the youth confesses his sin; A[sic], the father gives orders to the servants for fresh clothes; C, the servants obey; D, the fattened male calf is slain; E, the feast is made ready; and F, the older son shows up angry—but the father placates him. The eye flutters across the scene like a feather blown by the narrative breeze.

In the distance behind F the sun (unlettered) appears to be either rising or setting. Two horizon dots appear on the face of the shining orb. They may very well be boats; but the modern viewer, conditioned by signs and sights of our day, might fancifully construe them as a pair of eyes peeking over the scene. It is obvious that most of the characters, having experienced the parabola of the story, are having a good day. The son who was lost has been found. The family has been reunited. The rude Pharisees are implicitly invited to make of the story what they will. Our four-part annotated meditation for the Saturday after the Second Sunday of Lent is complete, and we are invited to fast or feast and make of it what we will.

SABBATHO POST DOMIN. II. QUADRAG.
De Prodigo Adolescente.
Luc. xv.   Anno xxxiij.

66

xlij

A. *Ad Bethabaram poſt Encænia*
   IESVS docet.
B. *Contra inhumanitatem Phariſæ-*
   orum Chriſtus parabolam dicit.
C. *Venit ad patrem adolescentior*

vecors filius, petit ſuam partem
ſubſtantiæ.
D. *Congregatis omnibus, diſcedit à*
   patre peregre in Regionem lon-
   ginquam.

Bern. Paſſ. Rom. inu.   Corol. de Mallery Sculp.

EODEM SABBATHO.
Profundit omnia Prodigus Adoleſcens.
Eodem cap.   Anno xxxiij.

67

xliij

A. *Arripit primam occaſionem lux-*
   uriose, profuseque viuendi:
B. *Ita per luxum coſumptis omnibus,*

extruditur à meretricibus; à
paraſitis deridetur; ab omnibus
deſeritur; fit miſer.

B. Paſſ. Rom. inuent.   Corol. de Mallery Sculp.

46 A–D

Hieronymus Natalis (also known as Jerome Nadel)

De Prodigo Adolescente (1595)

Four engravings from *Adnotationes et Meditationes in Evangelia.* Drawn by Bernardino Passeri and Marten de Vos. Engraved by Adrianus and Johannes Collaert and Carolus de Mallery.

46 A (right)
De Prodigo Adolescente
[Concerning the Prodigal Son]

(6 x 9⅜ ins.)

46 B (left)
Profundit omnia Prodigus Adolescens
[The Prodigal Son spends everything.]

(6 x 9⅜ ins.)

46 C

Fit subuclus

[There is a little pig]

(6 x 9⅜ ins.)

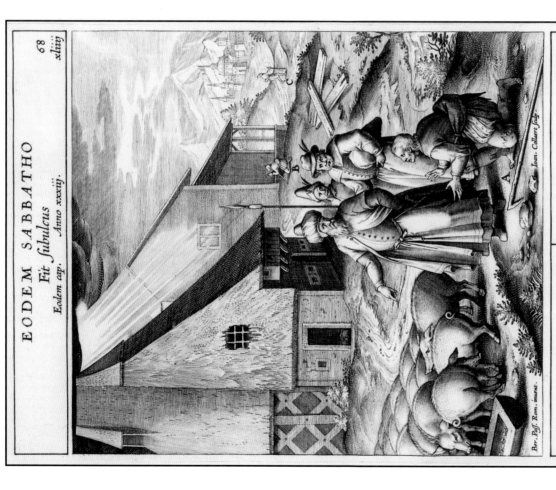

EODEM SABBATHO

Fit fubulcus

Eodem cap.   Anno xxxiij.

68

xliiij

Br. Paff. Rom. inuent.   J. Ioan. Collaert fulp.

A. *Ad fummam egestatem redactus,*
    locat fœde fuam operam pafcen-
    dis porcis; & ne ibi quidem vel
    filiquis poteft explere famem.

B. *Redit ad fe tandem ; meditatur*

    reditum ad patrem, & verba
    quibus illum obfecret.

C. *Deferit ærumnofam vitam; per-*
    git ad patrem.

EODEM SABBATHO.

Accipit illum pater benignissime.
Eodem cap. Anno xxxiij.

69
xlv

A. *Occurrit ei pater longe; ruit in amplex-*
um; filium ofculatur.
B. *Dicit fupplex patri adolefcens; Pater*
peccaui, &c. Nec patiuntur vfcina
patris totam eius orationem audire.
A. *Iubet eum veftiri, & ornari, & ap-*
parari conuiuium.

C. *Afferunt ferui ftolam primam, calceos,*
annulum.
D. *Vitulus faginatus occiditur.*
E. *Conuiuium inftruitur.*
F. *Redit ex agro fenior filius. Is rem cog-*
nitam indignè fert. Egreffus etiam ad
hunc pater, benignè rogat & placat.

Born. Beff Rom. inuent.
Adrian. Collaert, fculp.

46 D

Accipit illum pater
benignissime
[The most kind father
receives him.]

(6 x 9⅜ ins.)

Sheep farmer comes home to a great feast

During the course of his investigation in the case known as "Silver Blaze," Sherlock Holmes made two telling observations. The first, which almost everybody knows, had to do with the curious incident of the dog in the nighttime. The lesser known, but equally trenchant remark was this: "Let me recommend to your attention this singular epidemic among the sheep." If Sherlock Holmes were a docent discussing this serigraph by John August Swanson (b. 1938), his remark about the sheep would be singularly appropriate.

In the fourth panel of Swanson's work our attention is drawn to the Prodigal Son, down on his luck, tending sheep—not feeding pigs. The caption to the panel claims that the son is now poor, hungry, and ashamed. But to most roving eyes he would appear to be standing somewhat diffidently in a tilled field among eight placid sheep; his left hand is gently extended to stroke the nose of a horned and docile ram. One might speculate that Swanson—either naively or wryly—borrowed these sheep from the previous parable in Luke (15:3-7).

This fanciful but reverent scene fairly represents Swanson's interpretive approach to biblical narrative. In an artist's statement Swanson once indicated that he wanted to speak to us in everyday terms, pulling from old roots to make a new thing. Sheep instead of pigs, a four-toed youth standing in his field among a brace of birds like a prototypical Saint Francis, the sun shining with benign intent on what looks like a prosperous farm: These images do indeed pull from old roots to make a new thing. The playful but thoughtful construction entices us to see aspects of the Prodigal story in a fresh way.

Something similar is going on in the fifth panel. The son—his missing toe, like his fortune, now restored—is warmly received by the father, in the midst of a busy farm scene. A field hand is plowing in the background; a servant escorts a pair of goats (not a fatted calf) in the middle distance. A palpably jubilant sister (not an older brother) rushes to greet the returning lad. A striding goose, with neck coiled, participates in this scene of gracious abundance. And, spelling out for our mind what we can readily see with our eyes, the text tells us there is rejoicing and that there will be a family feast.

This bountiful portrayal of homecoming is a rich tableau, a pair to an equally lavish depiction in the first panel, the leave-taking. Told by the text that the young man is out to make his fortune in a distant city, we can see the family homestead bursting with life and activity. Mother and father wave goodbye, the latter sporting a fuller fringe of facial hair than in the closing panel. A sheep wanders in the middle of the scene surrounded by all manner of walking birds. The departure appears neither sorrowful nor joyful. It is just an accepted fact, something about to happen; everyone, including the birds and animals, are unruffled, calmly reconciled to the act of leave-taking.

In the second panel, we see the youth standing on a cobblestone pavement with arms outstretched, awed before the bustling city. Someone from a farm in South Dakota or from a small town in upstate Connecticut might likewise stand amazed at first encountering a big city like Minneapolis or New York. With those women waving and playing instruments in various windows, though, we might deduce that the young man is not there to attend a concert or go to a museum. And sure enough, in the middle panel we see him surrounded by wine, women, song, cards, and a strutting peacock. The latter frequently symbolizes immortality in Christian art, but in this context the peacock may more likely represent vanity or the vice of pride. Or, consistent with Swanson's playfulness, it may just be a peacock strutting on the tile floor.

In any event, that bird leads our eye forward to the scene of the son in the field, now poor, hungry, ashamed, and in the company of the aforementioned non-biblical sheep. The story of the parable (though not the whole story) is recapitulated in these five panels. It is a story Swanson deals with at least twice more—and in vivid color. (See page 131 and page 157.)

Swanson is a sunny artist. Overall, his vision is bright and summery. In this work, as in others, the sun shines a lot. Except for the star-studded scene of genteel debauchery, the sun shows its face in four of these five panels.

From beginning to end the artist invites us to accompany the son on his odyssey; because of Swanson's insight we envision leave-taking, amazement, foolishness, shame, and rejoicing. Anyone who has gone forth, experienced some of the sweet and the bitter of life, and returned home can appreciate the alluring arc of Swanson's storytelling. In agreement with our docent, the great detective, we might conclude that Swanson's perceptive art is by all accounts elementary, my dear viewer.

47

**John August
Swanson**

The Prodigal
(1970)

Serigraph (five panels,
in one frame—
working copy)
(40 x 10 ins.)

The story of the Prodigal in bright colors with a circus

While this serigraph by John August Swanson (b. 1938) is a richly textured and highly nuanced work, there is definitely something childlike about it. It is likely Swanson would concur, because he enjoys engaging children and having them enter into his work. He intentionally invites young people into a dialogue with his peculiar envisioning of the biblical narrative. Sensitive to his audience, the artist listens to their discoveries and responds to their reactions. What might a child looking at this version of the story of the Prodigal Son notice?

Well, over there on the roof of the house where all the people are waving: just look at that rooster crowing. He sure would wake anybody up if they were going off on a trip. Then, over there by the fountain, see that juggler? He's really neat. It looks like he is juggling six, no seven, balls at once. No wonder the boy is impressed. Can you see all those people playing instruments? I like the guy who is hitting the little bells with his hammer by the candle. Now look at the starry night with the moon shining through the window behind them—you can see there are some shooting stars too! I wonder if the band is playing "Twinkle, Twinkle, Little Star"? Is that really a frog under the pig? He reminds me of Kermit, ribit, ribit! I like to see the boy and his daddy finally get together in the end. That makes me feel good. I wonder if there's a pot of gold at the end of the rainbow?

Grownups are invited to take a long look at and appreciate the five-panel scene as well. Adults are free to let their eyes roam from left to right and see how the horizontal bands of cloud and sky unite the five scenes, along with the diurnal arc of sun and moon. Looking at the central star and moonlit panel we see a card game in progress. But if we look closely, we see that most of the characters in this casino scene are wearing clothes patterned with diamonds, hearts, clubs, and spades. The son holds the cards in his hand for us to see, and we may wonder how it is that he is holding among his four cards two aces of spades.

Someone with a roving eye will look at this complex but playful scene and notice that Swanson actually tells the story of the Prodigal Son one and a half times. The first telling is in the five large panels with accompanying text. The latter half of the parable is depicted again in four lunettes atop columns that divide the panels, also with text. Between the third and fourth panels (in which the son cavorts first with gamblers and then with pigs, sheep, and frog) a circular picture shows us that, "The father and son speak to the angry older brother." That is a creative reconciling touch, for it goes beyond the letter (but not necessarily the spirit) of the story in Luke 15: 25-32. We surmise that the older brother is won over, for the next circular picture shows three characters sitting at table, sharing bread and wine.

Looking at the original of Swanson's serigraphs yields a visual reward that can only be hinted at in reproductions. A serigraph is a composite picture made up of forty, fifty—perhaps more—separate hand-colored stencils. These painted stencils are laid down in a very carefully controlled manner so that the flat images, especially when seen up close with a lens, are layered and even dimensional. Our delight is magnified as we revel in the depiction of scores of people and animals, birds, lush plant life, and rich atmospheric effects. It is an altogether yeasty landscape with nature naturing and people peopling. This vividly colored work from 2004 is worth comparing and contrasting with Swanson's earlier (and pigless) version of the story from 1970 (page 155).

Every child can tell you that the central character of the parable of the Prodigal Son is the Prodigal Son. Yet the child's observation of the clown, which we noted earlier, is astute and worth further consideration. The clown is not the key to unlocking the story by any means. Yet he may be a means for us to juggle all the pieces of this story—and others—that Swanson presents. (The artist has another series of work that deals with clowns and circuses.)

In an artist's statement from 1998 Swanson asks us to take another look at this figure who can make us laugh and cry. "[I]t has been the clown that has always been most important to me. He is the distiller of human experience—of our foibles, joys and sorrows. He is the rebel in us—standing up to the established order. When he trips and falls he shows us how to get up from the dust and join the parade. We see ourselves in his foolishness and can laugh at the self-image he flashes before us. He knows the secrets of our interior landscape."

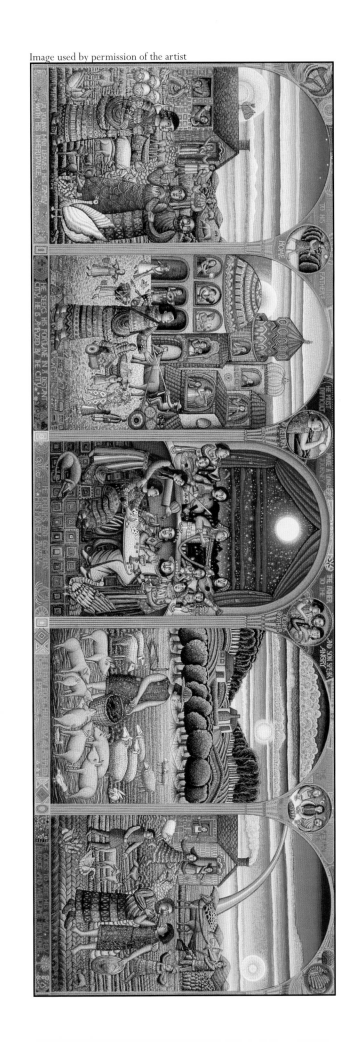

48

**John August
Swanson**

Story of the Prodigal Son
(May, 2004)

Serigraph
(40 x 13½ ins.)

An English Prodigal comes back from Japan

Regard for certain artists comes and goes like the ebb and flow of cultural tides. James Tissot (1836-1902) is such an artist. Though he was fashionable in England during the late nineteenth century, his reputation was in eclipse for most of the twentieth century. Recently, due to renewed interest in Victorian society, Tissot's work has emerged in a new light.

While his paintings and etchings are highly polished and crisp, Tissot's life is less easy to bring into focus. Wanting to picture modern life, he developed his own singular fashion, consciously eschewing the freer painting style of the Impressionists as well as the more regulated style of the academics. Though his work was popular, it was not free of controversy. He has been described as cool and passionate, carefree and neurotic, arch and sincere, sophisticated and superstitious, sociable and reclusive.

Tissot's life story suggests that he might have been a conflicted man. He was born and raised in France and was an accepted exhibitor at the Salon. However, in his mid-thirties he took up residence in England, thus becoming an ex-patriot. Soon after, he began living with Kathleen Norris, thus establishing a life style at odds with his strict Roman Catholic upbringing. It is not unlikely that his paintings and prints relating to the Prodigal Son reflect something of Tissot's conflicted experience, for in his own mind he had left his native country to live abroad; by the standards of the day he was living in sin.

The subject of the Prodigal Son was a popular one in British art, being related to works like Hogarth's *The Rake's Progress* from the early eighteenth century. Nor was it a new subject for the middle-aged Tissot. He had painted Prodigals twice in the 1860s: once as a German medieval costume drama and another in an Italian Renaissance setting. Here, in this series of prints released in 1882, Tissot depicts the subject with a lavish blend of Victorian sensibility and biblical seriousness.

The initial print in the series—*The Frontispiece*—is dated 1881; it reveals an open, well-worn Bible with tassels, page markers, and tattered pages. Most, but not all, of the text of the parable from Luke 15 is reproduced and categorized in four sections. Overall, the series of etchings is unified by such visual devices as background bodies of water and bright reflected light on various surfaces. For example, radiant light shines through the windows of *The Departure* and glances off the highly polished table on which the son sits. Through the window shades the bars of the windows take on the symbolic

form of crosses. Further symbolism may be inferred from the fallen flower blossom on the table, emblematic of the soon fallen and straying son. One of the cats beneath the table blithely strays from the litter, further underscoring the theme of departure.

The next print, *In Foreign Climes*, shows the son wasting his fortune in far away Japan. The influence of Japanese prints (like those of Hokusai) is apparent here. Japanese art and culture were popular in the late nineteenth century, as evinced by the musical production of the *Mikado* in 1885. However, Victorians tended to view the Japanese culture with a degree of ambivalence. On the one hand it was seen as exotic and beautiful, but it was also regarded as hedonistic and irresponsible. The well-dressed son is sitting in a teahouse with slumped, perhaps inebriated associates. This setting and his absorption in the suggestive line of fan dancers illustrates the immoral lifestyle of this irresponsible man in a foreign clime.

In *The Return* the prodigal wears shabby clothes. He kneels on the wet boards of a busy wharf and clutches intensely to his bent and forgiving father whose embrace is so enthusiastic that his hat falls behind him. The only reference in this series to the son's sojourn among pigs is the background where men are unloading pigs and other cattle. The impassive older brother with a female companion stands on the right, looking on stiffly from the shadows.

In the final scene, *The Fatted Calf*, this elder brother openly remonstrates with the father. The father returns the stern look while pointing at his recovered son who self-assuredly sits sharpening the knife, ready to carve the roast. We are left to ponder the wisdom of the father, the smugness of the returnee, and the justice of the older brother's claim. One thing more: There is a satisfying visual *inclusio* in this scene. The blooming flowers in the trellis in this scene echo the flower fallen from the vase in the opening scene. What had been separated then is now united in full flower.

While we live in a time vastly different from the sedate and proper world of the Victorians, we can still take pleasure and instruction from this series of prints. They had a salutary effect on Tissot; soon after he completed this work he began his ambitious project of illustrating the New Testament (from 1886 to 1894), and later the Old Testament (from 1896 until his death in 1902). Having faced the issues of sin and alienation, the artist went on to deal with matters of repentance and redemption. Such a course of reflection is available even today for those who care to look and see.

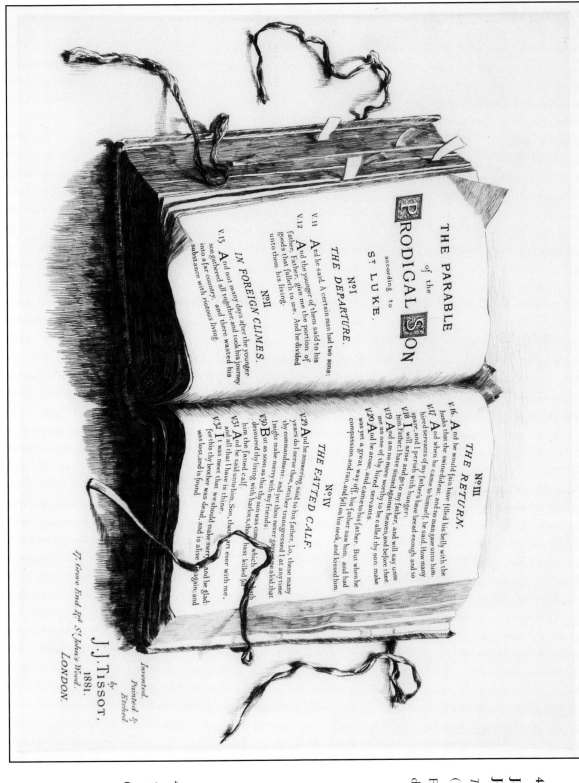

49 A-E

**James Jacques
Joseph Tissot**

The Prodigal Son
(1882)

Five etchings with
drypoint

49 A

The Frontispiece
(13¾ x 17½ ins.)

49 B

The Departure

(14½ x 12 ins.)

49 C

In Foreign Climes

(14½ x 12 ins.)

49 D

The Return

(14½ x 12 ins.)

49 E

The Fatted Calf

(14½ x 12 ins.)

The son sails home

He has stolen Nature's secret; whatever she produces, Vernet can recreate." Thus the great French encyclopedist, Denis Diderot, described the seascape paintings of Claude-Joseph Vernet (1714-1789).

While Vernet painted many realistic sea storm pictures, he specialized in colorful harbor scenes with calm seaports, hills and rocky bluffs, lighthouses and old fortresses. His paintings often contain features in classical architecture and a rich cast of characters working or enjoying the moment. Vernet's pictures were frequently copied (with permission) by other artists, for patrons wanted to have those pleasant views on their walls. His maritime scenes were also made into engravings, another means for disseminating his works, thus enriching the viewing public as well as the artist.

One of these works, a "Kupferstich," a copper engraving, was etched by Jerem.[sic] Wachsmout and released by the Parisian Printing house, chez Rosselin, in 1750. A first look at this print reveals a winsome harbor view, typical of the marine scapes of the artist. Even though it is a print (and therefore lacking both size and color) it is similar to Vernet's Italian works of this period, like *Ruins near the Mouth of a River* (1748), in the Hermitage, or his *Imaginary Italian Harbor Scene* (1746), now in the Minneapolis Institute of Arts.*

We find ourselves looking along a winding body of water flanked by a rocky mass on the left. It contains one structure that looks like a fortress and another that might be a lighthouse. To the right of this curving harbor is an elaborate quay that is more like a balustraded plaza. Beneath a generous tree people are dancing, conversing, and gesturing grandly. Behind the balustrade one couple is engaged in cozy conversation while next to them a young man excitedly looks out at us and doffs his hat. Out on a ledge another young man, head uplifted in awe or prayer, extends his arms with open hands. In front of him, on the water, a canopied barge is being rowed to the left and out of the picture. On the shingle at water's edge a husky half-clad man is busy with his fishing gear.

It is a picture bursting with activity and energy, a marine scene that is refreshing to look at on its own terms. Yet, by the writing at the bottom of the print, we see that something else is going on. In several languages we read the text of Luke 15:20-22 where the happy father throws a party for his Prodigal Son. Without this reference we might not have interpreted the figures in the lower right as signifying that event. Without the text to guide us we might be seeing an exhausted guest arriving by boat, late for the merry-making. Or we could be looking at a fisherman down on his luck, unlike the husky other off to the left. What prevents ready identification with the parable is that we know the rebellious son in the story returned by foot, not by boat.

Since artists can be interpreters of the truth, however, who is to say, in the larger sense, that this interpretation of the story is not true? Even though we know that the father's manse was not located in a harbor and the son did not arrive by boat, the picture still spirals out and makes sense. Those revelers on the rialto are making merry because the son has returned. They might have seen him in the distance while his skiff was making its way under the cloudy sky along all those other boats in the harbor. The word doubtless went out in time for the musician to tune his lute and the dancer to strap on her castanets. There was ample time for the three men to gather behind the father to help haul the boat to a safe berth among the rocky ledge. And there was time for the mother to hear the news and position herself on the balcony like the captain of a boat overlooking the scene.

Vernet in his painting and Wachsmout in his engraving of it have captured a scene that appeals to viewers on more than one level. Overall, the work is a picture of waterfront activity, complete with the eye-filling pictorial elements that make Vernet's paintings so pleasing. On another level this engraving is an unexpected depiction of a biblical story. That is, we see a harbored interpretation of the story, in effect, a nautical Prodigal. We see that the man has rowed the boat ashore, hallelujah; we behold the lost son as he debarks and kneels to be welcomed by the father. Altogether it is an unexpected return in an unexpected way at an unexpected place—just like God's grace.

*The following information appears at the lower left of this engraving: *I. Vernet peint la Vue Tardieu les figures.* (J. Vernet painted the scene, Tardieu the figures). This inscription raises an interesting question. Since Vernet was not noted for being a narrative painter, was the original work by him a calm harborscape to which Tardieu added numerous figures, thus turning a relatively open scene into a densely populated "return of the Prodigal Son"?

Collection de Vernet.

Evangelium. Luc. XV. v. n 32.

N.VI

Urget longa fames urget miserabile fatum:
Unica fpes miferi fubfidiumque pater,
Noch hoher fann fein, ihm der Jammer mag,
nicht fteigen:

Dum redit, (in coelis refonant fie jubila coelis)
A patre felivis plaufibus excipitur;
Es hrevislet die freibliblich durch Wald Gefang
und Lieber

Si se leva donc et vint vers son pere, et comme il étoit encor loin, son pere le vit, et fut touché de compassion, et courant à lui se, ietta a son cou, et le baisa. Mais le fils lui dit: Mon pere, j'ai peché contre le ciel et devant toi; et je ne fuis plus digne d'êbre appellé ton fils. S. Luc. C. 15. v. 20-22.

50

Jerem. Wachsmout

Nach I. Vernet [After Vernet]
(about 1750)

Copper engraving by
Jerem. Wachsmout,
after Claude-Joseph
Vernet. Printed by
chez Rosselin, Paris
(12 x 9¾ ins.)

A dreamy son gets dressed for the party

(right) Completed *Prodigal* window as installed in St. Bernadette Roman Catholic Church, Northfield, New Jersey. Window is about 3 ft. by 8 ft. *Photo by Adam Brusic*

Biographies are valuable to the reader because of their attention to the detail of the subject's life. Illuminating insights into someone's youthful and formative experiences can give readers a fuller understanding of that person's later adult activities. In a similar way, early studies for works of art can enhance the viewing experience when they enable us to catch glimpses of the creative process at work from initial concept to final state.

David Wilson's *Drawing for the Prodigal Son* window in the Church of St. Bernadette, Northfield, New Jersey, allows us the intimate pleasure of seeing a small, preliminary work stand on its own. But happily we are also enabled to double our pleasure if we track the work to its finished state as it appears in the nave of the church itself. In this way we can see how this work, modified by the artist (and doubtless by the ecclesiastical patron), grew from early stage to completed form.

The hand-colored drawing has a smoky graphic quality. The sketchy background, heightened by a ribbon-like sweep behind the figure's head, gives that effect. The face, penciled in, has a neutral quality, while the slender fingers—with a large blue ring on the ring finger—add to the linearity of the richly dressed son. His green kimono-like robe, which reaches to mid-shin, contains an array of patterns, making it a coat of many colors.

The languid lad wears a pair of fancy shoes that bear a visual resemblance to the suede boots that were popular in the 1970s and 1980s. The figure stands on a checkerboard platform tilted up to create a skewed perspective at the bottom of the picture. A note from the artist recalls that the "Prodigal Son looked after pigs." That temporary vocational stint is suggested in this sketch by the profile of a gray-brown pig in profile behind the son. The drawing contains a balance of stationary architectural forms and fluttery decorative patterns.

If we compare this preparatory work with the final window—or, better, if one takes a trip to Northfield, New Jersey, to view the window in context—we can see how the work has "matured." For one thing, the difference in scale impresses, for the drawing is 15½ inches high and 8½ inches wide while the window measures 8 feet by 3 feet—more than six times larger. The etched glass of the window is orange, crisp, and luminously bright; when the light streams through, we get an illuminated impression of this bedecked son.

For another thing, the fluttering ribbon (which the artist considered a symbol of flamboyance) is gone. The ring, stroked now by the son's less lithe fingers, is on his little finger. The suede boots are simply dark brown shoes.

The robe, which is now ankle length, contains a shoulder-to-hip belting that looks a little like a bandolier. Three decorative swatches incorporate a total of ten white forms that suggest clouds in the sky. This feature is an intentional act of symbolism by Wilson who calls them a "clouds in robe" motif, because "his (that is, the son's) head had been in the clouds."

In the window, as in the drawing, the surrounding architectural features and the "checkerboard" base bring the son down to earth. Most notable in the final work, however, is the elimination of the pig in favor of a stylized calf's head. One gets the impression that, while the slaughtered calf *is* a part of the story, churchly sensitivities favored a head of beef over a side of pork.

In contrast to the sketch the son now looks out with a nuanced expression that suggests a number of things to anyone with eyes to see: introspection, pensiveness, wistfulness, the dawning of wisdom. This soulful work is located in the church so that it directly faces a window of Mary Magdalene, another forgiven sinner. Anyone who walks down the center aisle (or sits anywhere in the cruciform nave for that matter) confronts—and is confronted by—the gaze of either the Prodigal Son or Mary Magdalene. Together these colored glass figures silently suggest that those who wish to receive the means of grace are obliged to take forgiveness into account. The Prodigal and the saint look mutely but suggestively on all hungry sinners who enter the church seeking nourishment.

Image used by permission of the artist

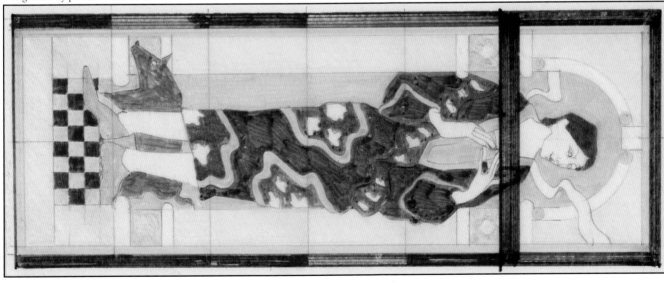

51
David Wilson

*Design drawing for the
Prodigal Son window,
St. Bernadette Roman
Catholic Church,
Northfield, New Jersey*
(1986)
Hand-colored sketch
(8½ x 15½ ins.)

Sister Helena Steffensmeier

"Pleasure is a freedom song, but it is not freedom."
(1970)

Fabric, stitchery and appliqué
(70 x 46 ins.)

Steffensmeier used a sentence from Khalil Gibran as the starting point for her work depicting the Prodigal Son.

Artist: Sister Helena Steffensmeier, OSF (1900-1997) © School Sisters of St. Francis

The Prodigal Son "Off the Wall":
Further Works of Art Inspired by the Parable of the Prodigal Son

by Robert Brusic

An art fancier with eclectic tastes was once heard to say: "Paintings and prints may be the meat and potatoes of the art world, but there is a lot of great stuff that doesn't hang on the wall." Doubtless most museum and gallery goers fancy the pictures, but many people also show up for other forms of art as well. With respect to art inspired by the parable of the Prodigal Son, the most eye-catching part may be the paintings. Still, many captivating artistic expressions exist that don't hang on the wall.

The Evenrud collection contains numerous examples of art that are neither paintings nor prints. Many of these latter works are musical and literary; sometimes they are works of a more ephemeral nature. In this essay we discuss these "off the wall" artistic expressions in four categories: music, literature, related arts, and ephemera. While the categories are somewhat arbitrary and the works selective, the examples suggest the wealth and range of artistic expression inspired by the parable of the Prodigal Son. They open our eyes (and ears) to the depth and breadth of the parable's influence on the imagination. The appendices to this book, though selective, amplify the prodigal sweep of works stimulated by Jesus' story as related in Luke 15.

On the score: Musical works inspired by the Prodigal Son

Though venerable, this uplifting sentiment from an eighteenth-century oratorio is not the oldest musical expression in the collection based on the parable of the Prodigal Son. That position goes to a Latin oratorio by Marc-Antoine Charpentier, dating from about 1690. This work emerges from the spirituality of Ignatius Loyola, the founder of the Society of Jesus. Charpentier's dramatic motet is an Ignatian meditation on the virtue of forgiveness: The Father is not just lavish with his forgiveness, he is actually impatient to bestow it upon his errant but penitent son. Even the older son (in a departure from the original account) agrees to join in the feast and make merry.

Free adaptation of the biblical narrative is quite normal in these musical works—as it is in the graphic art. For example, Arthur S. Sullivan in *The Prodigal Son: an Oratorio*, from 1869, depicts the Prodigal Son as a buoyant youth, tired of the monotony of home; Sullivan omits any musical reference to the older brother. This work was composed when Sullivan was only twenty-seven. The music floats between the musical-oratorical world of Mendelssohn and Sullivan's later association with W. S. Gilbert; that is, this Victorian oratorio musically reflects what was and what was yet to come for this prolific composer.

Composed only fifteen years later (in 1884), Claude Debussy's *Rome Cantata, L'Enfant Prodigue* is a spare work radically different from Sullivan. The cantata (or *Scène Lyrique*) won the Premier Grand Prix de Rome for the twenty-two-year-old French composer. The work is scored for three voices: The mother (named Lia) laments for the departing son (Azael), while the father (Simon) gives stirring praise when the son returns. The trio that concludes the work is an exultant scene in which all three give glory to God.

Other major composers have written musical works based on the parable. In the midst of World War I Darius Milhaud wrote a stark, expressive cantata, *Le Retour de L'Enfant Prodigue*. This musical conversation piece (1917) incorporates

Begin—each tuneful Voice employ,
With ev'ry Pow'r of Music join'd
To spread abroad, in Sounds of Joy,
This welcome Truth to all Mankind:

When Grace on guilty Minds hath Beam'd
And Sinners leave the wicked Way,
Devoutly bent no more to stray,
Celestial Thrones with Transport ring,
And Angel-Choirs exulting sing
A Man reclaim'd, a Soul redeem'd!

Concluding chorus from Hull and Arnold's oratorio *The Prodigal Son* (1773)

Twentieth-century musical expressions encompass musical styles that range from "classical" to jazz, rock, rap, and the Broadway musical. It is no surprise, therefore, that the Prodigal Son has been adapted to these styles. Robert Elmore wrote a "Sermon in Swing" in 1940. Thomas Steven Smith produced *Can You Tell Me the ZIP of That Far Away Land: A Youth Musical about the Prodigal Son* in 1983. Ballad rock was the musical style for Jon Anderson's *Prodigal* in 1996, while *My Green Eyes, a Rock Opera: A Story of Love, Sibling Rivalry, and Organic Farming* made its debut in Minneapolis to enthusiastic audiences in 2006.

The works considered above are generally theatrical pieces; that is, they are intended for performance by vocal and instrumental forces on the stage. Many of them were created for special occasions and were well received, though they are rarely if ever performed today.

Another vein of musical expression inspired by the story of the Prodigal Son

the text of a book by André Gide (*Le Retour de L'enfant Prodigue*). In 1928 Sergei Prokofiev composed his Ballet in Three Scenes. Prokofiev modified the parable to make it more "balletic." The older brother is eliminated in order to make space for a seductive female character, the Siren. This work was based more on a prose tale by Pushkin than on the biblical text. The ballet was revived in 1978 for a memorable television production which was choreographed by the septuagenarian George Balanchine (who worked on the original production in 1929). The 1978 production introduced the young Mikhail Baryshnikov to America audiences.

The parable was also the basis for a concert suite, *Den förlorade sonen*, by the Swedish composer Hugo Alfvén who utilized folk paintings (perhaps bonader) as the basis for his ballet. The Norwegian composer, Egil Hovland, composed *Gud Synes On Deg* in 1978, while the Finnish Kari Tikka wrote an oratorio for choir and orchestra, *Tuhlaajapoika*, in 1996. In the United States the beloved Norwegian-American F. Melius Christiansen wrote *The Prodigal Son, A Sacred Cantata*, in 1918.

Benjamin Britten

The Prodigal Son (1968)

(10½ x 14 ins.)

In this opera Britten used Islamic art as the unifying motif for the costumes. Britten dedicated this work to Dmitri Shostakovich.

Joe Cox and Jody Lindh

Welcome Back, Billy Best: A Roaring Parable of the Twenties (1995)

(8½ x 11 ins.)

is hymns. Scores of hymns and songs about the Prodigal have been composed and sung. Anthems, a square dance, and even a Prodigal Son rap have also appeared, some examples of which are included in the appendix. Whether sung or played, danced or observed, music has variously interpreted the parable and has endeavored to carry out the sentiment voiced by Hull and Arnold: "To spread abroad, in Sounds of Joy . . . A Man reclaim'd, a Soul redeem'd!"

On the Page: Literature based on the Prodigal Son

Young man, come away from Babylon,
That hell-border city of Babylon.
Leave the dancing and gambling of Babylon,
The wine and whiskey of Babylon,
The hot-mouthed women of Babylon;
Fall down on your knees,
And say in your heart:
I will arise and go to my Father.

From *God's Trombones* by James Weldon Johnson (Penguin Twentieth-Century Classics)

Near the end of his mournful reflection in the book of Ecclesiastes the Teacher wryly observes: "Of making many books there is no end." If that is true in general, it is certainly true of the books and other written works derived from the parable of the Prodigal Son. One can only pause in wonder at the number of sermons that have been written and preached on the parable. Someone once said that if the texts of all those Prodigal Son sermons were laid end to end, they would probably paper the road the son traveled from his father's house to the distant country where he squandered his property in dissolute living—and back again. What an incalculable amount of preaching about pigheadedness, penitence, forgiveness, hospitality, and grace! Some of these sermons are in the Evenrud collection.

The collection contains other writings as well: poetry, drama, and numerous books. Some of the poetry is both dramatic and cautionary, like the retelling of the parable in James Weldon Johnson's *God's Trombones*. Johnson tells the story of the boy who was stubborn in his head and haughty in his heart. The poet recognizes that there comes a time when every young man looks out from his father's house, longing for that far-off country. But he also issues a clear warning: "Young man—Smooth and easy is the road that leads to hell and destruction."

Soon after the turn of the twentieth century, St. John Hankin, a well-known English dramatist in his day, wrote *The Return of the Prodigal: A Comedy for Fathers*. It opened in London in 1905 and was well received. Hankin focused on the returning son, placing him in Edwardian England. While the play was based on the biblical story, its over-riding theme was the morally corrupting effects of capital and political power.

Kenneth Bailey, a highly regarded biblical scholar, wrote an extended study of Luke 15, *The Cross & and Prodigal*. Bailey considers the parable from a Middle Eastern perspective, and his book concludes with a compelling drama, *Two Sons Have I Not*. The play, a response to Muslim criticisms about the cross and forgiveness, deals with conflicts implicit in the parable: law vs. love; servanthood vs. sonship; preservation of family honor vs. restoring family fellowship. In the play the latter is stretched to the breaking point, for the angry brother neither accepts the returning brother, nor does he understand the father's act of forgiveness.

Other imaginative works offer insights into the parable, like Andre Gide's *Le Retour de L'Enfant Prodigue*. This existentialist reflection provided the basic narrative for Darius Milhaud's cantata of the same name. The parable is such a deep well that many have drawn from it, producing a wide range of reflective works. Some of them are books offering psychological insight,

James Weldon Johnson

"God's Trombones" (1927)

Drawings by Aaron Douglas

The poem begins, "Young man! Your arm's too short to box with God!"

"Illustration" by Aaron Douglas, from *God's Trombones* by James Weldon Johnson, copyright 1927, The Viking Press, Inc., renewed (c) 1955 by Grace Nail Johnson. Used by permission of Viking Penguin, a division of Penguin Group (USA) Inc.

Many books have used the theme of the Prodigal Son. Illustrated here are *Batman Prodigal* (DC Comics, 1997), *Vom Verzeihenden Vater* by Emil Maier (Stuttgart: Verlag Katholisches Bibelwerk GMBH, 1978), *Tus Tub Loj Leeb* (The Prodigal Son) (Saint Paul: Concordia University, 1996), *The Return of the Prodigal Son* by Henri J. M. Nouwen (New York: Doubleday, 1992), and *The Cross & the Prodigal* by Kenneth E. Bailey, originally written in English and here translated into Dari for an Afghani readership. The cover of the Nouwen book feaures the Rembrandt painting of the Prodigal Son that now hangs in the Hermitage in Saint Petersburg.

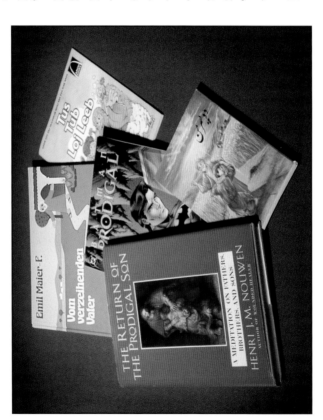

like Sue Thompson's *The Prodigal Brother;* some are theological reflections, like *The Waiting Father,* by Helmut Thielicke; some are scholarly interpretations, like *Prodigal Son/Elder Brother: Interpretation and Alterity in Augustine, Petrarch, Kafka, Levinas,* by Jill Robbins. Marilynne Robinson's recent bestseller *Gilead* (2004) is another contemporary version of the story of the Prodigal Son.

Some writers assume that the negative connotation of prodigality is something with which everyone is familiar. Thus, merely using the word *prodigal* is

Other authors capture the reader's imagination by similar association, tapping into latent cultural and verbal familiarity with the term. For example, Philip High creates a work of science fiction in which a foster child of a distant planet returns to earth. Commingling the Superman legend with the biblical parable, his book is entitled *The Prodigal Sun* [sic]. P.G. Wodehouse wrote a Sherlock Holmes parody in 1903 called "The Prodigal." In this short work Wodehouse teasingly brings the detective back to his homeland after his journey to a distant land (and his presumed demise at the Reichenbach Falls). Another work of popular fiction that makes an association with the parable is *Batman Prodigal*, in which (as the back cover tells us) Bruce Wayne "has asked his 'prodigal son' to return and take up the identity of Batman—perhaps forever." One must read through two- hundred-seventy-two pages in this heroically illustrated and imaginative work to discover just how this particular version of the story of the Prodigal Son plays out.

The Prodigal Son narrative has been told and re-told numerous times in children's books like *Der Verlorene Sohn, The Father Who Forgave,* and the Hmong version, *Tus Tub Loj Leeb.* These publications introduce children to a story they will encounter many times and in many guises throughout their lives.

The story of the Prodigal Son is paradigmatic. It may connect only by invoking the term *prodigal*. Or it may stir the imagination to faith, scholarship, and fantasy. As James Weldon Johnson reminds us, it is a story that can call us to "come away from Babylon; fall down on your knees, and say in your heart: I will arise and go to my Father."

Elsewhere: The Prodigal Son depicted in related arts

Every generation reads those parables over and over again in terms of its own questions, and in every case the freshness, the shock of Jesus' teaching, rocks us over and over again. . . . Take the old Jewish father . . . [who] does what was an incredible thing in a Jewish family. . . . [He] reversed the traditional reverential distance between father and son.

Every Jew who read that said, "Come on, that's no way for a Jewish father to behave." But that's exactly the way Jesus wanted it. Do not therefore read the parables as slick little stories of the ordinary; read them rather as they turn the ordinary upside down."

Joseph Sittler, *Gravity and Grace* (Minneapolis: Augsburg, 1986), p. 45

sufficient to evoke associations with the biblical story. For example, Marvin Olasky's *Prodigal Press: The Anti-Christian Bias of the American News Media* has virtually nothing to do with the biblical story. Yet the author builds his argument by early planting the term *prodigal* in the reader's mind. In the introduction Olasky states his case this way: "American journalism is one of Christianity's prodigal sons. . . . Journalists influenced by anti-Christian humanism and pantheism abandoned their Christian heritage and ended up wallowing among the pigs.""There are no significant references to the parable in the rest of the book.

One of the engaging aspects of public radio's *All Things Considered* is that the program delivers what its name implies. That is, as listeners we can expect to hear something about the big stories of the day, yet we are surprised by a wide range of ordinary but interesting things as well. Similarly, the Evenrud collection invites us to view the story of the Prodigal Son in colorful paintings and prints. But we are also surprised by how the story is told in related arts, such as sculpture, calligraphy, ceramics, commemorative medals and stamps, and fabric.

Sculptors like Jacques Lipschitz, Ivan Mestrovic, Leonard Baskin, and Auguste Rodin have told the story of the Prodigal Son in works of bronze, wood, and stone. These works, generally quite large, are displayed in museums and sculpture gardens throughout the world. Some modest sculptural works are in the Evenrud collection. One of them, *Prodigal Parent*, was executed in 1985 by the Minnesota sculptor A. Malcolm (Mac) Gimse. Now retired from the faculty at St. Olaf College, Gimse created a large bronze sculpture of the Prodigal Son in 1988. An earlier work in the Evenrud collection is only seven inches high, yet it possesses a monumental quality. It shows a seated nude figure leaning back in an anxious gesture. This Jewish father has indeed reversed the traditional reverential distance between father and son. Sculptural works by Britt Wikstrom, Roman Sledz, and George Hagale are also in the collection.

Prints sometimes contain text that enhances or explains a picture. (We have seen this use of text in the works of such artists as James Gillray and Marten de Vos.) Calligraphic works, on the other hand, are primarily or solely text. The calligrapher Timothy Botts has scribed hundreds of images that reflect verses of the Bible or lyrics of popular hymns. The Evenrud collection features a work (see next page) that is a condensation of the Prodigal Son story in script. Botts has penned the story in colored ink on a gridded, tan ground. The text often interprets the narrative. For example, "Wild living" is penned in a large purple scrawl that reflects the son's willfulness; and "we must celebrate with a feast" bursts out with large letters in green, red, blue, and purple interspersed with golden confetti-like dots. The collection also contains calligraphic works by Joan Bohlig and Kristin Malcolm Berry.

Image used by permission of the artist

Text illumination is another way in which the Word is made visible. In a copy of the Gospel of Luke from The Saint John's Bible Luke 15 is accompanied by a dramatic illumination that includes the New York Trade Towers. (See page 179.) The text tells us of the father's welcoming the son; the illumination of the Trade Towers seeks to elicit a similar action on our part. Text-with-towers becomes a calligraphic challenge to our capacity to love our enemies.

Pictorial representations sometimes take old-fashioned forms. The Evenrud collection includes a set of twelve fine and rare creamware dessert plates from the Paillart et Hautin factory at Choisy, France, circa 1820. The plates

A. Malcolm Gimse

Prodigal Parent
(1985)

Bronze sculpture
from the Kyrie
Miserere Series
(6 x 7½ ins.)

Of this sculpture,
the artist has said,
"Extravagant
wastefulness is not
limited to children.
Sons and daughters
have found many
parents to be poor
stewards of earthly
resources as they live
the American dream
without regard for
tomorrow."

Timothy Botts

The Prodigal Son text in

Luke 15

(2000)

From *The Holy Bible in full-color calligraphy* by Timothy Botts

(21¾ x 11 ins.)

The artist has crumpled the paper around the verses

("when he finally came to his senses . . .") in which the Prodigal discerns that he has messed up his life.

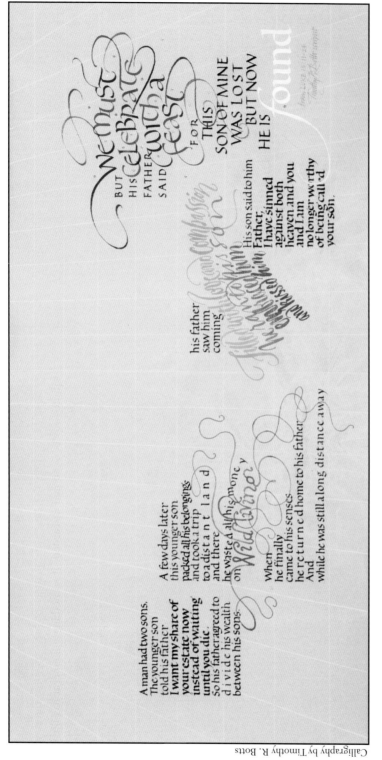

Calligraphy by Timothy R. Botts

depict twelve stages in the story of the Prodigal Son. Each plate has a scene that is a self-contained anecdote, imaginatively interpreting the progress of the son from departure to return. For example, Number 7 in the series, "The humiliation of Arael sharing the food of the pigs," depicts a tattered, beggarly youth being scorned by a well-dressed dandy. A villa, a variety of trees, and a brace of pigs form the background to this moral scene. No doubt the story would be doubly appreciated if one saw it gradually unfold beneath a serving of Gâteau Saint-Honoré or Crème Brûlée. The collection likewise includes a plate with an oriental scene in which an aged father in an elegant kimono welcomes his miserably poor son in front of a bamboo glade. The scene is from the *Lotus Sutra*, a Buddhist work that affirms the realities of daily life and encourages an active engagement with others and the whole of human society. Some observers see in this tender scene a Buddhist parallel with the biblical narrative.

Examples of commemorative art appear in the collection. In 1988 the

Society of Medalists struck their one hundred seventeenth issue, a relief of the Prodigal Son by the sculptor Leonda F. Finke. The society's descriptive material draws the viewer's attention to the pivotal role of the woman in balancing the relationship between the father and the Prodigal Son. A large empty space tells of breaking away and loneliness. On the reverse side three entwined figures depict the family reunited in love, an image that displays tenderness and great strength.

Philately is likewise represented in the collection. Since 1937, eight countries have issued stamps depicting scenes from the parable of the Prodigal Son. Old Master paintings by such artists as Rubens, Guercino, and Rembrandt are reproduced on the face of each stamp. The countries, dates, and artists of these stamps are listed on page 176.

Tapestries depicting scenes from the parable hang in many museums, such as the Walters Art Gallery in Baltimore, Hospices de Beaune in France, and the Minneapolis Institute of Arts. Several modern textile pieces are in the

Evenrud collection. A colorful fabric, stitchery, and appliqué piece by the American artist, Sister Helena Steffensmeir, OSF (d. 1997), depicts the parable in five scenes. (This work is illustrated on page 168.) The son is reckless, then he is contrite; the pigs are as round and fat as balloons; the reunion is musically merry. Stretching across the surface of the piece is its title, one that is both apt and philosophical: "Pleasure Is a Freedom Song But It is Not Freedom." This work stands in the company of about ten other fabric pieces by such artists as Edward F. Summers, He Qi, and Jeanette Paulson.

The works of art considered in this section (sculpture, calligraphy, ceramics, commemoratives, tapestry) cohere with the observations of Joseph Sittler: They are not slick little stories of the ordinary; they turn the ordinary upside down. Paper, fabric, glass, words—the ordinary things in life—are transformed by the artist; and their works challenge us to see a fresh meaning in an old story.

Here today, gone tomorrow: Prodigal Son ephemera

And the younger of the sons went to his father and said, "Father, give me the portion of goods that falleth to me. I will take them and travel unto the Twin Cities, where I shall make merry with strange people and finance expensive body art and sleep through my classes until they are nigh over."
And the father said unto his son, "No."
And that was the end of all that nonsense.

A student's contribution in a creative writing class taught by Garrison Keillor, quoted Minneapolis Star Tribune, Wednesday, February 7, 2001

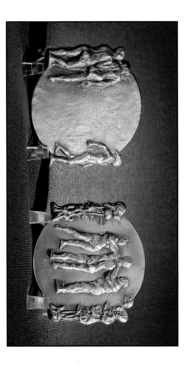

By definition something that is ephemeral is something that is transitory, a short-lived thing. Ephemera are matters of brief life, like the newspaper quote—to be read and discarded. If something ephemeral has life beyond its intended limited span, it is only because some collector clips and saves. Otherwise it is "here today, gone tomorrow."

The Prodigal Son has been manifested in ways that are both long-lasting and ephemeral. In certain contexts the mere mention of the word prodigal suggests an association with the wayward son. We see this, for example, on the cover of the November 1990 Minnesota Monthly. There we observe a smiling gray-haired man. Across his chest are printed the words: "The Prodigal Senator—After falling from grace, can a repentant Dave Durenberger regain the public's trust?"

One need not be a native Minnesotan to get the gist of the lengthy article inside—which makes no further reference to the biblical story. There need not be, because the reader implicitly understands something about the senator merely by the prodigal reference on the cover. A similar point was made on the cover of the May 13, 1996, issue of Time. There we see the evangelist Billy Graham with his son and successor, Franklin. Looking at the pair, we know what to expect in the feature article pointedly titled, "The Prodigal Son—the story of his redemption."

Perhaps proleptically, the Billy Graham Association released a film in 1983

Leonda F. Finke

The Prodigal Son
(1988)

A bronze medal (shown front and back) struck by the Medallic Art Company for the Society of Medalists (One-hundred-seventeenth issue)
(2¾ ins. dia.)

Unknown artist

Lotus Sutra plate
Made in Hong Kong
(9¼ ins. dia.)

This scene from the Lotus Sutra suggests a Buddhist parallel with the Prodigal Son story.

Russia used the iconic image by Rembrandt on a stamp issued in 1970. The original painting is in the Hermitage Museum in Saint Petersburg.

In 1971, Sweden issued this stamp honoring Master Amund, a medieval painter (c.1494) known for his humorous wall paintings in churches in Värmland. Here the Prodigal is blowing a horn while two pigs butt heads.

In 1969 Rwanda issued this stamp featuring a painting by Peter Paul Rubens. The original painting, of which these horses are only the lower left corner, is in Antwerp.

In 1969 the then-new Republic of the Maldive Islands issued a stamp honoring human rights. The stamp shows an image of a statue (1884) of the Prodigal Son by French sculptor Auguste Rodin.

Many countries have issued postage stamps honoring artwork inspired by the story of the Prodigal Son. Besides those illustrated here, Romania (1969) used a work by Bernardino Licino; Yemen (1968) and San Marino (1967) used a work by Guercino. In 1937, France issued a stamp featuring Auguste Rodin with his 1884 bronze statue, here seen on a stamp from the Maldive Islands. The United States, to date, has not issued any stamps with this theme.

entitled *The Prodigal*. The advertisement for the movie depicts a young man in a blue blazer. Striding purposefully forward, he carries a brace of tennis rackets in a bag on his back and a boom-box in his left hand (in all likelihood, he is not Franklin Graham). The panel text over the young man's head declares: "He walked away from his family . . . their lifestyle . . . their God." Another film with the same name is the 1955 Hollywood biblical spectacular. That this work is different from the Graham film can be seen in the passionate words spoken by voluptuous Lana Turner to the smitten son, played by Edmund Purdom: "I am the high priestess of Astarte; I belong to all men."

Many diverse and ephemeral images of the Prodigal Son have shown up—and wound up in the Evenrud collection. A calendar issued by the American Bible Association for 2001 contains a richly colored illustration of the Prodigal Son for the month of November by Esben Hanefelt Kristensen. The 1988 Calendaro Ecumenico from Caracas, Venezuela, contains monthly scenes from the parable. Greeting cards and posters—here are more than a dozen of the latter in the collection—regularly feature scenes from the Lukan story.

Even the fatted calf plays an ephemeral role. The Basilica of Saint Mary in Minneapolis promoted its 1997 Block Party with this announcement: "It's like the party for the Prodigal Son except we're substituting bratwurst for fatted calf." In a vintage 1928 advertisement for the National Rifle Association, a picture of a drooling, toga-clad figure slices into a platter of (presumably) eponymous calf. "Anyone who has been around the world very much appreciates a fatted calf [the ad states]. Not wishing our prodigal brothers in the shooting fraternity to miss a chance at a fatted calf we are telling you in this menu what awaits your return to the game for 1928."There follows a list of six "dishes" including such mouthwatering enticements as a full year's membership in the NRA, personal advice on where to hunt, and the promise of a continued battle to protect the subscriber from vicious "anti-firearms" laws. In many and various ways is the parable invoked and interpreted.

The Prodigal Son has provided fodder for other diverting and ephemeral expressions. In March, 2001, the *Metro Lutheran* (Minneapolis) provided its readers with a Word Search puzzle. Readers were informed that a box of scrambled letters contained seventeen words (like *falsefriends, fattedcalf,*

pigpen, and *oldperson*); people were invited to circle the words and gain insight into the parable of the Prodigal Son.

Prodigal humor has arisen in many places, like political and *New Yorker* cartoons. Newspaper comic strips frequently refer to the parable for a laugh and perhaps a bit of instruction. In recent years the Prodigal Son has been invoked in such strips as *Doonsbury,Wildwood, B. C.,* and *Peanuts* (see page 178), examples of which are in the collection.

Some years before the class exercise at the head of this section, Garrison Keillor dramatized the parable on public radio for listeners all over the country. The parable, broadly interpreted, amused and instructed an audience of folks who may or may not have had any previous knowledge of the parable. That evening, however, people heard Wally (the son who went off) mix his parables by encountering five foolish virgins who were low on oil. Soon the lad was drinking cheap wine with an appreciative Wanda who regarded him as "such a tremendously vital person." After an internship among the swine Wally returned home, where he admitted: "It was a big mistake, leaving, but I'd like to say that everything worked out real good in the end." Coincidentally, Keillor reprised (and rewrote) the parable for his

Alfonso Santoni

Calendario Ecumenico 1988: El Hijo Prodigo.
Caracas, Venezuela
(8 x 12 ins.)

The calendar tells the story of the Prodigal Son with cartoon drawings.

X ANIVERSARIO ACCION ECUMENICA
Caracas/Venezuela

CALENDARIO ECUMENICO 1988

Fourth of July (2006) television show, where the "Parable of the Prodigal Sister" featured Meryl Streep.

Final Thoughts: Off the wall

It is difficult to find a literary figure as ubiquitous as the Prodigal Son. Other literary figures like Sherlock Holmes or Don Quixote have captured the imagination of numerous artists and pundits. But Holmes and Quixote are characters with names while the Prodigal Son is anonymous. (Interestingly, the cognomens of all three have contributed words to the English language.) However, the detective and the Don, while iconic, do not have such a "prodigal" reach in the arts. Each of the three characters has taken on a life far beyond the intention of their creator, and they have achieved a permanent place in our imagination. But the Prodigal Son occupies a unique place on and off the wall, in works of art that are both long-lasting and ephemeral.

While many things are here today and gone tomorrow, we might discover, if we look, that the truth dwells even in the ephemeral.

As this essay has shown, the story of the Prodigal Son has serious ramifications in music, literature, and related arts. The story also has a broad impact on popular culture—in politics, comic strips, advertising, and other aspects of contemporary life. In the end the parable of the Prodigal Son is an inspiring story for all seasons with an artistic message for all media. It is truly difficult to imagine our world without the story of the Prodigal Son.

Charles Schultz

Peanuts

Minneapolis Star Tribune
November 5, 1996

PEANUTS: © United Feature Syndicate, Inc.

Donald Jackson

Detail from Luke Anthology, The Saint John's Bible (2002)

Donald Jackson, with contributions from Sally Mae Joseph and Aidan Hart

(Page is approximately 9½ x 15 ins.)

This page from *The Saint John's Bible* illustrates Jesus' Lukan parables. The parable of the Prodigal Son is illustrated in the second diagonal stripe up from the lower right corner. The father runs to welcome the returning son with a colorful coat in his hand. In the background the Twin Towers appear in gold leaf.

Appendices

Appendices

Appendix A: Exhibits of the Prodigal Son collection

Art for Faith's Sake: An exhbit of art inspired by the parable of the Prodigal Son (Luke 15) from the collection of Jerry A. Evenrud has been displayed in the following venues. The collector would like to thank all those who visited these shows.

1986	Central Lutheran Church	Minneapolis, MN
1989	All Saint's Lutheran Church	Minnetonka, MN
	Immanuel Lutheran Church	Eden Prairie, MN
	St. Luke Lutheran Church	Park Ridge, IL
1991	ELCA Churchwide Office	Chicago, IL
1992	Luther Theological Seminary	Saint Paul, MN
	United Theological Seminary	New Brighton, MN
	Central Lutheran Church	Minneapolis, MN
1993	Fourth Presbyterian Church	Chicago, IL
	Second Annual Heritage Art Show	
	from Lutheran Churches	
	Trinity Lutheran Church	Starbuck, MN
	Wartburg Theological Seminary	Evanston, IL
		Dubuque, IA
1994	Fall Homecoming, Luther College	Decorah, IA
	Library & Faith and Life Center	
	Interfaith Spiritual Art Gallery,	
	Cathedral Heritage Foundation,	
	Cathedral of the Assumption	Louisville, KY
1995	Hope Presbyterian Church	Richfield, MN
	Bethel Lutheran Church	Madison, WI
	Crossview Lutheran Church	Edina, MN
	Dordt College	Sioux Center, IA
	National Conference on Islam,	
	Luther Seminary	Saint Paul, MN

1996	Our Savior's Lutheran Church	Sioux Falls, SD
	Lutheran Theological Seminary	Gettysburg, PA
	Bloomington Covenant Church	Bloomington, MN
	United Theological Seminary	New Brighton, MN
1997	Dadian Gallery,	Washington, DC
	Wesley Theological Seminary	
	Brauer Museum of Art,	Valparaiso, IN
	Valparaiso University	
	Interfaith Spiritual Art Gallery,	Louisville, KY
	Cathedral Heritage Foundation	Louisville, KY
	Republic Bank and Trust Company	Minneapolis, MN
	Plymouth Congregational Church	
1998	Christ Lutheran Church	Preston, MN
	Steensland Art Gallery,	Northfield, MN
	Saint Olaf College	
1999	ALOA Lutherhostel	Eau Claire, WI
	Wisconsin State University	Richfield, MN
	Oak Grove Lutheran Church	
2000	Michael Dunn Memorial Gallery,	Waverly, IA
	Cornwell-Reed Fine Arts Center,	
	Oakland City University	Oakland City, IN
	Rockford Art Museum	Rockford, IL
	Waldemar A. Schmidt Gallery of the	
	Fine Arts Center, Wartburg College	
2001	Institute of Theological and	Saint Paul, MN
	Interdisciplinary Studies, Macalester College	Willmar, MN
	Willmar Arts Fair, Bethel Lutheran Church	Sioux City, IA
	Sioux City Art Center	

Appendix B: Operas and musical productions based on the parable of the Prodigal Son

Alfvén, Hugo. *Den fölorade sonen*, Concert suite from the ballet. 1957. Stockholm Philharmonic Orchestra, Neeme Järvi, BIS-CD-455.

Anderson, Jon. *Prodigal, A Musical Journey (ballad rock)*. Dubuque, IA: Center for Youth Ministries, 1996.

Bairstow, Edward. *The Prodigal Son: A Choral Ballad for Chorus and Small Orchestra*. London: Oxford University Press, 1939.

Baker, Randy, and Doug Weatherhead. *My Green Eyes Rock Opera: A Story of Love, Sibling Rivalry, and Organic Farming*. Unpublished. 2006.

Britten, Benjamin. *The Prodigal Son, A Parable for Church Performance*. London: Faber Music, 1968.

Charpentier, Marc-Antoine. *Filius Prodigus, A Latin Oratorio (or Dramatic Motet)*. ca.1690. Edited by Janet Beat and Watkins Shaw. Oxford: Oxford University Press, 1987.

Christiansen, F. Melius. *The Prodigal Son: A Sacred Cantata*. Minneapolis: Augsburg Publishing House, 1918.

Cox, Joe, and Jody W. Lindh. *Welcome Back, Billy Best! A roaring parable of the twenties*. Garland, TX: Choristers Guild, 1995.

Debussy, Claude. *L'enfant prodigue, scène lyrique*. Paris: Durand et Cie, 1884.

Elmore, Robert. *The Prodigal Son: A Sermon in Swing*; The text from "God's Trombones" by James Weldon. New York: The H.W. Gray Co., 1940.

Fragerolle, Georges. *L'enfant prodigue, poème et musique en sept tableaux*. Paris: Enoch & Co., 1894.

Green, Keith. *The Prodigal Son Suite*. Chatsworth, California: Sparrow/ Birdwing Music, 1983.

Horvitz, Wayne. *Prodigal Son Revisited: Jazz Variations*. 1990. The New York Composers Orchestra, New World Records, NW397-2.

Hovland, Egil. *Gud Synes om Deg: Gudstjeneste for store og små barn*. Oslo: Norsk Musikforlag, 1978.

Hull, Thomas (words) and Samuel Arnold (music). *The Prodigal Son: An Oratorio*. London: J. Bell, 1773.

Lloyd, Tracey (words), and Herbert Chappell (music). *The Prodigal Son Jazz*. Melville, NY: Belwin Mills Publishing Corp, 1971.

Marohnic, Chuck. *Desert Spirit, Concerto for Jazz Piano and Orchestra* (based on the Parable of the Prodigal Son). Apache Junction, AZ: Superstition Music, 1999.

Marsh, Donald F. *Barbecue for Ben, A Musical for Young Voices based on the Parable of the Prodigal Son*. Carol Stream, IL: Agape, 1977.

Milhaud, Darius. *Le Retour de L'enfant Prodigue*, Cantata. 1917. Accord, 201902.

Parker, Alice and Brian Marsh. *The Prodigal, An improvisational musical play*. Unpublished, 1995.

Prokofiev, Sergey. *The Prodigal, Ballet in Three Scenes*. 1928.

Self, Adriane (music) and David Orme (words). *The Prodigal Son Cantata*. London: Oecumuse, 1982.

Smith, Thomas Steven. *Can you tell me the ZIP of that faraway land?* A youth musical about the Prodigal Son. Grand Rapids, MI: Singspiration Music, 1983.

Spiritual Chants of the Russian people. *Parable of the Prodigal Son*. The Sirin Choir, Andrey Kotov, LCD 288 073.

Sullivan, Arthur. *The Prodigal Son, An Oratorio*. New York: William Pond & Co., 1869.

Tikka, Kari. *Tuhlaajapoika*, Oratorio for choir and orchestra. Helsinki: Finnish Music Information Center, 1984; 1996.

Willett, Ernest Nodall (words) and Frederick C. Nicholls (composer). *A Prodigal Son or Gleaners of Life*, An opera in two acts. Liverpool: Lee & Nightingale, c. 1900.

Wormser, André. *L'enfant Prodigue*: Pantomime in trois actes de Michel Carré fils. Paris: Biardot, 1890.

[no author]. *Der Verlorene Sohn*. Stuttgart: Deutsche Bibelgesellschaft, 1997.

Appendix C: Selected bibliography of books based on the parable of the Prodigal Son

Baden, Robert. The Father Who Forgave. Saint Louis, MO: Concordia, 1983.

Bailey, Kenneth. The Cross and the Prodigal: A Study of Luke 15 through the Eyes of Middle Eastern Peasants. Downers Grove, IL: Intervarsity Press: 1973, 2005.

————. Jacob and the Prodigal: How Jesus Retold Israel's Story. Downers Grove, IL: Intervarsity Press, 2003.

Chick, Jack T. The Brat. Chino, CA: Chick Publications, 1992.

Davidson, Alice Joyce. A história do Filho Pródigo. Lisbon: Edições Paulistas, 1992.

Dixon, Chuck, and others. Batman Prodigal. New York: DC Comics, 1997.

Fernández, Domiciano. The Father's Forgiveness: Rethinking the sacrament of reconciliation. Collegeville, MN: Liturgical Press, 1991.

Gide, André. Le Retour de L'enfant Prodigue. Paris: Nouvelle Revue Française, 1907. (Peter L. Kjeseth has translated this work into German.)

Graham, Lorenz. How God Fix Jonah (African retelling of biblical stories). Honesdale, PA: Caroline House, 2000 (original copyright, 1946).

Graham, Ruth Bell. Prodigals and Those Who Love Them (Poems and diary entries of the prodigal years of her two sons). Colorado Springs, CO: Focus on the Family Publishing, 1991.

High, Philip E. The Prodigal Sun (A science fictional tale mingling the Superman legend with the Prodigal Son). New York: Ace Books, 1964.

Johnson, James Weldon. God's Trombones. New York: Viking, 1927.

Maier, Emil. Vom Verzeihenden Vater. Stuttgart: Verlay katholisches Bibelwerk GMBH, 1978.

Olasky, Marvin. Prodigal Press: The Anti-Christian Bias of the American News Media. Westchester, IL: Crossway Books, 1988.

Piper, John. The Prodigal's Sister. Wheaton, IL: Crossway, 2003.

Robbins, Jill. Prodigal Son / Elder Brother: Interpretation and Alterity in Augustine, Petrarch, Kafka, Levinas. Chicago: University of Chicago, 1991.

Shaw, Luci. Listen to the Green. Wheaton, IL: Howard Shaw, 1971.

Thielicke, Helmut. The Waiting Father: Sermons on the parables of Jesus. New York: Harper & Brothers, 1959.

Thompson, Sue. The Prodigal Brother: Making peace with your parents, your past, and the wayward one in your family. Wheaton, IL: Tyndale, 2005.

Tus Tub Loj Leeb (The Prodigal Son). Saint Paul, MN: Concordia University, 1996; 2000.

Appendix D Selected list of songs, hymns, and anthems based on the parable of the Prodigal Son

Song	Date	Lyricist/Composer
"A Beggar Is Walking the Highway"	1978	words, Britt G. Hallquist; music, Egil Hovland
"Behold the Wretch . . ."	n.d.	words, Isaac Watts; music, William Billings
"Come Back Home"	1981	words and music, Daughters of St. Paul
"Come In from the Cold, My Friend"	1993	words and music, Daniel Charles Damon
"Come, Prodigal, Come"	n.d.	words, Mabel C. Frost; music, Ira Sankey
"Doggone Son"	1988	Trad. American, arr. by Lyn Howe
"Far from Home We Run Rebellious"	1993	words, Herman Stuempfle; Tune, LIBERTY
"Father, I Have Come"	1998	words and music, Doug Norquist
"Father, I Have Sinned"	n.d.	words and music, Eugene O'Reilly
"Forgive Me, Father, I Confess"	1994	words, Rae E. Whitney; music, David Ashley White
"Frälsare, du som äger lakedom"	1938	words, K. H. Aagaard; music, Oskar Lindberd
"God Is Calling the Prodigal"	1889	words, C. H. Gabriel; music, Jack Boyd
"God Who Built This Wondrous Planet"	1986	words, Jaroslav Vajda; music, Thosmas Leeseberg-Lange
"Gonna Have a Party"	1982	words and music, Warren McKinnon
"Help Me, Please"	n.d.	words, John Ylvisaker; music, Slavic tune
"How Deep Is Your Compassion"	n.d.	words and music, Bob Stromberg
"How Far Away Is Heaven"	2001	words, Richard Leach; music, Carson P. Cooman
"I Believe I'll Have to Go Back"	1968	words and music, Mary Grissom
"I Will Arise"	1981/17th c.	words, anon (1874); music, RESTORATION (1835)
"My Father's Hand"	1977	words and music, Kari Tikka
"My Father's House"	1928	words and music, Chalvar A. Gabriel
"New Beginnings"	1983	words, Brian Wren; music, attr. Louis Bourgeois
"Oh The Shame That Fills My Heart"	n.d.	words, Matsumoto; music, Lewis [Japanese melody]
"Prepare the Banquet, Laugh and Sing"	n.d.	words, Herb Brokering; music, Carl Schalk
"Our Father, We Have Wandered"	1989	words, Kevin Nichols; music, Hans Leo Hassler
"Poor Child of God, Rise Up"	1982	words, Madeleine Marshall; music, Kevin Vogt
"Prodigal"	1980	words, Renato Getti; music, Paul Creston
"Prodigal Son"	n.d.	words and music, Charles Culbreth
"Prodigal Son"	1992	words, Josiah Moore; music, Square-note song
"Prodigal Son Rap"		words, Trilby Jordan; music, Albert Zabel

"The Lord Is Full of Compassion"	1952	words and music, F. Melius Christiansen
"The Penitent"	1892	words and music, Beardsley Van de Water
"The Penitent's Vision"	17th c.	words, Luke 15; m, WERDE MUNTER
"The Prodigal Child"	n.d.	words, Mrs. Ellen H. Gates; music, W.H. Doane
"The Prodigal Comes Home"	1977	words, Chris Rogers; music, Peter D. Smith
"The Prodigal Daughter's Return"	1894	words and music, Lincoln J. Pollack
"The Prodigal Girl"	n.d.	words and music, Emmet G. Coleman
"The Prodigal (Now! Now! Now!)"	1999	words, Richard Leach; music, Curt Oliver
"The Prodigal's Reprieve"	1962	words and music, Carl Edward Anderson
"The Prodigal's Return"	n.d.	words, John Newton; music, arr. Ira D. Sankey
"The Prodigal Son"	n.d.	words, *Baptist Harmony*; music, E.J. King
"The Prodigal Son" (keyboard solo)	1995	music, James Biery
"The Prodigal Son"	1914	words, Thomas O. Chisholm; music, George C. Stebins
"The Prodigal Son"	1977	words and music, John Greenwood
"The Prodigal Son"	1994	words, Gracia Grindal; music, Daniel Kallman
"The Prodigal Son"	1959	words, William Albert Luce; music, Martin Broones
"The Prodigal Son"	1976	words, adapted from Luke; music, Joe Wise
"The Prodigal Son"	1854	arr. Harry C. Watson
"The Prodigal Son"	n.d.	words, JohnYlvisaker; music, Traditional English
"Rejoice, I Found the Lost"	1994	words, Gracia Grindal; music, Wayne L. Wold (arr.)/ Rusty Edwards
"Sät en ring på hans hand"	1975	words, Anders Frostenseon; music, Knut Nystedt
"Tennessee"	n.d.	words, John Newton; music, Chapin
"Where Is My Boy Tonight?"	1919	words and music, Robert Lowry

Appendix E: Selected books containing pictures of Prodigal Son representations

[no author]. *J.B. Speed Art Museum Handbook*. Louisville: J.B. Speed Art Museum, 1983.

On page 68, there is a photo of a Prodigal Son tapestry (Flemish, 1475-1485), which is a companion to a tapestry in the Walters Art Gallery in Baltimore.

Adelson, Candace. *European Tapestry in the Minneapolis Institute of Arts*. New York: Abrams, 1994.

Chapter 4 discusses and illustrates "The Prodigal Son Sets Out" (Flanders 1517-1530), a tapestry owned by the Minneapolis Institute of Arts.

Arneson, H. H. *Jacques Lipschitz Sketches in Bronze*. New York: Praeger, 1969.

Several "sketches in bronze" of the return of the Prodigal (1930-1931) appear on pages 83-85. A finished sculpture, *Prodigal Son*, (44 inches tall) is illustrated on page 19. It was completed in 1931.

Bach, Friedrich T. *Constantin Brancusi 1876-1957*. Cambridge, MA: MIT Press, 1995.

On pages 130-131 is illustrated Brancusi's *Prodigal Son*, his earliest (1914/1915?) wood sculpture surviving in its original state. The sculpture is owned by the Philadelphia Museum of Art.

Digby, Wingfield. *Victoria & Albert Tapestry Collection*. London: Her Majesty's Stationery Office, 1980.

Plate 57 illustrates a Flemish tapestry (sixteenth century) that might have the return of the Prodigal Son as its subject.

Eric Gill, the Engravings (edited by Christopher Skelton). Boston: Godine, 1990.

Page 804 illustrates the Prodigal Son story (1931) as a wood engraving to illuminate the word "and" in Gill's editon of the *The Four Gospels* on which he collaborated with Robert Gibbings, a fellow engraver.

Erlandi-Brandenburg, Alain. *Musée National du Moyen Age Thermes de Cluny* (Guide to the Collection). Paris: Réunion des Musés Nationaux, 1993.

A photo of a 1520 tapestry showing the departure of the Prodigal Son appears on page 183.

Joffe, Irma B. *The Sculpture of Leonard Baskin*. Westford, MA: Murray, 1980.

Prodigal Son, bronze (55 ins. tall), 1976, is illustrated on pages 186-187 and discussed on pages 184-185.

Jussin, Estell. *Slave to Beauty: The Eccentric Life and Controversial Career of F. Holland Day: Photographer—Publisher—Aesthete*. Boston: Godine, 1981.

The Prodigal, a photographic triptych (1909), is illustrated and discussed on pages 191-192.

Miller, Malcolm. *Chartres Cathedral*. New York: Riverside, 1991.

On pages 79-81, the author discusses the Prodigal Son window in the north transept of the cathedral.

Newdick, Jane. *Flower Arranging*. Surrey: Colour Library Books, 1989. Illustrated on pages 138-139 is the dressing of a well (a Celtic custom) with the theme of the Return of the Prodigal.

Schmeckebier, Laurence. *Ivan Mestrovic: Sculptor and Patriot*. Syracuse: Syracuse University Press, 1959.

A sculpture, entitled *Prodigal Son*, appears as plate 187. It is plaster, 2 ft., 3 ins. tall, 1954. As of the printing of the book the sculpture was in the collection of the artist.

Wayment, Hilary. *King's College, Cambridge: The Great Windows*. Cambridge: King's College, 1982.

On page 54, there is a discussion and photo of window 19, section B, the *Return of the Prodigal Son*, probably seventeenth century.

Wisloff, Carl. *Norsk Kirke-Historie*. Oslo: Lutherstiftelses Forlag, 1971.

The dust jacket has a picture of the mosaic of the Prodigal Son's homecoming created by Emmanel Vigeland for Gjerpenkirke in 1920.

Wray, Naomi. *Frank Wesley: Exploring Faith with a brush*. Auckland: Pace, 1993.

Wesley was a distinguished Indian artist. His painting, *Forgiving Father*, is illustrated and discussed on pages 44-45.

Appendix F: Contributors to the collection

The collection has been enriched by contributions of art and artifacts from these people and institutions.
The collector is also grateful to those who attended his docent-led tours of the collection.

Parker and Katie Adelmen
August Anderson
Jutta Anderson
Kenneth E. Bailey
Mark Bangert
John Becker
Kirsten Malcom Berry
Al and Pete Bine
James L. Brauer
Sandra Bowden
Herbert and Lois Brokering
Phillip and Carolyn Brunelle
Adam Brusic
Fran Burnford
Bruce and Cynthia Burnside
Bob Cray and Wade Johnson
David and Merrie Dahlgren
Linda Marie Delhoff
Alan and Ruth Dietz
Kevin D. Dietz
Helen C. Dreiling
Keith Eiken
Robert Elmore
Chris Engstrom
Duane and Marlene Engstrom
Robert George
Kathy Handford
Lutz and Lyse Haufschild
Joy Heebink
Elizabeth Downing Heller

He Qi
Marilyn Zutz Heurer
Robert Holtz
Egil Hovland
Don Hunt
Jack and Helen Hustad
Roberta Joern
Brian Johnson
Ed Knippers
Kathyrn L. Koob
Kosuke Koyama
Lois Kremer
John and Ginny Kruse
Alice T. Larson
Stephen and Rebecca Larson
Otis and Kathryn Lee
Robert E. A. Lee
Diana Lewandowski
Rob Marchand
Chuck Marohnic
Martin E. Marty
Marie McCord
Gloria Mellon
Daniel Meyer
Dean and Anita Moe
David Morgan
Henry Nouwen
Curt Oliver
Richard C. Parkow
James and Joan Peterson

Carroll and Carol Procter
Bob and Gretchen Ravenscroft
Kirsten Marie Evenrud Ringo
Leland B. and Pauline Sateran
Bunnie Tetlie Sather
John S. Setterlund
Craig Swager
Lislie Morman Silko
Morgan and Mary Simmons
Vera Slabey
David and Mary Sterling
Marcel and Hannah Suliteam
John August Swanson
Magdalena Velesquez Swanson
Lee and Pat Thoni
Bruce Thorpe
Kari and Eeva Tikka
Craig Vista and Gloria Svare
Gunnel Wennerholm
Bill and Sally White
David Wilson
Edwin Wolf II
John Ylvisaker
James Quinten Young

Bethel Lutheran Church, Madison WI
Luther College, Decorah, IA
Valparaiso University, Valparaiso, IN

Appendix G: Index of artists whose work is illustrated

About the authors

Richard H. Bliese joined the Luther Seminary faculty as academic dean and associate professor of mission in July 2003. He was elected president of Luther Seminary in 2005. Previously, Bliese served as the director of graduate studies and Augustana Heritage associate professor of global mission and evangelism at the Lutheran School of Theology at Chicago (LSTC).

Robert Brusic is seminary pastor emeritus at Luther Seminary in St. Paul. He has nurtured a lifelong love of the fine arts through course work, reading, and frequent museum attendance. He has written for *Word and World*, *Lectionary Homiletics*, and *ARTS*. He also contributes to Sherlockian publications.

Jerry A. Evenrud is a retired church musician who has an avocational passion for the visual arts. This book is evidence of his Prodigal collection. He also has a collection of art inspired by Old and New Testament narratives. From 1955 to 1976, while he was serving as director of the ministry of music at Grace Lutheran Church, Eau Claire, Wisconsin, he was a member of the "Art for Faith's Sake" committee that developed a biblical collection. This led him to develop a biblically inspired collection of art for the churchwide office of the Evangelical Lutheran Church in America in Chicago. Evenrud is a distinguished alumnus of St. Olaf College in Northfield, Minnesota.

Sarah Henrich, a pastor in the Evangelical Lutheran Church in America, has taught New Testament at Luther Seminary since 1992. Her commitment to the visual arts is expressed in docent work at the Minneapolis Institute of Arts and in her love of quilting. In addition to many Bible curricula and essays, her publications include *Great Themes of the Bible*, published in 2007.

David Morgan is Phyllis and Richard Duesenberg Professor in Christianity and the Arts, and professor of humanities and art history in Christ College, the undergraduate humanities honors college of Valparaiso University. He has taught at Valparaiso University since 1990. Morgan served as chair of the department of art from 1990 to 2000. The history of religious images, American religious and cultural history, and art theory are Professor Morgan's major interests.

Wilson Yates is professor emeritus of religion, society and the arts at United Theological Seminary of the Twin Cities. He is president of the National Society for the Arts in Religious and Theological Studies and editor of the journal *ARTS, The Arts in Religious and Theological Studies*. He has published in the areas of theological education and the arts, the church and the arts, and theology, spirituality, and the arts. His most recent publication, co-edited with Kimberly J. Vrudny, was *The Arts, Theology and the Church: New Intersections*.